HOW TO RUN A FOOTBALL CLUB

JIM KEOGHAN

HOW TO RUN A FOOTBALL CLUB

FOOTBALL CLUB

THE STORY OF OUR NATIONAL GAME

First published by Pitch Publishing, 2020

Pitch Publishing
A2 Yeoman Gate
Yeoman Way
Worthing
Sussex
BN13 3QZ
www.pitchpublishing.co.uk
info@pitchpublishing.co.uk

ISBN 978 1 78531 644 9

Typesetting and origination by Pitch Publishing

Printed and bound by TJ International, Padstow, UK

Contents

Acknowledgements

I WOULD like to say a big thanks to everyone who agreed to be interviewed. Each person featured has been exceptionally generous with their time and I hope that they're satisfied with the outcome.

Special thanks need to go to Rotherfield Football Club who allowed me to intrude on their weekly matches and training sessions and plague their coaches with more questions than they probably bargained for.

Several sites and publications have been kind enough to allow me to reproduce their work, for which I would like to say thanks. These are: Pitch Publishing, *The Warm Down*, *The Blizzard*, *Training Ground Guru*, *The Sunderland Echo*, *The Chronicle*, *Lynn News*, ESPN, *That's Liquid Football* and *The Bootiful Game*.

At Pitch Publishing I'm grateful to Paul and Jane for giving me this opportunity and would like to thank everyone else there who has been involved with the creation of the book.

On a personal level, my children, Emma and Jamie, have provided a welcome and much needed distraction from the daily grind of writing. They probably don't realise it but being around to hear about their days remains one of the greatest perks of working freelance. Through researching this book, I have even managed to introduce Jamie to the attractions of non-league football, albeit with the additional bribe of a pre-match, half-time and post-match Mars Bar.

But I save my biggest thanks, as always, for Nicky, without whom there would be no book. You have helped me throughout the process, fact-checking, reading over a subject area upon which you have zero interest and patiently correcting my appalling grasp of grammar. It's been a long slog, with its fair share of ups and downs, but I could not have got through any of it without the love and unconditional support you provide every single day.

Introduction

IT all started with dog s**t. Or to be more specific, with lots of dog s**t. A few years ago, after being endlessly nagged by my son to come and help out his football team, I reluctantly caved in and offered my (admittedly limited) services.

Memories of my own days of junior football were obviously child-centric, a world of playing for fun, of stress-free games, an administration- and responsibility-free age of joy. It never occurred to me just how much work went into those games, the admin, the coaching sessions, the dealing with 15 hyperactive budding scallies, each with the attention span of a goldfish. What for me was nothing but a laugh must for the coaches have been one long, continuous headache.

And then, of course, there's that dog s**t.

One of the downsides of our grassroots game is just how much of it is played on municipal fields. They are open to all, including those who choose to walk man's best friend upon them. And while many owners are good, wrapping up their dog's steaming productions in a plastic bag, others are just arseholes, leaving said productions out there, like a landmine waiting to spoil someone's morning.

How many coaches have picked up how many such landmines is a figure beyond me. But judging by my own experiences, the number must be significant. I can tell you from the heart that there is nothing less likely to get you in the mood for coaching a football game than leaning down and picking up your third dog turd of the morning. There might be a plastic bag separating your skin from the mushy mess being collected but that does little to stifle what for me has become a gag-reflex-inducing horror show.

It was while picking up one such deposit that the idea of this book came to me, as I thought to myself 'I wonder if Pep Guardiola has ever had to do this?'

As soon as football in this country stopped being about one village trying to kick an inflated pig bladder into the neighbouring village's church and instead began to morph into the sport that we recognise today, the game has always been, in its heart, about two teams trying to best each other. And yet, how a coach training U10s on a Saturday morning, a manager running a side in county football, or a Premier League owner experience the game are often so far removed from one another to almost make you think that there is nothing to link them beyond the simple fact of kicking a ball.

In my 40 (mumbles) years involved with football, watching it, playing it, writing about it, I'd experienced my fair share of these different mediums. I'd played junior football, university football and Sunday league, I'd followed a top-flight side for decades, I'd watched local sides grind it out in the unforgiving world of non-league football, I'd coached the game where it first begins and

I'd reported and written about all kinds of different clubs, right across the pyramid. And through it all, it's clear that as much as there is a uniting similarity in the matches that take place, there is also so much that sets them apart.

And it was this that I wanted to explore, to journey through our national game to see just what it takes to run a football club, how the experience differs from the bottom to the top.

It's an exploration that has taken me up through the pyramid, from kids starting out on their football journey to the bright lights of the Premier League. Along the way I have not just seen how and why the sport we love keeps going but also witnessed how it is changing. Because although there are unquestionably parts of English football that are not what they once were, suffering under growing indifference and financial constraints, there are also new parts that are thriving. The pyramid might not be the structure it used to be, but that's not necessarily a cause for concern. A different structure is taking shape, one more inclusive, more innovative, better suited to our world today.

And through this journey I have got to appreciate just how much of the sport is dependent on one simple thing, the sheer love of the game. English football has its paid positions, the people whose job it is to run academies, to manage sides, to keep clubs ticking along. But across the pyramid, so much of the game is dependent on those who give their time for free, simply because they love football. That love is there in the coaches sacrificing their Saturday mornings to coach kids, it's there in the groundspeople keeping non-league pitches alive and it's there in the owners putting their hands in their pockets, sure in the knowledge that it's money they might very well never see again.

It's fair to say that without them the game as we know it today would be very different. England is blessed with such a vast network of clubs because so many people love this sport, so much so that they collectively underwrite it with their time and their income.

And it's easy to see why. It's been two years since I relented to my son's incessant nagging, two years of midweek training and Saturday morning matches. Two years of trying to get 15 excitable kids to do one thing they're meant to. Two years of tying soggy laces on a cold morning, of waterlogged pitches, driving rain and biting winds.

Would I change any of it? Would I go back in time and recommend to my earlier self that I resist his pleas? Of course not. It's football. Come Saturday morning I'll be out there again, tracksuited up, game plan in hand, giving my time for nothing.

When my dad first took me out in the garden, flyaway football in hand, and introduced me to the game, he started a love affair that has lasted since. And no amount of dog s**t will ever change that.

Chapter One

Jumpers for Goalposts

IT'S a gloriously sunny September morning in the heart of the East Sussex countryside. On a pitch as manicured as a lawn tennis court, Spartak Rotherfield U10s take on their local rivals, Jarvis Brook Tigers. Both teams are resplendent in new kits (a long season of grass stains and machine washes yet to take their toll), supportive parents stand behind respect barriers and coaches in matching, club-coloured tracksuits pose questions in measured tones from the touchlines. It's like a scene from an FA promotional video.

The kids play with the levels of enthusiasm and hunger you would expect from those still in the first throws of love with the game. But there is technique and method there too. Some DNA might remain from those early days, when fledgling footballers taking their first steps in the game chased the ball en-masse, like a pack of animals hunting down its quarry, but it is a mere memory. Years of coaching, of Saturday morning sessions, of drills, games and instruction have moulded them, developed them, brought out the footballer within. The ball is moved with precision, players exploit space, positions are held.

The two sides are neatly balanced, with every outcome on the table. Rotherfield take the lead, Jarvis Brook level. Rotherfield pull away again, only for their opponents to haul them back. If the coaches and the parents are feeling the tension, they hide it well. The days of grown men screaming from the touchline seem consigned to another age.

You would expect the players to tire as the game progresses, for legs to become heavy. But it doesn't happen. If anything, as full time edges closer and the prospect of a narrow win becomes more tangible, they seem to find hitherto unknown reserves of energy. Although the outcome does not matter (we are still some way off points and league tables), this is like watching the closing stages of a vital cup tie. The players are throwing everything they have at each other, desperate to secure that telling goal.

In the dying seconds of the game, with the minute hand approaching 30 and the scoreline still even, a ricochet from the centre circle sends the ball high over the heads of the Jarvis Brook defenders. One of Rotherfield's wingers is the fastest to react, sprinting beyond them, just about controlling the ball with a half-decent first touch. He knocks it forward and bears down on goal, two defenders giving chase, gaining ground with every millisecond.

With time running out, the keeper advancing, his angles closing and the breath of the chasing pack on his neck, he decides to let rip. A rare bobble on the pitch lifts the ball up invitingly and he smacks it with everything he has; accuracy thrown to the wind. For a moment, it's as though time has stopped, the coaches, the parents, the players frozen, with only the ball exempt. Both sides watch as its trajectory beats the despairing keeper's outstretched arms and ... smashes against the crossbar, ricocheting safely out of play behind. And then time unfreezes. Groans ring out amongst the home side's parents and coaches, a palpable sense of relief evident within the away contingent.

When the final whistle blows not long later, it's a mixture of handshakes and high fives all round and mutterings of 'well played' and 'good game'. The Rotherfield players trot back to their side of the pitch, gather round the coaches and collectively break down what's just happened. The white board comes out, questions are raised, answers given by the kids. The parents are there too, encircling what is going on, not just spectators but part of the process. At the end of the team talk, one will step forward and give their opinion on the game, a positive spin on everything that has happened, one last boost to the self-esteem of the kids.

For every player who makes it, and the millions who won't, this is where it usually begins. This is where an interest that began with watching football on the tele, kicking a ball around the back garden with your mum or dad, playing down the park with your mates, turns into something else. It blossoms into a love affair, one that will last longer than many marriages. The kids here today will likely not go on to realise their dreams of playing in the Premier League, but through football they will develop themselves, physically, emotionally and cognitively and at the same time form lasting memories.

For the kids playing at Rotherfield and the many others lining up to play for their teams on a weekend morning, football has always been about love. It's about longing to get on the ball. It's about counting the hours until the next game. It's about waking up on a Saturday morning, looking out the window at the horizontal rain and thinking, 'I can't wait to get to training'.

It's also an enduring love of the game which ensures that when those kids make it to that pitch, there are people and clubs there to welcome them. Because, more than anything else, junior football in this country is defined by its volunteers. Without the people who give up their time to run the administration of the country's many clubs, to coach the players, to even make the tea in the clubhouse, places like Rotherfield FC would not exist.

'I run the U10s and to do it properly can be a time-consuming job,' says Andy Garrett, who has been coaching at Rotherfield since 2014, getting involved not long after his son joined the U5s.

'I'd played semi-pro locally for years but had given it up when my son was born and had sort of consigned myself to a life without football on a Saturday. But that love of the game never really leaves you and not long after he began here, as I watched the kids from the touchline, I could feel the urge to get involved, like something was drawing me back. I asked them if they needed any help and they bit my hand off.'

What started off as a casual involvement for Garrett has, by his own admission, become something of an all-consuming passion.

'Coaching is a challenge. But I love it and want to do it right. We've got 31 kids here, across three teams, and I see it as my job to give them the best football experience possible. That means ensuring that training is as much fun as it can be, that it stretches them to become the best player possible and that they leave here on a Saturday feeling good about themselves and wanting to come back. And to do that takes a lot of work. Planning sessions, tailoring player development, liaising with parents, it's very time consuming. In fact, sometimes my partner thinks it's too time consuming!'

While a small proportion of the millions of children playing some form of football each week will receive their coaching from professionals within the academy system, the majority will undertake their football journey at clubs similar to Rotherfield – small, FA-affiliated community clubs staffed and run by volunteers.

'The whole system of junior football is completely dependent on volunteers, people good enough to give up their time during the week and at weekends,' says Garrett. 'Without these people,' he continues, 'and it's most often parents like me being persuaded to pull on a trackie and get involved, then the whole thing would collapse. And I don't think that's always appreciated by the wider football world. Without us, and the time we commit, the football journey our kids take would be very different.'

This emphasis on creating the best 'football journey possible' for kids currently lies at the heart of the FA's coaching philosophy, England DNA; a strategy that runs right through the development period of the game.

'One of the most important things for us, particularly in the Foundation Stage, which goes up to age 11, is to get children to fall in love with this game. We want them to have positive memories of playing football and to engage fully. And even if they decide that football isn't for them later on, we want to create sports people, people who will have a lifelong involvement with sport,' says Pete Sturgess, FA national development coach.

The England DNA philosophy is tasked with bringing an end to the 'command and control' approach that many of us of a certain age will vividly remember from our youth, an approach defined by static drills, children being the pawns for the grand tactical vision of a coach, and it being OK to scream things like 'Get Stuck In!', 'Play the Way You're Facing' and 'Who Wants This?' at nine-year-olds.

Thinking back to those days, it's amazing how long some of us stuck it out playing junior football. I wince at some of the names players got called in the teams I played for, shudder at the advice we were sometimes given (usually centred around knocking it long and exacting revenge) and look back with frustration at how that environment limited us as players. It's perhaps a testament to how alluring the game can be, that participating was still an attractive prospect.

'Under the new philosophy, there is much more emphasis on giving the players ownership of the game. By this we mean encouraging them to explore as they learn, by us asking questions, posing challenges and seeing how they react and develop. We are trying to move away from coaches simply telling their players what to do. By making football a more collaborative experience, by giving players ownership, not only will you create better footballers, players who think for themselves, you'll also have better odds of retaining kids because there is more chance of them being engaged with what is going on,' says Sturgess.

Along with giving players more ownership, there is also a shift away from static drills, the kind of repetitive training that would often see children doing the same activity again and again.

'We try to make our training "game related" practice as much as possible,' says Andy Garrett. 'The idea is to make what we do relatable to the matches they will play in and also to almost make them feel like it's not a teaching environment. They get enough of that in school all week, so they don't need it at the weekend too. I can remember from when I played as a kid, training could be really boring, because it was so repetitive. It's not a surprise that some kids never bothered turning up and some ended up walking away from football. You're asking for a big time commitment from them and if a part of that is tedious, you can't be surprised if some aren't keen.'

Key to initiating this new approach to grassroots football is the education of coaches. For those clubs seeking FA Charter Standard status (something that gives them access to funding from the FA), all youth sides need to have at least one FA Level One accredited coach for each team. And it's through the Level One qualification that coaches are introduced to the England DNA.

For coaches, the qualification is more about 'how to coach' children, less about 'what to coach'. It uses constructionist learning ideas, rooted in the thinking of PE guru Muska Mosston and his spectrum of teaching styles. The spectrum incorporates ten styles of teaching, based upon the degree to which the teacher or the student assumes responsibility for what happens in the lesson. It's essentially a continuum where at one extreme is the direct teacher-led approach (command and control) and at the other end lies a much more open-ended and student-centred style, where the teacher only acts in a facilitatory role. What the spectrum offers is more choice, opening teachers, or in this instance coaches, to different ways of learning, each with its own implications for development.

'Under the new coaching environment, you are thinking more about how children learn,' explains Rob Selby, a Level Two coach at Rotherfield. 'When I played football as a kid I was just told what to do through seemingly endless drills. While there's always a role for a bit of command and control, you've got to get the kids thinking for themselves. That's what keeps them engaged, makes them better decision makers, and ultimately better footballers. So, we try and keep that in mind when devising sessions. Sometimes this even means getting the kids involved with what we are doing, asking them what went well, what didn't work and what we could do better.'

Allied to these coaching methods, the new approach also takes into consideration the 'whole' player via the 'Four Corner' model. This breaks development down into four areas: technical/tactical, physical, psychological and social.

'It gets you thinking that there's more to a player's development than just what he or she does with a ball,' Selby continues. 'It brings in other considerations to mind, such as how well they work with others, how well they deal with challenges, how they understand the game. After all, what exactly is a "good" player at this age? You can be good on the ball but a poor team player. You could need work on the ball but excel in other areas, like psychological strength or sportsmanship. Our approach is to take all four areas into consideration during the development stage, with the aim of making these kids the best they can be by the time that streaming might occur at a later age.'

But the new way to coach is not the only method by which the FA has sought to change the culture of the game and make it more about 'positive experiences'. There has also been a concerted effort to make Foundation level football (and sometimes also ages beyond) less competitive.

'By this,' explains Pete Sturgess, 'we don't mean no competition. Football is, by its very nature, a competitive sport. And children need to learn that. The overwhelming majority probably like that part of it too. But, what we don't want to see is coaches running young sides for results. If that happens, as it often did in the past, then you just end up with needless streaming, kids being sidelined, kids dropping out and development coming a distant second to results. And that's not doing anything to create positive memories for *everyone* involved.'

The Respect League in Manchester is the perfect embodiment of this new approach. Developed by local coaches, the league operates on a principle of development first.

'The league has a set of guiding rules, which cover things like equal time for every player, silent sidelines, playing kids in every position and, perhaps most importantly of all, mixed ability. Everything is about long-term development and not about short-term results. The Respect League is great because it gives you the perfect environment to just let the kids play and have fun, which is what football should be about at this age,' says Ben Hamilton, who coaches with Respect League member Hough End Griffins.

What the FA and initiatives like the Respect League are trying to do is effect a sea change in what it means to experience junior football in England today. And, as with any sea change, the transition has not come without challenges. Take the current Level One, for example. As good as it might be, acquiring one doesn't come cheap. The fee varies from county to county but can range from around £140 to £190. And for those who want to progress to the more sophisticated and in-depth Level Two, the cost can range from £350 to £420, depending upon which county FA you learn with. For clubs and coaches, there is no fixed way to pay for this. Sometimes local leagues contribute, other times the club pays everything and there are many times when the coach has to fund it themselves.

This inconsistency and the significant cost involved is part of the reason why, in a recent survey into the grassroots game undertaken by the FA, only 27 per cent of coaches had a positive view on their opportunity to progress along the coaching pathway.

'For a lot of clubs, money is very tight,' says Peter Edgar of MHS, a junior club based in Huyton, Merseyside. 'And finding hundreds of pounds to put a coach through even a Level One course is beyond them. Sometimes, I don't think the FA appreciates how financially challenging running a grassroots team is. The Level One is a great course, and for what you get it's probably good value for money. But it's still expensive. I had to put my hand in my own pocket to pay for my course. And I'm not alone in doing that.'

And when it comes to the more 'progressive' football environment, one rooted in development and less focussed on results, not every club is so 'on board' with the approach. I caught up with Andy Garrett several months later, as his side were completing their season on a sunny spring morning in the Kent countryside.

'You look at this game today and it makes you feel so positive,' he explains. 'Neither side is streamed, all the kids are getting equal time and everyone is playing in lots of different positions around the pitch. Although the kids want to win, that's natural, development is still paramount. And, just as important, you saw there at the end that everyone left with smiles on their faces, irrespective of the result.'

He contrasts that with a game played a few weeks earlier that, despite the passage of time, still evidently frustrates him.

'We played a team, I won't say who, that did everything the opposite to what you see today; streamed, fixed positions, unequal time. They won the game easily. What upset me was not the result, but the fact that two of their subs barely came on. That's two kids putting in the effort to turn up and getting next to nothing back in return. And that's all just so the coach can get a win. How long are they going to stay in the game? We are meant to be creating an environment that encourages kids to want to come back, week-in, week-out. The look on their faces at the end of the match suggested to me two kids who were falling out of love with football.'

Rob Selby, who has had similar experiences, thinks that the problem is a generational one:

'People my age grew up with football being run in a certain way. It was results driven, quite tough and unyielding and, when it came to coaching, pretty reductive. I think a lot of people do the Level One because they have to but only pay lip service to the philosophy it preaches. I'd say that about half of the clubs we play stream at this age [U11], they put kids in one position and they play it long. They do this because the coach wants to win. And at this level, that kind of approach is brutally effective.

23

You see on the touchlines just how much it matters to them. I've seen some coaches absolutely lose their shit at times, acting like they are Jürgen Klopp or something. To change that mentality might take years. You might have to wait until the kids we are coaching today become coaches themselves, kids who have been brought up in a different environment.'

Despite the changes that have taken place in the game, as much aimed at attracting and retaining players as they are about creating better footballers, keeping kids invested in football is increasingly a challenge for grassroots clubs. Although millions of children are still playing, and football remains the highest participation team sport in the country, according to Statista, since 2010, the number of five-to-ten-year-olds participating in football (including five-a-side) has fallen by four and a half per cent, and those aged 11 to 15 by five per cent.

Part of this is cultural. Children now spend less time outdoors than their parents did. Recent research by the National Trust discovered that children are playing outside for an average of just over four hours a week. This compares unfavourably with the average of eight hours that their parents played outside each week when they were young.

And while outside, today's kids are also playing less and less sport, with one in three children in England, on average, doing fewer than 30 minutes of physical activity a day – half the amount recommended by government guidelines.

This trend can be attributed to a number of factors, including parental fears, lack of green spaces and the lure of digital technology, all of which have collectively led youngsters to lead increasingly enclosed lives.

'You can tell how much influence something like the Xbox has on kids by their goal celebrations,' says Rob Selby. 'When they are very young, and they score, they just leap about happy. By the time you get to our age group, it's a celebration they've learned playing *Fortnite*, *FIFA* or some other game. It's a huge part of their lives.'

But when it comes to football, the decline is also in part attributable to the experience on offer. As much as the FA has sought to improve the football journey of children through better coaching, the emphasis on enjoyment and the promotion of an environment centred on respect, the ability of so many clubs to attract and retain young players all too often falls down because of the facilities on offer.

To the casual observer, somewhere like Rotherfield, which is essentially a modest-sized community recreational field with five pitches (and a clubhouse attached) might not appear much. Yet, even something like the creation of this small, village football club has required years of continual hard work by the volunteers who run it.

Pete Ford has been involved, in some capacity, with football most of his life, playing and coaching with 13 professional and semi-professional clubs across Devon, Somerset and Sussex. His love of the game is apparent to anyone who talks to him for any length of time and it's a love that has helped transform Rotherfield over the past 25 years.

'I got involved with the first team back in 1992, eventually ending up as manager after I hung up my boots.'

Back then, the club and the 'rec' looked very different, as he recalls: 'There was no clubhouse, very few facilities, the current junior pitches were basically one big lake in the winter and our second pitch was an unusable bog. We had no junior club and so we were essentially a handful of senior teams who played on one decent pitch.'

Motivated by a desire to improve the facilities, Ford, and others, set about changing the club. 'First we added a junior section, something that helped us work towards FA Charter Standard status. Once we achieved this, it gave us access to Football Foundation funding, which was essential if we were to fulfil our plan of putting in better drainage.'

In 2006, ten years after it had begun the modernisation process, Rotherfield received £42,000 to improve the pitches from the Football Foundation, a funding body which uses money from the Premier League, the FA and the government to invest in grassroots football.

'We had to find £22,000 ourselves, which wasn't easy. It took a lot of hard work and fundraising. Once we had the full amount we could get started with "Operation Drainpipe", which took about a year. With that achieved we were able to not just offer a better quality surface, we could also expand as suddenly we had so much more space. Since then, we have doubled the size of our junior section and now have around 200 kids.'

Although in a better position, the costs facing the club have increased as a result of the modernisation that has taken place. Along with the costs involved in building and maintaining new facilities for the expanded membership (clubhouse), the pitches require plenty of tender loving care, as Ford explains:

'The annual costs for pitch maintenance are around £8,000, including equipment, grass seed, fertiliser, top dressing, verti-draining and pitch marking. We employ contractors to undertake some of this work, but the majority of the routine maintenance is completed by club volunteers (average of five hours per week all year). Without our volunteers, I don't think we'd be able to keep our pitches in such good shape.'

When it comes to facilities at grassroots, worryingly, stories such as Rotherfield's are becoming less common, a trend perfectly illustrated by a match taking place on another autumnal Saturday morning, 60 miles north in Tooting, south London. Or rather it should have been. On the morning I arrive, at the last minute, the game has been called off due to the appalling quality of the pitch.

'The problem we have,' says Matthew Pennington, U10 coach with Tooting Park Rangers, 'is that our facilities are not really for football at all.'

Tooting Bec Common is one of many open spaces that populate this part of the capital, a much-needed oasis of greenery amidst the urban sprawl. With indoor and artificial pitches limited, and often prohibitively expensive, it is, for many of those who want to play football locally, the only realistic option available. But, according to Pennington, it's also one that is rarely attractive.

'What you have here are just areas of the common that have been marked out. These are not fenced off football pitches. We share this space with the community, so that means anyone can walk over it. The result is that it is chronically overused, poorly maintained and totally unsuitable for football. Both matches and training are frequently cancelled and when they do take place, this is not a surface conducive to attractive football. In fact, it's safe to say that if Andrés Iniesta and Xavi were born in Tooting, they'd probably be fucked.'

Pennington is describing a football experience that will be familiar to many whose kids play the junior game. Across the country, grassroots football at this level is plagued with tales of postponed matches, of grass surfaces like quagmires, of sloping pitches, of molehills, of bumpy pitches, of crumbling facilities, of no facilities, of disappearing touchlines, of wonky touchlines, the list goes on and on.

'And don't forget the dog shit,' adds Tooting Rangers U7 coach Mike Quigley, 'lots and lots of dog shit.'

Was it always like this? I remember playing junior football in Liverpool during the 1980s and can recall some abysmal pitches. There was one near the Mersey in Speke that was so sodden in the winter that you'd need to adopt front crawl in the 18-yard box. Grassroots football in England has been poorly funded for as long as most people can remember. And for much of that time, it was sort of accepted. Football, from the top to the bottom, had a rough-and-ready quality about it. Just a casual look at some of the quagmire-like top-flight pitches from clips of *Match of the Day* in the 1970s and 1980s reveal that the gap between park football and Division One was not as big as it should have been.

But the telling difference for many coaches, when comparing today with the past, is the volume of postponed games.

'I've coached around Liverpool for decades, a city that gets its fair share of wet weather. But whereas in the past games might be called off now and then, in recent years you're getting games called off week after week, with kids sometimes not playing for over a month. And even when the kids do play, the surface is often shocking,' says Kenny Saunders. In his day, Saunders was a classic number nine, an old-fashioned target man who scored twice on his only appearance at Anfield for Liverpool Reserves, and then spent the remainder of his playing days regularly scoring for fun at an array of local non-league clubs. He also spent many of those days, and the ones that followed retirement from playing, coaching around south Liverpool.

'Through my years of coaching, I've got a first-hand perspective on what's changed. In recent years the situation has definitely deteriorated. You have kids around here, a lot of kids, who are playing on pitches that the Dutch wouldn't deem fit for grazing cattle. You have clubs who have no facilities for changing or storing equipment and you have kids having to piss in bushes because there aren't even toilets available. Against that, you have a top division in this country that has never been wealthier. Combined, the players at one club, like Manchester United, earn more in a year than we invest in grassroots football over the same period. How is that fair?'

Saunders's solution to the problems that clubs are facing is to take the money from those who have it, namely the Premier League.

'The campaign I launched is called "Save Grassroots Football" and it calls on the government to impose a five per cent levy on the Premier League's TV revenue, which is currently around £9bn for its most recent three-year deal. We have a petition on Change.org where we are trying to get 100,000 signatures of support in the hope of getting this issue talked about in Parliament.'

For Saunders, and his supporters, the juxtaposition within English football, the fact that a game which has never been wealthier is also suffering from chronic under-investment, is something that should not be tolerated.

'The Premier League blew well over a billion pounds in this summer's transfer window alone, so the money is there. All we are asking for is a tiny slice to ensure that the footballers of tomorrow have a much better football journey than they do today. In towns and cities across the country how can it be right that you have incredibly wealthy clubs and then often right next to them, kids playing football on fields that are basically useless?'

In its defence, the Premier League *can* point to the money it has given over to the grassroots game.

'Kicks is just one example of the great community work we do,' says Alistair Bennett from the Premier League. 'This programme uses the power of football to connect with young people in some of the most high-need areas of the UK. The youth outreach programme began ten years ago, with the aim to create safer, stronger and more respectful communities through the development of young people's potential, whilst providing access to facilities, coaching and mentoring.'

In its first decade, Premier League Kicks has engaged around 205,000 young people in weekly football coaching sessions held at local community centres across the UK. The programme is now run in 776 venues.

Alongside this it has also provided millions in infrastructure investment via the Football Foundation, which was established back in 2000. Since it was launched, the Football Foundation has awarded £1.5bn in funding to help improve around 3,000 grass pitches, to aid in the construction of over 800 artificial pitches and to assist in the building of around 1,000 changing rooms and pavilions – projects such as that wonderful pitch at Rotherfield.

'The money that we received from the Football Foundation was transformative. For small clubs like ours, raising the kind of money you need to make substantive changes to pitches and facilities is a real challenge. To do that without investment from the Football Foundation would, for many clubs, make the job even harder, and in many cases likely impossible,' says Pete Ford.

As was the case with Rotherfield, the Football Foundation typically does not provide all the funding. Although this approach is partly fuelled by limited funds compared to demand (and therefore a desire to make what cash is available stretch that bit further), according to Rory Carroll from the organisation, there is also the belief that asking clubs and communities to contribute has a long-term benefit to the facility provided.

'We have found, from our experience, that those who raise money to invest in pitch improvement or improvements to the facilities better appreciate the investment and tend to take better care of it. When the money is just handed out and no work is involved, do people have the same understanding of the value? We don't think they do.'

But not everyone agrees with the current funding strategy. Dave Horrocks is the academy development officer for Fletcher Moss Rangers, the little club tucked between a housing estate and a dual carriageway in the south of Manchester, where the likes of Marcus Rashford and Cameron Borthwick-Jackson first kicked a ball.

'We're in the process of trying to buy and then rebuild the facilities we have here off the council. At the moment they serve a purpose but they are not fit for purpose. We've got a leaky roof, not enough space and the whole building is looking tired to say the least. We could apply for Football Foundation funding, but even if we got it, that would mean the club having to raise a huge amount of money ourselves. For a club whose kids come from the less affluent areas of the city, that is going to be a challenge. When you think about how much money there is in the Premier League, and then consider how little they invest back into grassroots, does it seem right that the burden to invest is falling so heavily on clubs like ours?'

And the figures are stark. When it comes to fixing many of the problems facing junior football, for which the Football Foundation is the principal medium for change, for the financial years 2016–19, the Premier League invested around £71m. This equates to less than one per cent of the television deal for roughly the same period.

'These Premier League clubs are benefitting from our coaching too,' says Horrocks. 'It's clubs like ours who first develop young talent. And when the time comes for them to move on to a pro-club, those clubs get these kids free of charge. Pro-clubs do not recompense grassroots clubs. They effectively rape and pillage without any consideration for the future of grassroots clubs at all. They don't care how it affects our season or acknowledge the role we have played.'

Demands for elite football to provide greater support to grassroots have become widespread in recent years. Former FA chairman David Bernstein has called for a tax on the Premier League to improve grassroots facilities. Richard Caborn, the former sports minister, has suggested the establishment of a new formula for redistributing more of the top flight's television income. And the Labour Party, should it ever be elected, is committed to holding the Premier League to a promise, made back in 1999, that it would invest five per cent of its profits back into the grassroots game.

But to date, despite plenty of media attention and numerous campaigns on the issue, such as 'Save Grassroots Football', and 'Save our Game', a manifesto launched by *The Telegraph* back in 2018, little with regard to the Premier League has changed. And so the focus and frustration of many involved in football at this level has inevitably shifted instead towards the FA, the self-appointed guardians of the grassroots game.

Over the past few decades, it would be fair to say that when it comes to this guardianship, the FA has something of a chequered record. As recently as 2014, it lost £1.6m of public funding because it had done little to tackle a decline in the numbers of those playing football in England. While the sum was a small fraction of the FA's annual turnover, it was nevertheless a very public telling off.

For some of those who have been involved with grassroots football for many years, there has long been a sense of disconnect between the FA and the game at this level.

'I can tell you a story that perfectly sums this up,' recalls Dave Horrocks. 'A few years ago I was at an FA event and Trevor Brooking was there. Back then, Brooking was the FA's director of football development. So, we got chatting and I asked him, "can you do us a favour Sir Trevor, can you tell us what's your definition of grassroots football?" Without hesitation, he responded, saying it was, in his opinion, "academies and schools of excellence". I was gobsmacked.'

For Horrocks, it was a moment that perfectly captured the FA's attitude. 'It revealed a total misunderstanding of what junior grassroots football is. As far as I am concerned, grassroots football is a dad and lad kicking a ball about in the backyard. Then mum tells them to piss off and get to the park because they're ruining the grass. At the park they dodge round dog shit, burnt out cars and all sorts. As they're kicking a ball about a couple of other kids come along, and then a little game starts, next thing a little team gets made, then they join a league. That's grassroots.'

In the FA's defence, its approach to this level of the game *has* been characterised by a great deal more activity in the last few years and a growing realisation that its 'guardianship' extends further than 'academies and schools of excellence'. Alongside the revolution that has taken place in coaching (underwritten by investment in qualification provision and coach mentoring by the FA), there has also been an attempt by the organisation to try to tackle some of the problems that have beset grassroots football. Of late, the FA has become far more engaged with its responsibilities and far more willing to put its money where its mouth is.

'So now,' says Kelly Simmons, who was director of development at the FA from 2012 to 2018, 'we have increased levels of investment, in addition to our commitment to the Football Foundation. With this we have been able to develop an ambitious programme that is delivering meaningful change, such as improvements to more than 2,000 grass pitches across the country, creating 600 mini-pitches on school and club sites and a continued and sustained effort to significantly increase our national stock of 3G pitches.'

This greater level of commitment is best encapsulated in the FA's flagship 'Parklife' programme, part-funded by Sport England and the Premier League. Launched a few years ago, the initiative intends to establish a more accessible, sustainable model of grassroots football across 30 English cities and towns.

'Our "Parklife" hubs will provide floodlit 3G artificial pitches – which can be used all year round – new grass pitches, changing facilities and community spaces. They will be financially self-sustainable, open to all and flexible – catering for football activity, other sports and also other programmes such as education, health and wider community development initiatives,' says Simmons.

Despite the increase in investment, back in 2018 there appeared a tacit acceptance by the FA that more was needed. The organisation's attempt to remedy this shortfall was a bold one: the sale of Wembley Stadium to Shahid Khan, owner of Fulham FC and the Jacksonville Jaguars (of the NFL). The controversial plan, which was opposed by many involved in football, was thought to be worth around £600m, a significant part of which would form part of an ambitious long-term investment programme into grassroots football. Ultimately, the deal fell through, leaving the grassroots game no better off than it was before but with perhaps a more acute awareness of just how large the investment deficit in the sport is.

Irrespective of the shortfall, for an organisation that is frequently maligned, the FA has responded encouragingly and positively to its public wrap on the knuckles of a few years ago. There are hundreds of clubs around the country who have benefitted from its greater levels of investment, and long-term problems, such as a lack of artificial pitches and poor levels of coaching, are being addressed.

But for all the good it has done, despite the organisation's achievements, there is a sense that the FA is swimming against an increasingly difficult tide. And it is one powered by a singular telling statistic: the fact that 80 per cent of amateur football in this country is played on council-run grass pitches. And in the recent economic and political climate, that is a serious problem.

The reason for this can be summed up with one word: Austerity. The sustained reduction in public spending, which first began under the coalition government in 2010 and which has remained UK government policy under the Tories until very recently, has radically altered the public sphere right across the country. So severe has the programme been that a recent report by UN special rapporteur Philip Alston claimed that the UK government has inflicted 'great misery' on its people with punitive, mean-spirited and often callous austerity policies. These are polices that Alston claimed have driven millions into poverty, breached four UN human rights agreements and threatened the very fabric of society.

Although the cuts have touched almost every area of public spending, they have fallen particularly heavily on local authorities, largely through dramatic cuts in the Revenue Support Grant (money provided to local councils by central government). This, combined with a council tax cap (which has only been moderately relaxed in recent years) and rising demand for local authority services, particularly adult social care, has meant that many local councils have had no option but to slash their spending in 'non-essential' areas – areas, such as parks.

Overall, in the first six years of austerity, 92 per cent of park budgets were cut by local authorities in England, and some dramatically. Warwickshire County Council slashed its parks and green spaces budget by 87 per cent, Newcastle's has been cut by over 90 per cent and in 2018 Bristol City Council, which had already savagely hacked at its allocation for green spaces, flirted with the idea of making its parks budget cost neutral (eventually backtracking after public hostility to the plan).

A recent Freedom of Information request undertaken by *The Guardian* also revealed that in addition to slashing park budgets, many local authorities have been selling park football spaces to balance their accounts. The figures obtained showed that there were 710 fewer local-authority-owned or operated football pitches in the financial year 2017/18 than there were in 2009/10 – before the Tories' austerity project began. In England, the worst hit region was the north west, which lost 164 pitches during that period. Other heavily affected regions included London (54), Yorkshire (76) and the West Midlands (84).

'I completely understand why councils prioritise care for the elderly over something like parks. Some areas deserve priority. But that still leaves our parks bearing the brunt of the cuts. The problem with austerity is that it has meant that local authorities have been presented with choices that should not have to be made, choices like should we sacrifice the health of a town's or city's kids to pay for the care of a town's or city's elderly residents. It's a disgrace that those kinds of decisions have had to be taken,' says Kenny Saunders.

On the ground, the reality for those coaching junior football can be quite depressing, as Paul

Owens, who coaches girls' side Costello Vixens in Hull, explains:

'You have long grass or grass that's been cut and is just left on the pitch. You have slopes and parts of the pitch that are basically unplayable. Sometimes you don't really have markings, or markings so old that they are basically pointless. But perhaps worst of all is the fact that you simply don't have games. In the winter months games are just cancelled week after week. We had six cancelled in a row at one point. The surfaces aren't maintained properly, so the drainage simply isn't good enough.'

Every initiative brought in by the Premier League and the FA is laudable and the investment in infrastructure undertaken by the Football Foundation is welcome. But set against the unavoidable reality that so much grassroots football is played on pitches of poor quality and with facilities that are often dire or non-existent, it's questionable how effective it can be, something that Kelly Simmons acknowledges:

'In other European countries, such as Germany, the provision and maintenance of local sporting facilities is written into statutory law. By law, the local councils within these countries are expected to cater for the sporting demands within their communities – and are granted the funds to do so. That isn't the case here. So, our parkland has been hit. And that's frustrating for us because we are trying our best to improve the game in the face of an increasingly testing environment.'

Despite holding an iron grip on the country for the past decade, signs that austerity is nearing its end as a political force are now apparent. At the recent 2019 General Election, all the major parties (although some significantly more than others) expressed a desire to throw off the hair-shirt of the recent past and increase public spending.

Yet, depressingly, recent research by the New Economics Foundation revealed that at the current rate of change, it could take as long as a decade to return spending to 2010/11 levels. And even within this, there is no guarantee that local authority spending will necessarily recover completely. Much will depend on who governs and what their spending priorities are.

And locally, adult social care, a politically sensitive spending priority, will continue to consume more and more of available budgets. According to the Institute for Fiscal Studies, it is predicted to need billions in additional funding in the years to come, an outlay that might mean the continued squeezing of other services, such as parks.

Worryingly, the hostile environment that austerity has created over the past decade has not just resulted in poor quality pitches and facilities. It has also produced an environment that has become more costly for participants too.

One method employed by local authorities to shore up their park budgets has been to raise the prices for those that use park facilities, a trend that has afflicted football clubs right across the country in the form of increased pitch fees. In Birmingham, for example, some junior clubs have faced inflation rates of 45 per cent. In Wokingham, the figure has reached 60 per cent. And in Tunbridge Wells in 2018, some pitch fees for the town's junior clubs rose by nearly 70 per cent.

The historical context of just how much more expensive football is to play today compared to a generation ago was revealed by an *ITV News Central* investigation into the issue back in 2016. The broadcaster looked at the experiences of Sporting FC, who play in the Central Warwickshire Youth Football League. Back when the club was founded in 1994, it cost around £800 to hire its playing pitches for a season. In 2016 that figure stood at just over £10,000, with the cost rapidly escalating in recent years. Had the cost followed the rate of inflation since 1994, the figure should have been around £1,500.

And it's not just local authority playing fields that have been affected by this trend. School playing fields are often used by grassroots clubs, both as a place to play and train and as a place to run lucrative spring and summer fiestas. But increasingly less and less space is available at a reasonable cost as schools, under pressure to ease their own budget constraints, are either selling fields off or handing them over to private management companies (who appear to have no problem maximising profit from this asset).

One club who found out just how costly this trend can be was Ormskirk West End FC. For over a decade, the Merseyside junior club had been running an annual summer tournament for thousands of children on the playing fields of the nearby Ormskirk School. But in 2018 the school outsourced the letting of its facilities to School Lettings Solutions, including the field used for the tournament. When confirming the booking for its tournament in 2018, the club was astonished to find that the price had been increased from the previous year by over 400 per cent. Despite pleas from the club, School Lettings Solutions refused to reduce the price. The increase meant that the club had no option but to cancel its tournament, denying local children the chance to participate in a fantastic sporting event and costing Ormskirk West End a significant amount of its annual budget.

'Football is definitely becoming more expensive,' says Peter Edgar. 'All in, at the moment, to cover our costs, which include things like league fees, training session fees, refs' fees, equipment and kits, parents of players at our club are paying £30 per month. I think that's a staggering amount of money when I think back to what my parents used to pay when I played as a kid. Even with that money, it's been common for me to chip in from my own pocket to make up shortfalls when we have them. And I know for a fact that there are some parents who haven't been able to afford to pay what it costs to send their kids to play at this club. As a result, their child has had to walk away from the game. Which, in this day and age, is an absolute disgrace.'

There is a fear amongst some that even those well-meaning attempts to 'improve the game' could exacerbate the problem of rising costs. Take 'Parklife' for example:

'Inevitably, because you're talking about a high-end, artificial football experience, something like "Parklife" will cost more than a normal, local-authority-owned, grass pitch. If you rang up today to hire a full pitch for an hour in one of Liverpool's hubs, it would cost £180. Of course, for that, you're paying for reliability and quality. Games won't be called off very often and the surface you play on will be "perfect". But there is a worry that the hubs will start to just cater exclusively for those clubs and individuals that can afford it while those without the means will be priced out,' says Kenny Saunders.

There is a danger that the installation of 'Parklife' hubs, however welcome, creates something of a two-tier system locally, where the elite pay to play on high-quality surfaces and the rest are forced to remain on deteriorating park pitches.

'And how is that fair?' says Saunders. 'A big part of what the FA have done in recent years is to try and improve the football journey that kids experience. But there is a danger that what we are creating today is one fantastic experience for the better off and one inferior experience for those kids from poorer areas. How is the sense that you are getting a second-class experience going to encourage kids to stay in the game? Creating more artificial pitches is a good thing. But it needs to be done hand-in-hand with investment in our existing stock of grass pitches. At the moment, that just isn't happening.'

Focussing on artificial football runs further risks too. A huge amount of the football played by kids is informal, a kickabout on the school fields after the end of the school day or a bit of three-and-in down the local park on a weekend.

'There's a danger that with something like "Parklife", you're saying that football provision is covered, and increasingly local authorities can keep selling off park land and schools can keep selling off their fields. Everybody gets excited when a new artificial pitch opens up, but that is sort of negated by the fact that a lot of the open playing fields that we all grew up on aren't available anymore,' says Jen O'Neill, editor of *She Kicks* magazine.

Football has long prided itself on its accessibility. It might have become a turn of phrase that seems to mark its user as some misty-eyed romantic, rooted in the past, but 'jumpers for goalposts' perfectly summed up the simplicity of the game. Give them a ball and a few jumpers and kids could do the rest themselves. And even as their involvement became more sophisticated, with teams and kits, the barriers to entry were reassuringly low. But, for many that appears to no longer be the case. In Austerity Britain, the people's game does not apply to all the people.

'Over the weekend, I was watching games on other pitches and three teams – under-12s, 13s, 14s – only had nine players on the pitch; not even the full quota and no substitutes. And this is in Liverpool, a city that lives and breathes football. Even before the end of this season, in our junior grassroots game, thousands of kids will walk away from the sport and teams will continue to fold. Rising costs will play a part in this. As too will the quality of the pitches and the facilities on offer. Under investment is killing the game for these kids and these clubs,' says Kenny Saunders.

Since he founded 'Save Grassroots Football' back in 2014, Saunders has launched several petitions and has yet to reach his target. 'Which is frustrating,' he admits. 'It worries me that a lot of people are paying lip service to the campaign but not following through. This is a serious issue that is afflicting the football journey of our kids. And so, we need the government to act.'

But even if his campaign's efforts come to nothing, and no national action takes place, 'should we as fans not be saying to the clubs we support, "why aren't you doing more?"' he asks.

'Take this city,' he continues, 'we have two massive clubs in Liverpool, each with great community foundations. So for a while we've been asking them to do more. You're talking here of a game that brings with it all kinds of benefits to the community, which produces their stars of tomorrow and which is actually related to what they do as clubs week-in, week-out. A few million quid, for example, is nothing to the likes of Everton and Liverpool. But for the grassroots game on Merseyside, having that amount invested each year would be transformative, revolutionising the football lives of thousands of kids in the process.'

And there are signs, in that city's case at least, that clubs are starting to listen. In November 2019 it was announced that Liverpool and Everton were committed to investing £75,000 a year into a Grassroots Football Development Fund, done via their respective community foundations. The investment would be there to provide equipment, training opportunities and pitch-time for clubs, leagues and families who may face financial barriers.

'I think it's definitely a step in the right direction,' says Peter Edgar, 'one which all Premier League clubs should be participating in with the amount of money being thrown about. Hopefully it can be put to good use and get more pitches playable during the winter, get more kids involved in football, help those parents who can't afford for their kids to play and also improve the quality of the kids coming through the system in years to come.'

Football, at all levels of the sport, is dependent on the junior game. It is from its ranks that the players of tomorrow will emerge, whether that's those turning out for sides in the glamorous top flight or the millions who play Saturday and Sunday football. But more than just those who play, it is also from their ranks that future coaches will emerge, future referees, and those who administer the game, whether at leagues or at clubs. Junior football is the production line for adult football. And it is one that needs to be affordable and attractive to those participating.

But, increasingly, for many it's not, turning instead into something of a lottery.

'And that shouldn't be the case,' Saunders argues. 'There is enough money in the sport to ensure that every kid in this country who wants to play football should be able to do so at an affordable price, on decent pitches and be taught by well-qualified coaches. That isn't the reality though. And unless something changes more and more kids are going to drop out of the game and more clubs will fold. I think people look at the Premier League and just assume that English football must be in good health. But down at the bottom, the game is sick. And it needs help desperately.'

Chapter Two

Out With the Old, In With the New

A COLD winter's morning on Hackney Marshes. It is, for many, the spiritual home of Sunday league football, an area that oozes grassroots authenticity.

The Marshes boom, in football terms at least, came in the years immediately after the Second World War. When London got round to clearing up the extensive debris created by the bombed out and bulldozed areas of east London, collective local authorities decided to dump the majority of rubble on the open lands on the edge of Hackney Borough.

'After it became grassed over, some of the first pitches were laid out on the foundations of this rubble, and before you knew it people were flocking with footballs and impromptu goalposts. With all the debris beneath, providing perfect drainage, it was one of the best surfaces in the city,' says Johnnie Walker, chairman of the Hackney & Leyton Football League.

Walker has been coming to the Marshes to participate in Sunday football since the late 1940s. 'I first played here in 1948, when I was in my mid-teens, probably 15 or 16,' he says. 'If you can believe it, the team I first played for was called Islington Queens! It didn't mean the same thing back then as it does today.'

In those days, the Marshes would host over 100 matches at a time, with thousands of footballers from all over London converging on the area, bringing with them supporters drawn from the ranks of friends and family members.

'There were about 120-odd pitches,' remembers Walker. 'There was so much demand to play in those days that if you could find a spare bit of grass, it was marked out. There were times, if you didn't look around, that when you took a throw in or a corner, you could find yourself on a different pitch!'

Seventy-odd years on, the Marshes remain the largest collection of pitches in London, a social and cultural phenomenon. To the uninitiated, the sight is a breathtaking one, a wide vista of amateur football. The air around is punctuated by the thuds of the ball, the shouts of players, the peep of whistles. And undercutting everything, the familiar stench of Sunday league: sweat, dirt and Deep Heat.

'There's no place quite like the Hackney Marshes on a Sunday morning. You look around and see all these teams competing, all these players turning up just for the love of the game and you appreciate just how important football is in this country. It's easy to just focus on the Premier League, that's where all the glitz and glamour is. But for me, this is real football, 22 players giving it everything, just because it's what they love doing,' says Joe Lodge, who manages local club Bocca Albion.

There is a feeling of permanence about the Marshes that would resonate with anyone who has ever played Sunday league. It's been 20-odd years since I last turned out on a Sunday (a penchant for weekend lie-ins and the easily accessible joys of five-a-side curtailing my less than stellar career) and yet, even though time and geography separate my experience from those playing today, there is a sense of familiarity that bridges the divide.

The language helps. How we speak in the wider world might be in a state of constant flux, but in the world of Sunday football time appears to have stood still. 'Where's the Talking?', 'It's Still 0-0', 'We've Gone Quiet', the familiar refrains that have seemingly always rung out across pitches ring out today. Two decades might have passed, but even now when I hear the shouts of 'Out!', I have a near Pavlovian response to leg it upfield.

But as key as the sounds are, just as important are the sights. The handful of players turning out in unwashed kit, the evident hangovers, the crafty ciggies at half-time. Coaches still deliver bollockings from the touchline, good goalkeepers remain gold-dust, and some tackles continue to verge on the X-rated. On watching, I'm transported back to my younger years, freezing my knackers off at left-back, lining up against the pub teams of south Liverpool, horizontal rain whipping in from the Mersey, sometimes wishing, as the old joke used to say, that I was 'left-back in the changies', or 'right-back at home in bed'.

But, although the feeling exists that the Marshes have, in many ways, stood still, there is undoubtedly change evident too. This is no 'preserved in aspic' notion of

English grassroots football. For a start, the demographics mirror that of modern London, a slice of the multicultural city at its best.

'Years ago, when we first got all-black teams in the league, there was a little bit of trouble. But that's all long passed now. We have teams from all kinds of different communities and we all just get along and play the game. That's what I like about football, it brings the whole community together. We all get on great. We're all friends. And everyone respects one another,' says Walker.

And the football looks different too, visually and stylistically. Coloured boots appear the norm, tricks and worldies (not always successfully) punctuate the play and you even see a few players adopt the 'Ronaldo stance' on free kicks (a move made slightly ridiculous when the free kick balloons into a different borough).

'The pace of the football is different as well,' admits Walker, a hint of regret in his voice. 'It's faster now, but probably gentler too. It was a lot more physical years ago. You used to get stuck in, "no quarter given, no quarter asked," they used to say. Some players today don't seem to like that part of football anymore.'

But although the Hackney Marshes remain impressive, they are not what they once were. Today, there are just over 80 pitches to play on, many lost as slivers of land have been shaved off over the years. Most recently, the Olympic Park has encroached on the parkland, with several pitches lost to associated developments.

Along with this shrinkage, there are also fewer clubs using the pitches than was once the case. Although Walker cites several factors for this – restricted car parking, cuts to bus routes, the limited number of (albeit better quality) dressing rooms – part of it simply mirrors a trend that has affected Sunday league football across the country, one that has seen clubs fold at an alarming pace and players walk away from the game in droves. In fact, the Hackney Marshes have done well to remain so robust. The marginal decline in the number of teams playing there on any given Sunday is dwarfed by what has happened elsewhere.

A recent study commissioned by the FA found that 2,360 grassroots football teams had folded in a three-year period between 2012 and 2015, many from the ranks of Sunday football. Alongside this statistic is an equally depressing one – around 180,000 players aged 16+ had dropped out of the game since 2005.

The conveyor belt that once worked so seamlessly, transporting juniors to Sunday league, has broken down. Fewer and fewer are coming through, and for those who do the hunger for the game that sustains them through junior football no longer appears strong enough to sustain them during adulthood.

'Clubs have always come and gone. That's the nature of Sunday football. Often clubs are just a group of mates who start off with enthusiasm, which then wanes as time goes by and the grind of Sunday league hits home. But what's happened recently is something different. You're seeing more established teams go under and you're seeing fewer teams coming through to replace them,' says Walker.

So great has the exodus become that many leagues have been forced to close down, a problem that has affected the whole country, illustrated by the recent closure of the Chichester and West Sussex Sunday Football League after 51 years, the Middleton Sunday League in Manchester, which folded after 50 years, and in the North East the closure of the Middlesbrough and District League, which once boasted 42 teams in its heyday and held the honour of being the oldest Sunday league in the country. These are just a selection of the many leagues that were once so vibrant and which have now disappeared because the clubs and the players are simply no longer there.

The folding of the King's Lynn and District Sunday League in 2019 represents a familiar tale. The league first began in 1963, and, although teams often came and went, participation remained healthy. Just a few years ago, the league ended the season boasting 21 teams.

But a sharp decline in participation precipitated a crisis. At the end of the 2018/19 season, just five sides remained. After further withdrawals and no new arrivals, by June of 2019 it was evident the league would be forced to close due to lack of interest. Fifty-six years of local football history down the drain.

League spokesman Rob Bunting told the *Lynn News* that, 'we have tried anything and everything over the last three or four years to increase numbers, being very pro-active to try and stave off the inevitable. We introduced equalisation fees on referees so everyone paid the same over the season. We offered free kit initiatives. We've even been lenient on administrative fines to keep costs down.'

The league also established a fund for new teams to help with start-up costs, but it received no interest. The players and the clubs were just not there.

Why this nationwide decline has occurred has its roots in a number of factors that have increasingly made it a challenge to run football clubs at this level.

'For a start, the culture isn't for everyone,' thinks Adam Hurrey, author of *Football Cliches* and a long-time Sunday league devotee. 'It's perhaps not as aggressive as it once was, but it remains very "masculine", which often clashes with modern sensibilities. It still amazes me how perfectly reasonable people get so angry in Sunday league football. I think a lot of it is just habit. We just sort of accept that football is a sport where people can behave like that. You see it on the terraces and you see it in Sunday league. And I doubt any "respect" agenda will stop that completely. It just seems that's the way it is. And you can appreciate why it might turn some people off.'

The football experience matters when this medium of the game is trying to compete for the attention of adults who, because of wider societal changes, are increasingly viewing playing weekend football as an activity less and less deserving of their diminishing free time.

According to a recent Active People survey from Sport England, 57 per cent of UK adults have played no sport at all in the last month, the highest proportion of inactivity in a generation. One reason suggested for this is the way that we now work. UK workers currently put in the longest hours in Europe, averaging 42 hours per week, up from around 37 hours back in the 1980s. Set against this, it is perhaps unsurprising that sporting participation has declined, as time-poor individuals find it a challenge to find a place for sport within their work/life balance.

A time-hungry pursuit like traditional 11-a-side football was always likely to suffer in light of this trend. But even amongst those who *do* want to regularly participate in sport, the appeal of this form of football has declined. Recent research by the University of Kent revealed that for these adults it is sports like athletics and cycling, those where the time and location of the activity is very much in the hands of participants, that are taken up in place of team sports like football, rugby and cricket, where the opposite is the case.

Then there is also the idea of a person's 'football fix' being delivered in other, more accessible means. The digital revolution that has taken place over the course of the past few decades has both transformed people's appetite for football, and at the same time changed the way we consume it. Given the prominence of online gaming and social media, which have become increasingly accessible through our consoles, phones and TVs, more and more of us are getting our football fix via non-physical means. The lure of Sunday league is perhaps not so appealing when you could dedicate those same hours to getting to Division One on *FIFA*, watching the highlights from Saturday's top-flight games on Sky, or building your squad on *Football Manager*.

'I've found that it can be a real struggle just to get eleven players on a Sunday. Teams that I've played in around London have had to use Gumtree just to get enough players out. One time we ended up with a 5ft 2in Ecuadorian goalkeeper. And another time we got a player who had an ankle tag and claimed he was Neymar's cousin. You do spend occasions lamenting why you don't have eleven friends,' says Hurrey.

Like their junior counterparts, those playing Sunday league also have to experience the appalling pitches and facilities that grassroots football has to offer.

'We had some ropey ones at away games, slopes, wonky lines, endless divots. At home, we mostly played Lower Breck – Breckside Park, Anfield. The council didn't cut the grass enough, and then you'd get a few idiots riding scramblers on them or lighting bonfires and ruining the grass. And, of course, there was loads of dog shit, which seems to be a given nowadays for Sunday League,' says Jim Taylor, who spent eight years managing Blackthorne FC in the Liverpool & District Sunday League.

The majority of junior sides, more often than not, arrive in kit and leave right away after the game has finished. Because of this, they tend not to experience the changing rooms and showers on offer at local-authority-run pitches. 'And that's probably just as well,' says Mark Hunnisett, manager of AFC Goring, who play in the Worthing & Horsham Sunday League. 'You do get some good ones, but there are some that are disgusting. Sometimes, the players just think it's preferable to go home muddy rather than chance using them.'

But at least these men's sides have access to facilities, even if they resemble something from a horror film. According to Katee Hui, founder of Hackney Laces, a community club for girls and women in Hackney, for women's teams, even appalling changing facilities are sometimes not an option.

'Pitches and facilities are as problematic in the women's game as they are in men's football. We encounter the same problems of poor facilities and pitches, but we have the added problem that in some places we can't even play in the first instance because there are no facilities for women at all. One of our sides was effectively barred from playing on Clapham Common because there were no facilities there. You know *why* this is the case, it's because there is barely enough money available to keep existing facilities going. But that doesn't make such an obvious example of discrimination any easier to take.'

Sunday league is competing for the attention of an increasingly disinterested demographic and doing so offering bumpy pitches, dog s**t and facilities that have embraced a 'POW-camp' aesthetic. It's little wonder that players are turning their back on the sport.

'And it's not helped by the rules and regulations that clubs face either,' says Sunday league stalwart and *The Athletic* sports writer Charlie Eccleshare. 'Right now, many of us playing the game feel like we are banging our heads against a brick wall, facing pedantic rules that seemed to have been created to deter people from playing football.'

'For example,' he continues, 'in the league I recently played in, every player had to send in a new passport photo before the start of each season. Who changes that much in a year? It might not sound much but managers have to spend their summers chasing people for passport photos in response to angry communications from the league telling them they are approaching the registration deadline. And that league was not uncommon in doing this. Surely things could be done better?'

And then there's what happens on the pitch. Amateur football is as codified as any professional game that takes place on a Saturday afternoon, and failure to adhere to these codes can result in a series of fines. The sums might be smaller than in professional football, but, as Eccleshare explains, their coverage is extensive:

'Alongside the obvious things, like fines for yellow and red cards, you have fines for things like the failure to wear numbered shirts, for not having a captain's armband, for wearing the wrong colour shorts/socks, for a late team sheet, for an incomplete team sheet, for a missing team sheet. And on it goes. If you have a game with a lot of cards, and some other violations, it can end up costing the club a fortune. And I question, considering this is only amateur football, whether some of these are necessary and whether they need to be so expensive.'

These fines are only adding to the escalating costs that many Sunday league teams are facing. According to research undertaken by Kitlocker, anybody considering setting up such a side, should account for the following costs (based on entry into the Sheffield Imperial Sunday League in 2017):

Area	Cost
FA Affiliation	£80 (Season)
League Affiliation/Entry	£88 (Season)
Pitch	£500–£1000 (Season)
Kit	£250–£600
Referee	£25–£35 per Game
Balls	e.g. 5 at £10 = £50

'The cost is becoming a big issue,' says Matt Hendrickson, whose Mendip Broadwalk Sundays FC side play in the Bristol Premier Sunday League. 'They are rising and it can be a struggle for teams with no backing. The game still has great appeal, having a laugh with your mates, win or lose. You can't beat the bond you have with your football lot and I wouldn't change it for the world. But there's no doubt that you're paying more and more to experience it. And for some clubs, it can prove too much.'

Of course, alongside spending, clubs have the ability to raise money. Paying to play, or subs, are the most obvious way of doing this. And most clubs have been compelled to put fees up in response to the rising costs they are facing. But as subs rise, players are understandably wary of fronting up cash without the guarantee of playing time.

'When it's so expensive to play in the first place, you can't really expect someone to pay the same as everyone else if they're going to be a substitute, or not even get picked that week. So, what we've done at our club is link the amount you contribute to the time that you play. And that way, if you're only on for the last 20 minutes, you'll pay less in weekly subs than someone who has played the full 90. You could collect more cash doing it the old way, but I guarantee that you'd soon alienate players, start losing them and before you know it, you can't put a side out. And there are plenty of other local clubs around here who have that problem,' says Mark Hunnisett.

In the past, it was common for Sunday league teams to be connected to a pub, often either being organised by the pub itself or emerging out of late-night boozy sessions amongst mates who, in a bout of drink-inspired over confidence, believed that they still had what it took to make it on the pitch.

'Pubs were always great outlets for raising money for clubs,' says Johnnie Walker. 'And that wasn't just with sponsorship. They were places to hold raffles, do spot-the-ball competitions and put on quiz nights.'

But according to the Office for National Statistics, the number of pubs in England has fallen dramatically, from 52,500 in 2001 to 38,815 in 2018. With so many closing, it makes it hard for the clubs that are left to raise the kind of money they need to simply stay afloat. And so, sponsorship from local businesses becomes more important. It means hitting the phone in search of leads, asking for help on social media, putting the feelers out locally. It's time that many don't have.

'The problem is that a lot of Sunday league sides are effectively a one-man band, one person doing the admin, the coaching, the finances. People are time-poor and not everyone wants to invest the hours into something like a football club. But the problem is, the more burdens you add, like having to scour the local area for sponsorship, the harder things become,' says Hunnisett.

And he thinks the organisational side of running a club plays a key role in whether it has what it takes to survive.

'To thrive at this level, you need to be organised. If everything is in place, and you have help, it's hard but it can work. When I first started managing here, I did it all, because I had to, and it was probably too much. If I'd kept going like that, then I'm not sure if the club would've survived. Now, I'm lucky enough to have someone to do the finances and an assistant manager who helps sort the admin and is also on hand to take training if I can't get there. I've had players come to us because we're run well. They like the fact that things are done properly, that training *will* take place, that we'll have the right equipment. It's part of the reason why, as other teams struggle to put out an eleven, we have more players than we can use.'

In contrast to the activity surrounding youth football, where the FA belatedly realised that it had a responsibility to do something about declining trends in participation, there is a feeling amongst many of those involved in Sunday league that their plight is met with comparative indifference.

'By the time you reach adult football, the FA almost disappears from view,' says Joe Lodge. 'They're there for disciplinary issues and occasionally might get in touch with the league regarding changes to formats, but there's no sense that anyone at the FA is bothered about our development, how we play or whether we're being coached properly. There seems to be a "hands-off" approach to Sunday league. I think there's a sense that there's nothing in it for them, because once we're adults we're no longer brimming with potential, so there's no sense funding us at all. We're essentially written off.'

In the FA's defence, as with youth football, the organisation can point to the investment it has continually provided via the Football Foundation, along with its recent additional investment into projects such as 'Parklife', as proof that the label of absentee landlord is not entirely justified. It also organises the annual Sunday Cup, open to Sunday league teams across the country to vie for the title of champion of England.

'Is that enough though?' argues Joe Lodge. 'Of the millions playing adult football each week, Sunday league represents a hugely significant part. And those involved are facing an increasingly hostile environment. If things continue the way they have been, you are only going to see more players dropping out, more clubs folding and more leagues closing. A few 3G pitches is not going to change that.'

But are *all* these players leaving Sunday league actually deserting the game? Although the sight of clubs and leagues closing is lamentable, and in some ways preventable, in part it is also attributable to a shift in tastes that has seen other forms of football blossom in recent years.

'One of the great appeals about five-a-side is the fact that you can keep going into your 40s, 50s and beyond.

When I was younger, I could get up and down the pitch and could probably have played 11-a-side. By my age now, 53, I can't manage traditional football. But five-a-side still works for me. I've lost that burst of pace and the ability to charge up and down the pitch. But I can still contribute by playing at the back, spreading the passes and reading the game,' says James Brown, author of *Above Head Height: A Five-A-Side Life*.

Small-sided football (five-, six- and seven-a-side) is now one of the most popular forms of the game in the country. This was confirmed by a Sport England participation survey in 2015, which estimated that just over a million adults play every week.

'The beauty of this sort of football is how accessible it is,' says Gary Huxtable, who runs a weekly five-a-side game near Tunbridge Wells in Kent. 'It's local, quick and easy to arrange. Sunday league takes a huge time commitment for those who play and a lot of organising for those who run clubs. There's no way I'd have the time or the inclination to run a Sunday league team. And there's no way most of the guys who play here could justify taking hours off from their families at the weekend to play Sunday league. But doing this, which pretty much just involves me sending round a quick query on WhatsApp to see who is available, and players dropping in when they can, is dead easy.'

A lot of small-sided football, like the game put on by Huxtable, amounts to little more than a few mates having a kickabout, a slightly more formal version of the park or street football that many of us played growing up – flexible, easy to arrange and with a standard that is reassuringly low.

'This is not football played at its beautiful best,' admits Huxtable. 'It's a group of mostly unfit men in their 40s playing as you'd imagine a group of mostly unfit men in their 40s to play. When it comes to quality football, for our games it's a case of the spirit is willing but the flesh is weak.'

But for those who fancy something with greater structure and often of a slightly higher standard, a plethora of leagues has emerged in recent years to sate this particular hunger. And many of these, such as Leisure Leagues, who boast 150,000 players and over 1,000 leagues, have become big players in the sport, with turnovers heading into the tens of millions.

'There are lots of people out there who like the competitive, organised league structure of traditional football but don't have the time or the inclination to play something like Sunday league. That's why you've seen such a rise in popularity of things like Leisure Leagues. People can run teams or clubs with minimum fuss and things like referees' fees and kits are taken care of by the league. All you do is get six mates together, which is easier than getting eleven, and pay to play,' says Andy Thorley of UK Socca, the domestic governing body for small-sided football.

Despite the growing popularity of the small-sided game, professional versions have never taken hold. A number of tournaments have come and gone over the years – most notably the Atari Soccer Sixes, which emerged in the early 1980s, morphing into the Guinness Sixes before fizzling out, unwatched and unloved, in 1991. The latest addition to this less-than-grand tradition is Star Sixes, a biennial competition that sees former pros, such as Michael Owen,

Daniel Amokachi and Dietmar Hamann, compete for their respective national sides.

Whether the sight of these ageing 'stars', with burgeoning guts and creaking knees, huffing and puffing their way through a game of indoor football, will add to the future growth of the sport is debatable. But what is perhaps more beneficial to the development of small-sided football is the support of the FA. In the past, the organisation was fairly hands off when it came to non-traditional mediums of the sport. But in recent years attitudes have changed, specifically in regard to futsal, the only FIFA and UEFA sanctioned version of five-a-side.

Born in Uruguay in 1930, futsal has become synonymous with flair and technique. The likes of Lionel Messi, Cristiano Ronaldo and Andrés Iniesta have all paid tribute to the beneficial effects of playing futsal in their youth.

'In places like Portugal, Spain and Brazil, futsal is something that young kids will likely play much more than "traditional" football. Their football diet growing up is very different to ours. And our version of five-a-side, playing off the wall with a fuzzy ball, is alien to them. For them, small-sided football is always futsal,' says Michael Skubala, head coach of the England national futsal team and the FA's futsal elite performance manager.

There are five principles that differentiate true futsal from hybrid versions of the 'old school' five-a-side. Futsal involves a bespoke ball (denser, smaller with a reduced bounce), taller goals (3m x 2m), a hard surface (largely indoors at top level), touchlines (not walls) and different FIFA laws of the game (four-second rule on kick-ins, set pieces and goalkeeper distribution).

'It's the constraints that are crucial for skill development,' Skubala explains. 'Unlike five-a-side, for example, you can't use the wall to get you out of trouble, so you start to develop strategies to get around this, maybe a skill or a neat one-two. The fact that it is played on a hard surface and not on astro or 3G is a constraint too as the ball moves faster. And the ball itself, which has less bounce, changes the way you play. It's a ball that encourages close control and short passing over just booting it forward.'

Today, futsal is played in more than 170 countries across FIFA's 211 member associations. It's estimated over 60 million people play futsal globally, equating to around 20 per cent of the number of people playing football worldwide (300 million).

Although the game has been around in England since the 1930s (there are pictures of it being played at the Hornsey YMCA in 1936), for most of the years that followed it remained a niche version of small-sided football.

'Like a lot of people who got into futsal years ago, I first played it at university, where it was quite established as a sport. When I got back home to Carlisle after graduating, the problem I found then was that there were absolutely no clubs, and so I sort of fell out of the game for a time. Outside of the university system, futsal was virtually non-existent in England back then,' says Al Tindall, chairman of the Carlisle Futsal Club.

Although the FA launched the Futsal Cup and established the inaugural national side back in 2003, the organisation's interest in this form of the sport inched along incrementally. The FA was perhaps held back by the glacial speed with which it shrugged off its decades-long attachment to route one, percentage football and the

POMO-obsessed theories of its former director of coaching, Charles Hughes, which dominated technical thinking longer than they should have. With Hughes's near-hostility towards unnecessary notions such as technical mastery, close control and trickery, for a long time the FA seemed diametrically opposed to a game like futsal.

'Before the FA really got involved, I think futsal was kept alive by people like us, people who took it upon ourselves to just start clubs up. It was very much a grassroots thing,' says Andrew de Santana, director of Helvecia, one of the country's leading futsal clubs.

Until recently, along with the university scene, a lot of the futsal played in this country owed its development to migrant communities, who brought their version of small-sided football into the UK.

'So Helvecia,' explains de Santana, 'came out of the large Brazilian community that lives in London. Brazilians coming to this country did not recognise the five-a-side game that people play here and wanted to establish a club where they could play the indoor football, or futsal, that they had grown up with.'

In recent years, the ad hoc development of the sport has finally been given more structure and support by the FA. This shift is embodied in the FA's 'Fast Forward With Futsal', a strategy for growth covering 2018 to 2024. It's an ambitious project that aims to make futsal the indoor sport of choice for footballers.

There are, according to Skubala, multiple reasons why the FA has chosen to get behind futsal. 'Nationally, we have great indoor facilities that we thought could be better utilised. Ours is a country blighted by poor weather, and in the winter lots of games in grassroots and lower level non-league football are called off. We thought if we could develop a competitive indoor form of the game, one with standardised rules, league structures and FA support, it would mean that grassroots clubs would have an alternative during the winter months.'

Allied to this is the development of a different kind of English player, something that is tied in with the England DNA.

'The FA, and grassroots coaches across the country, are all trying to build teams and players who play from the back, who are comfortable on the ball and who are intelligent decision makers. If we were trying to invent a way to do this, you probably couldn't do any better than futsal, which encourages all of the above. It's the perfect game,' says Skubala.

The FA strategy includes numerous ways to achieve its aims of making futsal a more popular indoor sport, such as embedding it in its support for schools' football, working with grassroots clubs to promote the game and investing to improve access to futsal facilities. Alongside this, the organisation is also working to increase the number of coaches.

'We need a skilled futsal workforce at grassroots level across the country, so coaches at clubs and teachers in schools can put on a futsal session for young players. Currently, we're delivering something like 3,000 futsal courses a year, so it is growing. But we want to move that number up across the' country over the coming years and really give our young players the best learning opportunities,' says Skubala.

Equally important for those playing the sport, specifically at a youth level, is the development of a clearly structured player pathway, something that 'FastForward with Futsal' is seeking to create. A key part of this has been the recent establishment of the National Futsal Series (NFS), which aims to catapult the quality of the futsal 'product' forward in England. The NFS is made up of two tiers. Tier One is a national division containing eight teams, the pinnacle of English futsal, with the winners granted entry into the UEFA Futsal Champions League. Tier Two is made up of two regional divisions, directly below the NFS.

'In other countries, people can choose to go and become futsal players. The infrastructure is there. We've not really had that in the same way. Now, increasingly, we do. If you want, you can decide to play futsal exclusively and the pathway is there for you to progress to one of the top clubs, like Helvecia and, if you are good enough, even represent your country. We have a tiered structure, just like we do in "traditional" football. It's not as big but it is growing,' says Skubala.

Despite the investment that has come from the FA, those involved in running clubs feel that there remain significant barriers to the sport's growth, as Mark Rutter, chairman of the Newcastle Futsal Club, explains:

'We face multiple problems that I know from talking to other clubs are shared across the game. Some of these are common within many mediums of football, like funding issues, rising costs, having enough volunteers. But we also have additional problems, such as there not being anywhere near enough indoor venues, coaching courses being difficult and expensive to access locally and a lack of support from some county FAs, a few of whom still don't seem to fully understand futsal. You want to attract as many kids and adults as possible to this sport. But that's not going to happen if clubs don't have enough qualified coaches or anywhere to put on matches.'

It is also a sport that, despite the FA's recent push, remains on the margins, as Andy Garrett of Rotherfield FC explains:

'Our kids play futsal midweek and they love it. But we're pretty much the only club around here playing it. If we had a competitive league to enter we could set up a Rotherfield futsal club, covering youth to senior level. But, as yet, the interest isn't there. I think part of the problem is that a lot of people still don't really know what it is. Although the FA have done lots of good stuff, there is still a long way to go. A lot of coaches of my generation still see "traditional" football as all that matters. For the sport to really flourish, you've got to change that mindset. And that might take years.'

When talking about football, whether it be youth football, Sunday league or small-sided games, the image of a player that often comes to mind, irrespective of gender, tends to exclude a significant proportion of the population. In our minds, understandably, football is a young person's game, and by 'young' I will generously stretch that definition to include people in their early 40s.

As someone approaching the extreme boundaries of that definition with a velocity I find uncomfortable, there was a time when your mid-to-late 40s, and the decades that followed, were assumed to be a time of your life that would, in terms of playing football, become something of a desert, as the knees gave in and the pace of younger players left you behind.

But that's no longer the case. The growth of small-sided football and the wider adoption of futsal are not the only examples of the inherent dynamism of the English grassroots game. In recent years, the sport has begun to innovate and develop new forms, in doing so reaching out to parts of society previously cut adrift.

'People want to continue playing for as long as possible, but want to do that against similar players in both ability and age. And that's where veterans', or "vets'", football comes in. A few years ago, we found that there was a growing demand from clubs around Liverpool to establish a vets' league as they had a lot of players who were ageing but who wanted to keep on playing,' says Stuart Carrington, FA Football Development Officer for the Liverpool FA.

Today the Liverpool FA boasts two 'vets'' divisions, one for over 35s and one for over 40s.

'When you're in your late 30s, you're still capable of playing weekend football physically but it's hard to compete against kids who are in their late teens or early 20s. And so, in the past, once you got to that age, that was it when it came to 11-a-side football. You were out to the knackers' yard. But with vets' football, you've got the chance to keep going into your 40s or even beyond. And one of the best things about it is the fact that you haven't got some nippy kid skipping past you. We're all of a certain age and so the playing field is level,' says Ste Coyle, manager of Liverpool's Abbey Road Veterans.

The innovations of the game for those of more mature years haven't stopped there. 'We have a version of vets' football, played at five-a-side, that has the added dimension of being non-contact,' says Paul Murtagh, chairman of the Birmingham Walking Football Club.

'Football was, until very recently, quite a limited game, in the sense that is was played a certain way, within certain parameters,' he continues. 'But that doesn't suit everyone, especially people who are over 40 and who perhaps are no longer able to cope with the physical side of the sport. There are plenty of people who want to play football but who don't want to endure sliding tackles, being elbowed off the ball, or the multitude of other ways that the game can impact you physically. By your 40s, the physical side of football can start to injure you in ways that can be tough to recover from. So, it makes sense to innovate and start offering forms of football that suit people's needs.'

The most popular of these innovations is alluded to in the name of Murtagh's club. To the uninitiated, walking football is exactly what it sounds like, the game played at walking pace.

'Since it first emerged a few years ago, walking football has boomed and is now the fastest growing sport in the country,' says Paul Carr, chief executive of the Walking Football Association (WFA).

'There were tens of thousands of people out there in their 50s, 60s and beyond who still wanted to play football but couldn't anymore because they were physically unable to cope with the games that were traditionally available. Walking football, with one simple innovation, has changed all that. Here is a game where you don't have to sprint alongside people half your age. You can play football at a much slower pace against people of a similar age and in similar physical condition.'

For an entire generation of people, male and female, the innovation of walking football has been transformative, as Peter Cribb, who plays for and runs the Grimsby Ancient Mariners, explains:

'It's hard to put into words how much it means to play again. But I suppose "magical" comes close. All of us doing this thought our days of kicking a ball were in the past, so it's wonderful to be pulling boots on again, getting out there and just playing this fantastic sport. And I can't tell you how much joy it gives me to see the look on the faces of the people at Sports Direct when I go in there, at my age, and tell them I need a pair of astro boots because I'm playing in a football tournament next week!'

Aside from the simple joy of 'pulling boots on again', the benefits of participating in walking football are manifold, specifically when it comes to health. Even playing football at a slower pace can improve levels of obesity and help tackle an array of chronic health conditions.

'Walking football is a great way to engage older adults and get them active again,' says Paul Kybert, chairman of Dexter Sports in Poole, which runs its own walking football side. 'But it's not just physical exercise where it can have a positive impact. There is also a social side to the game that is important too. It's a great way for older people to get together, to keep engaged with other people.'

According to the charity Age UK, over three million people above the age of 60 have depression, many of whom do not seek treatment from the NHS. Research by the Mental Health Foundation suggests that relationships are fundamental to mental well-being, but older men in particular are less likely to recognise their importance.

'Getting involved in a walking football club, or even some of the casual sessions that are put on by sports centres, can be a great way for older people to make new friends, to connect with people and develop a support network. It can also give you a sense of purpose, which is really important for people who have worked all their lives and suddenly face the uncertainty of retirement,' says Kybert.

To date, the rise of walking football has been a true grassroots success story in this country. Although the FA has got on board in recent years, working with the WFA on a set of rules and promoting the sport via county FAs, by and large this has been a bottom-up movement, one organised and fuelled by the people playing the game.

Jobe Berrington, founder and chair of the Brighton and Hove Walking Football Club (B&HWFC), is one such person.

'The whole thing's started quite informally,' he says. 'A few years ago I played in some walking football tournaments put on by Brighton and Hove Albion's community foundation and really enjoyed the game. But the city lacked a club. So, I advertised locally and put the word out that an informal session would be taking place in Preston Park one Saturday morning.'

Berrington hoped that he'd get a few interested people to come, just enough to make the session worthwhile.

'In the end, I'd been unnecessarily cautious in my hopes. I was inundated! Some were faces I recognised from the few games I had played in before but others were entirely new to me, people who I later learned had been hoping that something like this would be set up in the city.'

Three years on, the B&HWFC now has 50 members and two teams, the Dolphins and the Penguins. The club, which is mixed gender and mixed ability, draws from a variety of age groups.

'We have members as young as 50 and as old as 80,' says Berrington, 'all of them attracted by the idea of playing a sport that they thought they would never play again. It's this simple joy of playing football that really stands out as the main reason why our members keep coming back. Although the health aspect is great, more than anything people just love playing football for as long as they can.'

From small beginnings, not only has the B&HWFC grown, so too has the local walking football scene.

'We now take part in a monthly tournament,' says Berrington, 'that boasts 12 teams. These are great occasions. There's a real sense of camaraderie and great banter amongst those who attend. Although that's not to say that there is no desire to win. We might no longer be spring chickens but that doesn't mean, for some of us, that the competitive spirit has diminished.'

In just under a decade, walking football has expanded not just in England but across Europe too. So developed has the movement become that in June of 2019, the WFA hosted the European Nations Cup, a tournament featuring 160 players, representing eight different nations.

'We've come a long way in a short time,' says Paul Carr. 'Walking football is such a simple idea but it is one that has had a massive impact. I think it's a great example of what can be achieved in the sport if it is open to innovation. For a long time, football was very traditional, being played a certain way by certain groups in society. That is no longer the case and it should be celebrated. Innovation is changing the game for the better, making it much more inclusive.'

This sense of greater inclusivity is at the heart of another area in which the sport has innovated during the past few decades, an innovation that has brought the game to some of society's most vulnerable groups.

Justin Laidler is the chairman of South Tyneside Ability FC, a pan-disability football club that has been in existence in this part of the North East since 2011.

'There are a huge number of people out there who traditionally, because of their disability, would have been excluded from playing football, despite their desire to do so. In the past 20 years, more clubs like ours have emerged to provide these people with the opportunity to play the game that they love.'

From small beginnings, with just a handful of players training once a week, Laidler's club has gone from strength to strength and now boasts over 100 players, involved in three adult teams and two junior sides.

They are part of a wider trend that has seen participation in disability football expand over the course of the past 20 years. Prior to 1999, its development in England was limited, hindered by the absence of any coherent national strategy. That began to change as the new century dawned, first via the creation in 1998 of the English Federation of Disability Sport, an umbrella organisation for the eight national disability sports organisations, and then the establishment a year later of the FA's football development department, which led to the creation of the first disability football initiative: 'Ability Counts'.

'Since then, we have led the way in the promotion of the disabled game,' says Phil Heap, FA national participation manager (disability).

Today, disability football is embedded across the FA's most recent strategic plan (2016–20) and its associated strategic objectives, ensuring that the further development of this form of the game remains one of the organisation's key goals.

'Our philosophy is clear and guides all of our work within disability football. We believe that appropriate opportunities should be made available to all people irrespective of impairment, that, where possible, disabled people should be playing in mainstream football, and that player development pathways should be available from grassroots to the elite level for various impairment groups.'

The provision of mainstream opportunities is a more recent development but one that many clubs have embraced.

'Since we started with this age group about six years ago, we have had two children with disabilities play with us, one of whom is still with us in the under-11s. When I think back to when I used to play, kids like that would've been side-lined, probably out of the game altogether. It's great to see them today playing with their mates, having a good time and feeling part of the team,' says Rob Selby of Rotherfield Juniors.

Despite the support provided by the FA at both a national and a local level (the latter via specialised disability development officers), according to Justin Laidler, running a disabled football club still comes with manifold challenges, many more complicated that those facing mainstream grassroots clubs.

'Like any other club at this level we face the problems of poor pitches, poor facilities and a lack of volunteers. But added to this we have other issues that "traditional" clubs don't face. Our costs tend to be higher because our needs are more specialist. For example, we need a minibus to get to games, which is a significant expense for a small, volunteer-led club. We need specialist coaching, something that isn't really offered widely by the FA. And we also don't have access to local leagues. We take our players to tournaments instead, which are run around the country, something that again means more outlay.'

After nearly a decade of struggle, Laidler has finally got the club to a point of self-sufficiency. But it has been hard won.

'Funding is a constant problem for clubs like ours. There just isn't enough out there. The FA don't provide enough and local authorities simply haven't got the money to spend anymore. We've had to work so hard to get the sponsorship necessary to get our club to the position it is in now. But we can never be complacent. I know that costs will keep going up and up and that our sponsorship situation could change in an instant. You get into this because you want to simply coach football to kids who might be excluded from the game. But you end up almost spending as much time on the finances as you do on the actual coaching.'

Much of the football offered by grassroots clubs in this area covers pan-disability, providing an outlet to play within a medium that covers all disabilities. The resources often don't exist to offer more specialised forms of the game. For this, players tend to gravitate towards bigger clubs, often those in the Football League and the Premier League.

'We recognise that as a football club we have a responsibility to our community and so through "Palace for Life" we are constantly trying to provide services that enrich the lives of local people. In the area of disability football, that means establishing projects in schools, providing disability projects (and teams) that cover specialist areas, such as learning disabilities, powerchair or vision impairment, and making sure that anyone who wants to participate in football locally is not thwarted from doing so because of an impairment,' says Michael

Harrington, disability manager at 'Palace for Life', Crystal Palace's community organisation.

A good deal of the work undertaken by professional clubs via their community foundations, has been supported by the Disability Fund, a programme established by BT and the Premier League back in 2016, which has seen these two organisations invest to remove the barriers which at present mean that disabled people are half as likely to participate in sport as non-disabled people. The programme, which is delivered by 28 partner clubs, has so far reached nearly 36,500 participants, of whom about a third sustain their involvement over multiple sessions.

'You have to see it as a huge positive that through clubs like ours and the work that professional clubs do, the lives of those who would have previously been excluded from football are now enriched through involvement with the game,' says Justin Laidler. 'The innovations that have taken place in the sport over the past few decades have created this vibrant and growing part of football, one that will hopefully continue to grow in the future.'

The stories of clubs like South Tyneside Ability FC, the Brighton and Hove Walking Football Club and Helvecia illustrate that when people talk of a decline in adult football, the picture is not always as clear cut as is first apparent. For all the stories of Sunday leagues closing, of sides folding, of adults walking away from the game, it's also clear that alongside this, adult football is going through a period of innovation unmatched in the sport's history, one characterised not just by the creation of new formats but also by the sport reaching out to parts of the community for whom football was once something other people did.

And yet, despite the innovation and welcome broader appeal of the sport, there remains something undeniably sad about the decline of Sunday league. There is likely a generational perspective on this, a misty-eyed romanticism from those of a certain age, a demographic for whom six-a-side on a plastic pitch will always be a slight afront.

But, in reality, this form of the game was probably always on borrowed time. Austerity, and its accompanying savagery, might have hastened the decline, but for a while now Sunday league has been swimming against the tide.

'There was a time, back in our late teens and early 20s, when our Sunday league side was bursting with numbers,' remembers Steve Barnard, whose side, Romford Royals, used to play around the Essex town. 'And then, bit by bit, numbers dropped. A few had jobs that clashed, others had family responsibilities and some just didn't fancy the idea of getting the shit kicked out of you by some hungover meathead in the pissing rain, on a pitch that looks more like a ploughed-up farmer's field. And we're not alone. Most of the teams we played against are no longer around and the scene is not what it once was. Quitting didn't mean we'd fallen out of love with football. Enough of us, from lots of teams, still play five-a-side. But, bit by bit, Sunday league just lost its appeal.'

Chapter Three

For the Love of the Game

TO most, the names will mean nothing: St Francis Rangers, Gravesham Borough, West Witney, Jarrow Roofing, Glapwell FC, AFC Ludlow. There is a sense amongst football fans that the clubs we follow are permanent. They represent a certainty in our lives, an ever-present force that will always be there for us. And, of course, in the higher reaches of the pyramid this is largely true.

In their book *Soccernomics*, the authors, Stefan Szymanski and Simon Kuper, illustrate this point through the work of the economic historian Les Hannah. A few years ago, Hannah made a list of the top British companies in 1912 and researched what had become of them by the mid-1990s. He found that nearly half of these giants had simply disappeared, succumbing to a mixture of bankruptcy, nationalisation and takeovers. Amongst those that had survived, many had gone into new sectors, meaning that very few had managed to prosper within their original industry.

Considering that the time span that Hannah chose to look at included several recessions, a couple of depressions and two world wars, the fact that so many companies had suffered should probably not come as a massive surprise.

But over roughly the same period it would seem that the vicissitudes of the economic world didn't apply to English professional football. In 1923, the Football League consisted of 88 teams organised in four divisions. In the 2007/08 season, around the time the authors were researching the book, 85 of these still existed, 75 of them remaining in the top four divisions. Football seemed able to shrug off recessions, depressions and world wars in a way that no other industry could, as though the ebb and flow of market forces were of little consequence to the game.

There are many reasons for the uniqueness of football as an industry: the technology of the sport is unlikely to become outmoded, rivals from abroad are forbidden from entering a league and undercutting domestic clubs, and a team that fails to keep up with the competition can always survive in a lower league. The customers are different too. Put simply, supporters aren't 'normal' punters. When the business is failing and the team underperforming, most fans don't desert their club en masse. It's a form of brand loyalty that companies like Tesco and Asda must look on with a sense of awestruck envy.

But this sense of an industry inured to market forces, of one in which its participants can weather any storm they face, only really applies to the upper tiers of the game. Permanence, that feeling of a club always being there, is less evident near the bottom. Here, clubs *do* regularly disappear. And that's not because their supporters are less fervent in their following, that changes to the game are making them obsolete or 'rivals from abroad' are poaching their customers. It's simply because life down in the lower reaches of the pyramid is incredibly hard. So hard in fact that it's a surprise that there are so many clubs still going.

Stuart Daly is a man who lives and breathes amateur football. 'I've had decades in the game with this club and done the lot, player, manager, secretary, chairman, kit-washer, all over general dogsbody. I've experienced everything in football that you can imagine, the ups and downs, the frustrations, the heartaches, the moments of pure joy. But there's nothing quite like it. When the side lines up before kick-off on a Saturday, I think I'm as excited today as I was all those years ago.'

Daly's club, Roma, play in Division One of the Liverpool County Premier League, way down at Step 7 of the National League system. This is the structure for senior men's football that operates directly below the English Football League, stretching from the National League at Step 1 down to the various County Leagues at Step 7 (unrecognised 'Steps' continue below). The club is a stalwart of the local non-league scene, having been around for over 40 years.

In my youth, I had a mate who played for Roma, a player who was always a step above the rest of us. I can still remember the slight tinge of jealousy I would feel when his name would appear in the amateur pages of the *Liverpool Pink Echo*, the city's pink-hued Saturday sports paper. The exploits of my Sunday league side were never deemed worthy of inclusion, possibly because we were generally terrible.

Back then, Roma were plying their trade in the exotically titled I Zingari League, one of several Saturday leagues that catered for the city's near-exhaustive demand for football.

'The non-league scene in the 1970s and 1980s was massive,' Daly explains. 'There were teams everywhere and weekend football, on either a Saturday or a Sunday, was just a way of life for so many of us. People talk about Liverpool being a "football city". I think when they say that what they really mean is people following Everton or Liverpool. But for a whole generation back then it was about more than that. Football was something that you lived and breathed. It was something you followed *and* played.'

The *Liverpool Pink Echo* is no longer with us, disappearing in the early 2000s. The I Zingari went the same way too, merging with another league around the same time. The loss of both is symptomatic of a changing football culture in the city, one that Daly has experienced first-hand.

'Back in the 1970s, Roma had teams at every level, right through the junior game to the adult, sometimes more than one side. I think we boasted 15 teams at the club at one time. And now we've reached the point where there is just the senior side, and, to be honest, if it wasn't for me putting the effort in to keep it going it wouldn't even be around. It's sad to think that decades of local football heritage could just disappear once I decide to pack it in.'

Amateur football in Liverpool is not what it once was. 'It's a scene that's in decline,' says Jim Davies, who has been involved in amateur football in the city for decades and who, until recently, was the *Liverpool Echo*'s non-league correspondent. 'The number of clubs has dramatically dropped, leagues have shut down or merged. Twenty years ago there were three times as many amateur football leagues operating around here, with almost five times the amount of teams playing regular football.'

'And if that wasn't dispiriting enough,' he adds, 'the city is also seeing the demise of great local clubs. You only have to look at the recent demise of St Dominic's and St Aloysius, clubs that had been around since the 1930s, to see how bad things have become. Year-on-year, we're losing football history around here, as club after club goes to the wall and is lost forever.'

So lessened is the local amateur scene that 'Corinthian', the column that Davies had written for the *Liverpool Echo* for several years, and which under a variety of his predecessors had been a staple of the paper since the 1970s, disappeared in 2018. The *Echo* decided to take its non-league reporting in house, in the process massively scaling back its commitment.

What's happening in Liverpool is not unique. Across the country, in cities, towns and in rural areas, the same tale is told.

'Up here, we have lots of examples of grassroots clubs that are still doing well. Great clubs like Wallsend, one which always seems to thrive and remains well known for producing professional footballers. But equally, there are quite a few clubs that have disappeared and the amateur scene is perhaps not what it once was. Although every club that has gone tends to go for their own specific reasons, it's certainly the case that the environment for football clubs in the lower levels of the pyramid has got tougher around here in recent years,' says Mark Carruthers, North East non-league football writer for *The Chronicle*.

Most of us who play or who have played football generally experience the casual end of the sport: kickabouts with mates down the park, a bit of five-a-side. Even Sunday league, which requires a degree of commitment, does not demand high levels of fitness, massive amounts of travelling or even a particularly good level of footballing ability.

Although the lower levels of the pyramid are more akin to Sunday league, albeit a higher standard, in general, as you move up the pyramid, particularly as you edge closer to the National League, the difference in quality and what is expected of you as a player goes up and up.

Jamie Brotherton has been playing amateur and semi-pro football around the South East since he was 17, currently turning out for Saltdean United in the Southern Combination Football League (Step 5).

'Playing at this level is hard,' he says. 'You've got to put time into the gym and into training. It's physically demanding. People might look at our level, people who are used to watching football on TV, and think it can't be that tough. But it is. It's a huge step up from something like Sunday league, and to compete effectively takes effort and personal sacrifice. And I'm doing all of this for the love of the game because at Saltdean I'm not getting paid to play.'

Preparation, health and fitness. And all this while working full-time. Brotherton is not primarily a footballer, having worked as a teacher since leaving university in his early 20s.

'Like anyone working full-time, fitting in the demands of playing at this level is a challenge. There are lots of people who end up dropping out, good players, because their career comes first. You've got to appreciate that to compete we are putting in all this work and then training midweek and playing on a Saturday. And, on top of all that, we are also often travelling great distances on a Saturday too. The league I'm in now, the Southern Combination, covers two counties, so there are times when I could be doing a round trip of over a hundred miles.'

The very lowest reaches of the pyramid ask a lot of players, tapping into the same love of the game that powers Sunday league and junior football.

'When you're playing in the lower reaches of the National League system, and below, you're likely not getting paid,' says Stuart Daly. 'And often you're paying to play. So, that takes a lot of commitment. But the problem today is that attitudes are different to how they were in the past. When I played football years ago, people lived and breathed the game. But times change. Today, people seem less willing to put in what it takes to play as an adult at this level, particularly when they're not getting anything back in return. And so, it's getting harder and harder to get the players. You see teams struggle to get enough players, teams folding and even when new sides come along, they often don't last that long.'

The decline of football at this level mirrors that of Sunday league, in that the pool from which players have traditionally been drawn has contracted, a result of longer working hours, changing tastes and alternative ways to spend a Saturday afternoon. If increasing numbers of people are turning their back on Sunday league, it's perhaps unsurprising that the same has been equally true for a form of the game that asks considerably more of individuals.

But according to Jim Davies, there has also been a cultural shift amongst younger footballers that he feels has further eroded participation levels.

'The young lads who play football today are culturally not the same as the young lads who played football a generation ago. Back then, the manager was king and people respected him. That isn't the case now. Players do what they want. It's all, "I'll sign for these, see what it's like", "I'm not being spoken to like that, I'll jib this!" Players get dropped because they never showed up the week before and think "sod that I'll go and play six-a-side with my mates". Traits like loyalty, commitment and respect are declining. And it's undermining the fabric of the game. You need those elements to keep teams going, to keep leagues alive, to keep the sport thriving.'

But it's not just the decline in the numbers of those playing the sport that is leading to problems. The costs that clubs are facing are also escalating. Although in the lower levels of the pyramid wages are less of an issue, as you climb the National League system they increasingly become much more of a factor.

'You do get clubs around Step 6 and maybe even Step 7 that pay players, but it is less common,' says Matt Badcock, editor of the *Non-League Paper*. 'And even when it occurs, you're not talking about great amounts of money. From around Step 5 upwards, though, you begin to see more money enter the game. It's not the case that every club will pay players. You can have a club like Corinthian-Casuals, who play at Step 3 and don't pay their players anything. But those clubs become less common as you advance upwards. And those that are paying have found that wages are generally on the up. Non-league players, as a whole, seem to be better paid today than they were in the past. And for many clubs, that's a problem.'

But they aren't the only costs that clubs face. Irrespective of player wages, lots of clubs in the lower levels of the National League system try to cover the travel costs. And these can be quite considerable, as Bob Bacon, chairman of Binfield FC, explains:

'We don't pay wages but we do cover the expenses for our players. But the problem is that our senior team is probably covering about 2,000 miles a season, which is huge for Step 5. And then to add to that, our reserves are covering about 1,000 miles a season too. All in, I think we're shelling out about £1,400 a month on travel, which is a significant amount of money for a small club like ours to find. And what tends to happen is that as you advance up the pyramid, the leagues you are in begin to cover larger and larger distances, which means ever-escalating travel costs. So, when a club does well and wins promotion, it has to consider if it can actually afford to go up.'

Of course, costs are not restricted to travel and wages. There is also pitch/stadium rental, stadium maintenance, fees for officials, food and drink, County FA fees, public liability insurance, it goes on and on.

'Clubs have always faced a lot of costs. But the problem nowadays is that they seem to be going up and up,' says Stuart Daly. 'And when everything is going up like that, when your pitch rental is extortionate, when your official costs escalate rapidly, when you are getting charged a fortune for yellow and red cards, bit by bit it pushes you to the limits of what can be afforded. Take something as simple as kits. In my day you just wore the kit you were given. Today, everything has to be Adidas or Nike. And that can cost a minimum of £500. It's ridiculous. But it's the norm. There's probably no part of the game where the costs haven't just shot up in the last few years. It's no surprise that clubs go under.'

When it comes to the use of pitches and facilities, many of the clubs in the lower reaches of the pyramid are facing the same problems that those playing junior football and Sunday league encounter week-in, week-out, as local authorities and private providers raise their prices.

'Having a good relationship with a pitch provider is absolutely essential if you want to survive,' says Pete Ford of Rotherfield FC, whose senior side play in the Premier Division of the Mid Sussex Football League (Step 7).

Rotherfield are fortunate to have a long-standing relationship with the local Parish Council, who own the land that the club calls home.

'They grant us, which is essentially the Rotherfield Sports Club (covering football, cricket and bowls) an annual licence to use the land, which only costs £1. In return, we are responsible for ground repairs and maintenance. This isn't cheap, but that's largely because we want a good surface. Despite the costs involved, it's still preferable to the alternative, which could mean paying considerably more in pitch fees, having limited control over the costs we face and also being at the mercy of somebody else's maintenance priorities.'

The security and longevity of the relationship that Rotherfield has with the 'rec' that it plays on has also afforded the club the opportunity to develop it. And this isn't only in football terms, such as the development of a successful junior section. It has also, through the building of a clubhouse, been able to develop the site's infrastructure. Not only does this provide changing rooms and a place to store equipment, it also contains a bar and cafe, from which the club can make a few extra quid, specifically on its annual fun day, a small fiesta that brings in hundreds of pounds.

It's easy to forget when you follow a club in the higher reaches of the game that down at the bottom things like selling tea and bacon butties on a Saturday, having a bar where people can get together to watch football, owning a space that can hold events, could be the difference between a club surviving or a club going under.

To their credit, the principal players within the game are not blind to the benefits that such developments can provide to a club. Through the Football Foundation, millions of pounds' worth of grants are handed out to clubs each year to assist with the building or development of clubhouses and pavilions.

'We know that there's not enough money to meet demand, but where we can help we have. In the process we have transformed the fortunes and football experience of thousands of clubs across the country,' says Rory Carroll.

Clubs like Leicestershire's Bottesford FC have been helped, whose senior men's team plays in the Leicestershire Senior League (which covers Steps 7 to 9).

'A few years ago the club were trying to raise money to buy some land adjoining our junior pitches,' says club vice-chairman Nick Dobney.

Through Dobney's attempts to try and get some funding from the local junior league, he was alerted to the possibility of help from the Football Foundation.

'As I was telling the league board about our long-term vision for our club, someone mentioned that it was exactly the kind of thing that the Football Foundation and the FA would be interested in. It was about really improving our facilities and expanding the club way beyond what it was at the time. I got in touch with the Football Foundation, who through the FA sent people out to look at what we were planning. And that person from the league was right, they were very interested. Turning our meagre facilities into something more substantial and more sustainable was something they could get behind.'

The facilities that the club enjoyed back then were, as Dobney admits, less than salubrious.

'We had some knackered Portakabins. They let in water, had rats and were barely fit for purpose. We also paid £1,000 a year to rent a Portaloo. Nobody ever used it but we felt we had to offer something to our players and supporters. The club's infrastructure was exceptionally basic. To advance, we really needed a clubhouse.'

And that's what they worked towards. After hiring a consultant to navigate the funding process, Bottesford eventually received just over £500,000 from the Football Foundation to build a new state-of-the-art facility that includes four team changing rooms, two officials' changing rooms, a clubroom and bar, and a kitchen.

'We had to raise a proportion of the final cost of the build ourselves,' Dobney explains. 'A good part of that was raised by selling bricks, i.e. getting people to buy a brick in return for them getting their name permanently on it.'

The club also got help from local businesses to reduce costs. 'One local business donated all the doors and windows, which saved about £20,000. And another business gave us a free alarm system. The support from the local community throughout was tremendous.'

And through all this work, the club has been given strong foundations upon which to grow. 'Having good facilities enables you to put on events, it gives you a way to raise some income and provides the club with a focal point. Because of what we have got here, this club has thrived and expanded. Locally, I can't think of any other club that has grown in the way that we have in recent years. The majority have remained constant or declined. When it comes to our success, the facilities we have built played a big role in that.'

The higher any club progresses up the pyramid the more important having a permanent home becomes (ideally one that the club owns). Shropshire's Whitchurch Alport FC, who play in the North West Counties League at Step 5, have spent the last few years developing their ground, Yockings Park.

'In the last few years we have spent around £35,000 on the ground, installing new railings, a new lounge, a 75-seater stand and a play area for kids too. You have to do this to make sure that your facilities are something that will bring the community to your door. A great example of that is the kids' play area. There are mums and dads who want to come and watch a game but they can't because, understandably, their young kids don't want to sit through 90 minutes of non-league football. So, by us building that, and putting it alongside the new stand where the parents can sit, we are adapting to our community and showing them that we are a club that thinks about their needs,' says vice-chairman John Allman.

Over the past few seasons Whitchurch has played at various levels in the pyramid, at one point dropping a few steps below its current position. It's a journey that has really illustrated to Allman the importance of Yockings Park to the club.

'I look at the teams we have come up against in the last few years, in this league and others, and I don't know how they survive. Thriving at any level, but particularly down here, is a constant struggle. But having our own ground is a godsend. It's somewhere we can sell advertising space, earn money from the bar, use the facilities to generate income, from things like quiz nights, race nights and sportman's dinners, and also benefit from gate receipts.'

Although the ground comes with overheads, like maintenance costs and council tax, and if you advance up the pyramid, you'll likely have to improve aspects of your stadium to meet the FA's safety criteria at different levels, which can prove expensive, Allman would still prefer his club's situation to the alternative.

'If we didn't have Yockings Park and we were forced to rent somewhere, probably at ever-increasing prices, and we couldn't use that facility to raise as much income as we do here, then I'm not sure the club would still be around.'

The ability to survive at the lower levels of the pyramid can so often depend on a slice of good fortune: an accommodating local authority, a generous landowner, getting a grant to develop land. Hampshire's Tadley Calleva, who play in the Wessex League at Step 5, are one such example. It is a club that has had a great deal of good fortune in its short history and one that can show the benefits to grassroots football that can be achieved when businesses, local authorities, and funding bodies, local and national, work together with football clubs.

The club was reformed (an earlier incarnation had folded some years back) in the mid-1980s, back then just a group of mates having a kickabout on a pitch in the middle of a housing estate.

'Really, it was as basic as you can get in football,' says club chairman Sandy Russell.

In its early days the club trundled along, morphing from a casual endeavour into something more serious, joining the Hampshire League in the early 1990s.

'The real catalyst for our growth, and something without which I doubt we would be where we are now, was the decision in 1996 by the John Stacey Group, a local business, to donate an area known as Barlow's Plantation, for football and community use,' says Russell.

This led to the creation of Barlow's Plantation Environmental Trust Ltd (BPET), a body that would oversee the development of the former landfill site. One of the first actions of the newly established group, was to take advantage of the Landfill Tax Rebate Scheme, which generated £120,000.

A 99-year sub-lease on the site was granted to Basingstoke and Deane Borough Council, who provided a capital grant of £230,000 to develop the site, a sum that was augmented by an £800,000 development grant from the Football Foundation. In total, the project was able to secure £1.5m worth of external funding to create a senior pitch, a junior pitch, four mini-pitches, changing facilities and a clubhouse, spread over eight acres.

'In return for an agreement to fund the maintenance of Barlows Park, we were given access to a facility that is first class,' says Russell. 'Despite the overheads, it's helped make the club what it is today. Good fortune *has* played a part in this.

'However, without the amazing work of our members, both in obtaining funding and then working to make sure that stadium has continued to be improved upon, the opportunity that that slice of good fortune provided might have been squandered.'

It's great when everything works out as it did for Tadley Calleva. But 300 miles away in Horden, County Durham, a contrasting tale took place back in 2016, a tale characterised by misfortune, a breakdown in relations between a football club and the local council, and ultimately a club's demise.

Welfare Park had been the home of Horden Colliery Welfare (or Horden CW for short) since the club was founded in 1908. When you think of non-league football, Welfare Park is what would likely come to mind, a tired anachronism of brick and corrugated iron, nestled in-between terraced houses and local authority builds, a tiny oasis of green bursting forth from a Ken Loach landscape.

The Welfare Park's dilapidated appearance could speak as a metaphor for the area that surrounds it. The past 30 years have not been kind to this part of the world. Horden was once home to one of the country's 'super-pits', employing 4,000 people, 90 per cent of the area's working population. The closure of the pit in the late 1980s has seen Horden, alongside nearby Easington, Shotton and Seaham, blighted. Whether it's measures of poverty, unemployment or educational attainment, the community lies on the wrong side of national averages. This is one of the most deprived parts of the country, a place forgotten.

With the loss of identity wrought by the closure of the colliery, a football club like Horden CW increased in importance locally. It gave opportunities within the community to be part of something; kids playing in the club's youth teams, volunteers working the turnstiles, somewhere to collectively congregate on a Saturday afternoon. In short, it was exactly the kind of community enterprise that should be encouraged and supported by local government.

Back in 2016, the issue of unpaid debts, largely accrued by persons no longer associated with the club, led to a conflict between Horden CW (then playing at Step 7) and Horden Parish Council, the owners of the ground. The lease on the ground had expired in 2013, and in light of the conflict, the Parish Council was unwilling to negotiate a new one. The conflict eventually ended up in Newcastle Crown Court, where the right of the Parish Council to evict the club was established.

Despite a local community campaign to try to convince the Parish Council to reconsider, and efforts by the club to work on a plan to tackle the unresolved financial conflict, it was to no avail. Horden CW were evicted in February 2016, a move that sounded the death knell for that incarnation of the club.

Like all clubs at this level, irrespective of whether they own their own ground or not, the likes of Whitchurch Alport, Tadley Calleva and Binfield face seemingly ever-escalating running costs. Referee fees, travel costs, expenses (or in some cases wages), hospitality, programmes, rent, maintenance, utility bills, fines, council tax, coaching costs – it all adds up to make football a very difficult business in which to run clubs at a profit.

But although tough, clubs at this level are actually sheltered from the true costs of life in the pyramid. In the lower reaches of the game, and in fact much of the non-league system, an army of free labour shields clubs from life's financial realities.

'We, as businesses, are utterly dependent on volunteers,' says John Allman. 'At so many levels of this game, probably right up to the National League, clubs are only kept alive because they have people manning the turnstiles, running the bar, cleaning the place, who are doing it for nothing in return. Even the people who are on the board are giving their time for free. Collectively, if we didn't have this army of volunteers and suddenly had to actually pay people to do all these jobs, grassroots football in this country would probably look very different than it does today.'

And why do people do it? The answer for John is a simple one: 'In part it's because we love this sport. The game would be lost without that love. It's what motivates people to give so much of their time and energy for nothing back in return. But we also do it because these clubs matter to local communities. I think it sometimes gets forgotten that these are more than football clubs. They are community hubs, places that engage and help local people in all kinds of ways. They are places that do so much good that it's worth putting your time into.'

But even benefitting from this volunteer army, with depressing frequency the rising costs of the game still force some clubs to fold.

Gravesham Borough FC were one such recent example. Over its 90-year history, the north Kent club had rarely set the footballing world alight and perhaps its only claim to fame locally was its capacity for constant 'rebranding', which saw the club undergo a multitude of name changes. It was just an average club, eking out an average existence in the Southern Counties East League (Step 6). And its demise was just as average.

'Our club was never a rich one, but it had got by for the best part of nearly a century before the costs we faced in running it just became too much,' says former club chairman Scott Williamson.

In its quest for Step 6 football, Gravesham had been compelled to leave the borough and seek groundshares elsewhere in Kent. 'The facilities no longer existed in Gravesham,' Williamson explains. 'The only local ground was Ebbsfleet United, but that was too big for our needs and far too expensive. So, we ended up leaving Gravesham and sharing first with Rochester United and then with Chatham Town.'

Although necessary, the groundshares did not come cheap, adding yet another cost to a club that was already finding it hard to survive.

'Everything involved with football had become more and more expensive. Training midweek on 3G was costing us about £1,500 a year. Official fees were about £150 per home game. Then we had all the other costs you face as a club, like food on a matchday, fines, kit replacement, travel. When you added on the £5,000 we were paying to groundshare, it meant that the cost of running the club was going up and up and by the last year it was costing about £15,000 a season,' he says.

To cover this, the club had limited outlets. 'We didn't pay the players, which helped. But nor did we collect subs, because if we did, most of our players wouldn't have bothered turning out for us. We could collect a bit on the gate. However, because we were no longer in Gravesham, the numbers coming to watch us were generally low. Volunteering levels were decent, so that saved a bit of cash. But the volunteers, club members and the board didn't have the kind of incomes that other clubs have. Collectively, we just didn't have that much money to put in ourselves. This was a small, volunteer-led club, whose board was just made up of ordinary working people, like myself.'

And so, Gravesham ended up being reliant on external sponsorship to keep the whole thing going.

'As you can imagine,' explains Williamson, 'this can be risky. Sponsorship is not easy to come by at this level. You're asking people to kick in thousands of pounds for not a great deal of exposure. For a few years we were OK, but in the final season of the club's existence we just could not find anyone to help us out. We tried for six months, ringing round, talking to people, trying to get anyone who could put some cash in. But by the summer of 2018, it was obvious that it wasn't going to happen. And without that cash, it meant that we simply could not keep the club afloat.'

And just like that, over 90 years of local football history disappeared. 'Which is incredibly sad,' says Williamson. 'For a lot of us involved with the club, Gravesham Borough had been a big part of our lives. I'd personally played all my junior football with them and they were an important part of the local football scene. In recent years, things had been going well on the pitch too. We were building a good set-up, and had even entered the FA Cup for the first time in our history, playing in the preliminary qualification round. And then it was just all gone.'

Despite what would later unfold, Gravesham had done well to build a thriving squad at this level without financial inducement. For a lot of clubs, specifically those with small budgets, retaining players and building competitive squads can be a challenge because of the financial reality of the player market. Losing players because another club is offering more is not a problem confined to the higher reaches of the game.

Danny Dolan spent eight seasons managing Tadley Calleva and during that time did so with a playing budget that constantly put both him and the club at a disadvantage.

'Tadley are not a wealthy club. There was no benefactor with deep pockets who could just write cheques to pay players. And the ability for such a small club to generate money was limited too. Every year, just staying afloat was a challenge. As a manager, what the finances gave me was a very limited weekly playing budget. And all of that was eaten up by travel.'

Set against the fact that there are plenty of other clubs nearby who could offer better, sometimes in the form of more generous expenses, sometimes in the form of a small wage, inevitably Dolan's ability to keep hold of players was a real challenge.

'You are not talking about a lot of money,' Dolan explains. 'But at this level, when you're putting in so much time and effort into the game, it can be enough to turn heads.'

In response, Dolan had to offer something that money could not buy. 'So, support and development of players became central to what we did. A lot of clubs are just focussed on results. But we were a bit different, making sure players could still develop and improve themselves, no matter the age. I also put a lot of effort into the "dressing room", trying to create an environment that people loved being part of. It wasn't flawless and sometimes we did lose players. But I'm proud to say that in my last few years with the club I only lost one person, and that was because he emigrated to New Zealand.'

Of course, not every club is lucky enough to have a Danny Dolan in charge and there are occasions when so severe is the player drain that a club is faced with no option but to fold.

Back in 2015, Sussex-based St Francis Rangers, who played in the Southern Combination Football League, thought that being the worst football club in England was probably as bad as things could get. Bottom of the Premier Division after losing all 23 games, the club's goal difference was the stuff of nightmares, standing at – 111 (after the club had conceded 112 and scored just one).

And yet, as bad as that campaign was, at least the club survived. Just a few years later, it would not be so lucky. At the nadir of the 2015 losing streak, the club's chairman, Rob Ward, had considered winding things up but could not afford the fine from the league that would be incurred by doing do. Four years later, he had no choice. And the reason was simple, Rangers could no longer field a competitive side.

'We cannot attract local players when teams around us are paying players,' said Ward in a statement at the time. 'The players we have travel from a distance and get no expenses, so training sessions never have more than five to six players there. You cannot play a good standard of football without training. Player commitment in general is not what it was. They don't want to travel around the county to play and other commitments take priority over training and matches.'

Paying players at the lower reaches of the National League system is tempting for clubs. Even modestly improved playing budgets can have a dramatic impact on a club's fortunes. And for most clubs the only way that this can be achieved is by the arrival of a benefactor.

'The lower regions of the non-league world operate on exactly the same principles as the higher reaches of the pyramid, in that the more you shell out on a club, the better on average your footballing outcomes can be. And, the best way to do this is to get yourself a sugar-daddy. The non-league world is littered with examples of this taking place. Sometimes it can be someone just throwing a few quid at a small club with an aim of going up a few divisions, and other times it can be someone throwing serious money at a venture in the hope of the club powering up the pyramid. Some owners are there for the long haul and some don't hang around for that long. But either way, while they are there and spending, the effect can be transformative,' says Matt Badcock.

For many aspiring clubs and owners, one of the poster boys for what can be done in the non-league world with the right attitude and a few quid are Lancashire's Kirkham and Wesham FC, or, as they are known today, AFC Fylde. The club was originally formed in 1988 via the merger of Kirkham Town and Wesham, and for the best part of two decades they trundled along, just another small non-league outfit in the North West.

Back in 2007 the club was plying its trade in the second tier of the North West Counties League (Step 6) when it caught the attention of local businessman and lifelong Blackpool fan David Haythornthwaite.

'I wasn't looking to invest in a non-league club,' he says. 'First and foremost, I was a Blackpool supporter. From my first match at Bloomfield Road, when my dad had taken me to see Blackpool beat Newcastle 6-0 in the old First Division, I'd been hooked. I'd even named my company Tangerine Holdings in honour of the club.'

Haythornthwaite had twice tried to buy the Seasiders, first in 1998 and then again in 2005, but each time he'd been thwarted in his efforts.

'I believed I could make a difference at Blackpool and thought I had it in me to run a football club properly. But it looked like it wasn't going to happen, which was hugely frustrating,' he admits.

While he'd been trying to take control at Blackpool, further along the Fylde coast a good friend of his, Dai Davies, had been investing in Kirkham and Wesham.

'Dai came to the conclusion that what he was doing at the club could probably be done on a bigger scale if I got involved. Seeing as it wasn't happing at Blackpool, he asked if I was interested. And it made sense to me at that time. I wasn't enjoying following Blackpool, who had ownership problems. Everything about that club was frustrating me. I was annoyed at the players, the manager and the chairman. I was ready for a change.'

It was a decision that would have a dramatic effect on the club. In 2007, Haythornthwaite took ownership and immediately made his intentions known with a bold claim:

'It's the promise that the players have worn on their shirt sleeves since I took over, that by 2022 we would be members of the Football League.'

It was a promise that was met by raised eyebrows in some quarters when first revealed. And, according to Haythornthwaite, in fairness to the club's early detractors, it was easy to see why.

'We were playing in a field at the back of a pub in the village of Warton and were hosting the likes of Bootle and Leek County School Old Boys in front of really small crowds. Set against that, and the fact that it was my first time running a club, you can appreciate why my plan to get us into the Football League caused a bit of a stir. But, to be honest, it just spurred me on. It was a case of "let's prove to everybody we can do it".'

Since taking control, Haythornthwaite's bankrolling of the club has seen them power up the pyramid, and in 2019 they just missed out on promotion to the Football League via the National League play-offs. Had Fylde won the play-off final, it would have meant that the club had reached its lofty ambition three years ahead of schedule.

But despite the near miss, the club remains transformed, almost bearing no relation to the one that Haythornthwaite took over. Not only did it turn full-time in 2016/17 and change its name in 2008, today the club is an established member of the National League, playing its home games in a plush, new multi-million-pound stadium just outside Wesham.

'Mill Farm, our new home, is a modern 6,000-seater stadium,' says Haythornthwaite. 'It's a huge improvement on what we had before, a modern stadium for a club that is heading upwards.'

This stadium is built with the Football League in mind. And that's not just in terms of its size. With its hospitality and wider income generating potential (an 80-seat restaurant with roof terrace, a 40-seat café and multiple conference and event facilities), the stadium has been created to make sure that this club is able to compete financially in the Football League too.

Nearby the ground, Haythornthwaite has also invested in the state-of-the-art facilities at the Fylde Sports and Education Centre. The centre includes 3G pitches, a brand-new hockey pitch, two function rooms, classrooms, a canteen and a number of bars. As well as being used by the main club, the centre is also home to Fylde Hockey Club, AFC Fylde Academy and the AFC Fylde Community Foundation.

'The club today is almost unrecognisable to the one I took over,' says Haythornthwaite. 'We have gone from small, volunteer-led club, watched by a few hundred people, to a situation now where we are a full-time club, on the cusp of the Football League, followed by a couple of thousand people. We have a new stadium, an academy, a community foundation, everything in place to make this club a success when it eventually gets promoted.'

Although the club is arguably the extreme end of what is possible, AFC Fylde's recent history illustrates what can be done with money at this level.

'Money makes a difference,' says Daniel Magner, one of the authors of the non-league blog *Two Men in Search of the Beautiful Game*. 'Most people who are tempted to get involved in their local clubs probably don't have the time, the cash or possibly the imagination to power the club from somewhere like Step 7 to the Football League. But lots of people do it on a smaller scale, throwing a few quid and a bit of time at a project. And, by and large, while they remain committed, it does have an impact. When you are competing against clubs with miniscule playing budgets, or none at all, you don't need a great deal of cash to outperform them.'

The key word used by Magner there is 'committed'. The image of a football club becoming a 'plaything' for a wealthy individual is one that is often more associated with the professional levels of the game. So too is the image of the 'crisis club', the kind of club where the relationship has soured, and the owner in question has lost interest or lost the ability to fund the club. It brings to mind the likes of Leyton Orient under Francesco Becchetti, Bolton under Ken Anderson and Bury under Stuart Day.

But such tropes do not exist solely within professional football. They are just as commonly found further down the pyramid, albeit on a smaller scale.

'There are lots of examples scattered through the pyramid, examples of where someone with a bit of cash has come along and offered to change the fortunes of that club. There are times when this works out well, there are times when it works out well to begin with and then ultimately doesn't, and there are times when it doesn't work out well from the off. Although lots of these people have good intentions, there are probably some who shouldn't be allowed anywhere near a football club,' says Magner.

The temptation to open a club's doors to these individuals is often palpable. And it's easy to appreciate why. Life down in the lower levels is hard for clubs without benefactors. Making do on what they can generate themselves, however laudable, remains a constant challenge. As valuable as that volunteer army is, as beneficial as those raffles, sports dinners and quiz nights are, as much help as a decent cup run or a good crowd on matchday can be, none of it can hold a candle to the problem-solving capacity offered by the arrival of someone with deep pockets and a willingness to spend.

And it's not just a case of what they can do for those unpaid debts, those much-needed refurbishments, a pitch in dire need of some tender loving care. They also offer the chance, as AFC Fylde has illustrated, of rapid upward progression, bankrolling success on the pitch to achieve momentum up the pyramid. And, after all, isn't that what lots of fans want? People will get involved with local clubs because of the sense of community they offer and the chance to experience a form of the game freed from the rampant commercialisation so evident higher up. But they still want that club to do well. Few fans are happy with stagnation or decline.

So, clubs take risks. And sometimes these risks end up proving costly.

Back in 2018, East Sussex club Crowborough Athletic, which currently plays in the Southern Counties East League at Step 5, learned to its cost how damaging it can be when a club takes a gamble.

'Just before the 2016/17 football season, the club was approached by a benefactor who offered to develop the Crowborough Community Stadium to install a 3G pitch and additional buildings,' says current club chairman Clive Maynard.

The development was initially described as a gift to the community, but over time developed into an investment proposal where the benefactor would hold a majority stake in the club.

'Whilst preparing for this project and the remainder of his investment, the benefactor wanted the club moving in the right direction. So, a few changes were made. Some were cosmetic, like buying new kits for all age groups within the club, and others were more substantive, such as a significant increase in the playing budget, which saw new players from higher divisions come to us. The latter was part of an effort to get the first team to challenge for promotion,' Maynard continues.

As an act of good faith, the club part-paid for these changes by depleting its reserves. This was undertaken on the understanding that the cash would be repaid when the investment was completed.

'For a time, things were looking good. The club was doing well in the league and we had all these plans in place that were going to create this wonderful new pitch, complete with renovated buildings. And then, suddenly, it all changed.'

The club just missed out on promotion, an outcome that appeared to precipitate a crisis: 'It became clear that the benefactor wasn't going to come forward with the remainder of the promised investment, which came as a huge shock to all involved. There had been no indication that this was going to happen and everything had been proceeding in a perfectly normal way. Whether it was because the money wasn't there or because the club hadn't got promotion, we don't know. But the upshot was that the club found itself in a dire position.'

On the pitch, the squad was decimated as most of the players who had been recruited by the club left. The playing budget shrank to near zero, placing the club in a worse position than it had been prior to the 'benefactor's' arrival. Off the pitch, the outlook was even bleaker.

'The financial position was so bad that there was a real threat of the club folding,' explains Maynard, who was appointed chairman in response to the financial crisis.

For Crowborough and Maynard, the way back from the lows of 2018 has been a challenge.

'This is not a club that was great at generating income to begin with,' he explains. 'So, we have had to work hard on what we spend, squeezing every possible amount of value out of every pound. Alongside that, we have tried to improve our money-making ability. But it's hard. Small clubs like ours can only do so much. There are only so many quiz nights you can put on, raffles you can hold. But, despite this, we have managed to slowly turn the picture around and, perhaps more impressively, done all of this while retaining our league status, which is of absolute importance.'

You would be forgiven for reading this chapter and thinking that life in the lower tiers of the pyramid is fairly bleak, a land of clubs facing challenging odds just to survive. And partly that is true. Participation is down, costs are rising, clubs are disappearing every year, clubs that have often spent decades in the game. But the lower rungs of the pyramid are also a place filled with people like Stuart Daly, a man whose simple love of football has done so much to enrich the lives of those who have played for his club.

'Running a club is nothing but hard work,' he says. 'It takes up so much of my time that people think I'm mad to do it. But to me it's natural. From the first time I ever kicked a ball I have been in love with this game, and not being part of it doesn't make sense. And it's not the same for me to just support a team, watching from the stands or an armchair. I've got to be there, in amongst everything, living and breathing football. It doesn't matter how much hard work and frustration running a club causes me. When that whistle goes on a Saturday afternoon, it all makes sense.'

It's this simple love of football that still persuades people every year to start new clubs of their own. Despite the stories of clubs losing their homes, of clubs struggling with debt, of clubs going under, new clubs still emerge, run by people who think they have what it takes to do it well. And sometimes, these stories come full circle, with clubs that were once lost coming back to life.

On a balmy June evening, just outside Haywards Heath in West Sussex, Saltdean FC are playing a friendly against one such resurrected club. Their opponents are St Francis Rangers, once the worst club in England, now the latest club to come back from the dead. The architect of this Lazarus-style resurrection is Del Tobias.

'I was looking for a club that could provide a pathway for the kids that we have here at the LPA Academy, and St Francis Rangers made perfect sense.'

The academy, which currently provides weekly football coaching for over 5,000 young people across the South East, has been regularly producing graduates that have felt compelled to leave at the age of 18 in the pursuit of senior football.

'We have graduates of the academy scattered across non-league football at the moment. And that didn't make sense to me,' says Tobias. 'What I wanted was a medium through which these players could stay with us, an end point for kids to aim for when they joined, and also a way for them to continue to benefit from the coaching that we have been providing them during their football journey.'

Initially, he approached the previous owners of St Francis Rangers with an aim to take control of the club. The idea was to do this before the club had folded, thereby ensuring that it would've retained its league status.

'But this wasn't achievable in the end,' he says, 'and so we have had to take the punishment of being relegated. From one perspective, this is frustrating as we have to work our way back up. However, from another it gives us a chance to build from scratch. And because we are at a lower level, we can do this largely using players from the academy, which might not have been possible had we been higher up the pyramid.'

The emphasis on using academy players was certainly evident against Saltdean, where nine of the starting eleven were from LPA. By the final whistle, that figure had risen to eleven.

'Although we lost 3-0, there were lots of positives to be gained from the experience,' explains Tobias. 'Not only did we get our young players out into a senior team, we had lots of support from the local community, and that's really important to us. We have big plans for this club. This is not just a case of returning Rangers as it once was. Our plan is to create something very different. And the community are a big part of that.'

The old St Francis Rangers was a very traditional club, run by a small committee and focussed on its senior team. This new version is aiming to be a very different animal.

'We are organised as a community interest company (CIC), which means that we are a social enterprise that will use its profits and assets for the public good. So, although part of what we do will be about providing coaching and a pathway for academy players, we will also be initiating projects to benefit the local community. So, this could be something like the creation of a youth centre, an outreach programme to get isolated seniors to matches, educational schemes where local youngsters can learn skills in trades covering work in coaching, social media or groundskeeping.'

There are also plans to develop the stadium to provide better facilities for the community, including a 3G pitch and a revamped clubhouse, the former of which could be used for other sports.

'The football side of things *is* important. We want this club to rise through the pyramid and in the process provide an opportunity for our players to play senior football together. However, this is about more than football. We want St Francis Rangers to be at the heart of this community, operating as a hub for sporting clubs, for youth activities and for education.'

St Francis Rangers are not the only club to rise from the ashes. Hundreds of miles north in Durham, Horden CW has also recently come back from the dead, a new incarnation brought into existence in 2017 by many of those formerly involved with the old version of the club. It shows that despite the manifold challenges those who run football clubs often encounter, and the bitter experiences sometimes faced, people are still willing to roll up their sleeves and give it a go.

However, despite these resurrections, the concept of permanence still remains elusive down here. Had Szymanski and Kuper randomly picked 88 clubs from the lower reaches of the football pyramid in the 1920s and looked forward to today to see how many were still in existence, it is likely that the supposed permanence of English football would be nowhere to be seen. On the pyramid's lower rungs, life is tough.

But it's also a part of the game that reveals so much about English football too. Down here, the odds are stacked against you and are getting harder all the time. To an outsider, it must just look like one long struggle. The football isn't that good, the grounds are often tired and in need of renovation, and everything looks to be run on a shoestring, with clubs always seeming to be just a few bad decisions away from going under. And yet, from the simple love of the game, of players playing for little or nothing, of volunteers keeping clubs alive, of supporters going to watch these sides, exists this vast network of clubs. Constantly changing yes, but also, as a whole, constant too.

Chapter Four

Giant Steps

WITH the mercury plummeting, the nights drawing in and the weather grizzly and unforgiving, the Isthmian League South (Step 4) hosted its usual round of matches on a cold January afternoon back in 2015.

Or at least it nearly did.

Games at this level are no stranger to postponements. The weather, and its ability to freeze, waterlog or fog pitches out of use, haunts the winter schedule. It's rare that a season goes past without some matches needing to be rearranged.

But this time, the league's inability to complete its fixtures that week had nothing to do with the weather. Instead, it had everything to do with a friendly taking place thousands of miles away in Brazil.

Corinthian-Casuals should've been hosting Hastings United at King George's Field, its ground in Tolworth, south-west London. Instead, the club found itself lining up to face Corinthians Paulista, in front of 26,000 people at the Arena Corinthians, Sao Paulo.

'It's fair to say that the crowd was a fair bit bigger than the players are used to,' says current Casuals manager James Bracken.

Corinthian-Casuals was formed back in 1939, a merger between two giants of the amateur game, Corinthian and the Casuals. When it comes to the link with Brazil, it's the history of the former that matters. And to understand why, we have to travel back in time to Edwardian England.

Corinthian, established in 1882, was a product of the English public-school system, its players adhering fully to the amateur ethos that the likes of Eton, Harrow and Westminster prized so highly. It was an ethos that regarded professionalism as an anathema. Indeed, so wedded was the club to notions such as sportsmanship, fair play and playing simply for the love of the game, that Corinthian did not even regard penalties as part of football. As far as they were concerned, a gentleman would never foul an opponent deliberately. And so, if the side won a penalty, the captain would bally-well balloon the ball over the bar.

As England professionalised in the late-Victorian period, and fixtures became regimented within leagues and cup competitions, Corinthian, whose own constitution forbade entry into competitive games, began to tour instead, taking its message of 'football played the way it should be' across the globe, to places as far flung as South Africa, Germany, the USA … and Brazil.

And it was in Brazil that the historic connection with Paulista was forged, when Corinthian toured there in 1910. The visitors wowed the crowds with their style of play, ending the tour unbeaten. And, so the story goes, so impressive were Corinthian that five Sao Paulo railway workers met under a gas lamp in the neighbourhood of Bom Retiro and decided to form S.C. Corinthians Paulista.

It's not a bad legacy for a small amateur side: Paulista went on to become one of South America's biggest clubs, boasting 30 million fans across Brazil. Twice FIFA Club World Cup winners, the club's history is as long and storied as any in the world, with famous alumni including Rivellino, Dunga and Sócrates.

And it was in honour of the debt that Paulista owed to the London club that the invite to come over to Brazil was offered back in 2015.

'When you play at our level you don't expect to experience anything like that. My players are used to performing in front of a few hundred people at a level that barely gets any media attention. Over there, it was incredible for them. Not only were they playing in front of tens of thousands, they were treated like superstars, mobbed for autographs, in the full glare of the media. It gave them a taste of what life is like at the top of our game. Although they lost 3-0, the whole experience was something they will never forget,' says Bracken.

As the Brazilian interlude reveals, Corinthian-Casuals are not your average non-league outfit. Its international legacy aside, this is a club that boasts fans from all over the world, one whose former white strip inspired Real Madrid to adopt the same colour and whose alumni include legends of the Victorian and Edwardian game, such as Tinsley Lindley, a late-Victorian goal-machine, who famously wore brogues instead of football boots.

And if that wasn't enough, it is also the highest ranked amateur senior side playing in English football today.

Corinthian-Casuals represent just how far amateurism can take a club. As you edge up the pyramid, money creeps its way into the equation with every step. It starts small at the lower levels, expenses here and there. Then it becomes a part-time wage. Then a living wage. And on and on it goes, gathering momentum and size until you end up in the Premier League, a division where money is everything. It you want to resist that, hang on to the 'Corinthian' spirit of the past, then Step 3 is currently as far as it will currently take you.

'But it's very hard,' admits Stuart Tree, who sits on the management committee of the club. Tree had grown up an Arsenal fan, following the club avidly during the glory years of George Graham. But a casual decision one Saturday lunchtime back in the late 1990s changed all of that.

'I'd watched Kingstonian a few times with a mate of mine and enjoyed it, so I was getting more into non-league football. But I was still an Arsenal fan primarily. Then, one Saturday, when I was working in Tolworth, I thought I'd go down and watch the local club, who were Corinthian-Casuals. It was the best decision I ever made, because I was hooked from the start.'

Attracted not just by what he saw on the pitch but also by the relaxed, friendly and inclusive feel of the crowd, Tree began a process that has seen his footballing allegiances thoroughly shift.

'Over time I became a fan, and through doing so, I got more and more involved with the club. It seems like I've done most jobs here since: press officer, photographer, programme writer, the list goes on and on.'

According to Tree, thriving as an amateur side at this level of the game is a constant challenge: 'Surviving at

Step 3 is hard enough for most clubs. But it's ten times harder when you're an amateur club. If you want to put it in simple terms, think of this: we are competing in a league where plenty of players are on decent money. Wages are a really hard one to quantify. So many players like to inflate what they're paid. But we do know there are some pretty large wages in our league. A striker at a club close to us recently left having earned £450 a week. Some go higher ... it's not unheard of to see strikers pick up £600 to £800 a week at wealthy clubs at this level. Crazy really. By contrast, our playing budget is zero. So, what that means is that when we are recruiting players, the pool from which we can draw is significantly smaller than any other club at this level. Because we are essentially looking for players who are happy to play for nothing.'

The jump from county football to leagues at Steps 3 and 4, such as the Northern Premier, the Isthmian and the Southern League, is a significant one. At these levels, wages are common, playing budgets swell and the level of investment required by clubs to be competitive is more considerable than would be the case somewhere like the Combined Counties, the United Counties or the Southern Combination in the steps below.

'But it's not just finances,' explains non-league football writer Ian Townsend, author of Townsendaround.com, an independent football blog with a definite non-league bias, 'the quality of players is much higher too. At this level, you often get players who played higher up and have dropped down and players who will go on to play in higher leagues. The jump in fitness and knowledge of how to play is a considerable one. You can probably look at Steps 3 and 4, and particularly Step 3, as the level where the game starts to share some of its DNA with the Football League. That's not to dismiss the football lower down. But at Steps 3, 4 and above, the game starts, bit by bit, to better resemble professional football.'

Which makes the achievements of Corinthian-Casuals all the more remarkable. There are many clubs further down the pyramid with healthier playing budgets who remain unable to emulate what they have done without spending for success. And that gives rise to the obvious question: how has it happened? As so often is the case in football, a big part of that answer lies in smart recruitment and, in this instance, none smarter than the decision to appoint Bracken as manager back in 2015.

Prior to his arrival at King George's Field, Bracken had been coach of the reserves and the youth team at Sutton United, boasting an impressive record that had seen him amass 30 trophies during nine years there, seven in his last season alone. Although content at the time to stay with Sutton, an offhand comment by someone at the club precipitated a rethink.

'Someone there had sort of belittled what I'd done, saying that it was easy to win things at that level. That really annoyed me and made me want to go out there and show them exactly what I could do. And when it comes to hard jobs, roles that really challenge your coaching ability, probably none come harder than the manager's job here.'

When he took the helm at the Casuals, Bracken was ruthless in his appraisal. 'The squad I inherited was not up to the job. I told the board that I would be able to get them promoted into the top tier of the Isthmian but to do that I had to make a lot of changes, principally to the playing staff. I brought in a lot of new players in the summer, many of those from my last job at Sutton.'

Other changes were also made behind the scenes, such as the hiring of new strength and conditioning coaches, a nutritional expert and the introduction of video analysis.

'I also changed some simple things too. When I got there, we had players turning up for training in Arsenal and Chelsea kits. And our tracksuits were these horrible waterproof things that rustled as you walked. I made sure they had proper training gear and tracksuits. It was all part of a general process that was bringing a more professional approach into the club.'

And it was one that yielded results. In the 2016/17 season, the club reached the play-off final and came agonisingly close to going up, losing 4-3 to Dorking Wanderers on penalties. The season after, Corinthian was there again, this time against Walton Casuals. Although luck appeared to desert the side for a second time after Walton clinched promotion in the shoot-out, Bracken's men were not to be denied. The club were promoted to the Premier Division after Thurrock resigned from the league, gaining the position by being the play-off finalists at Step 4 with the highest points-per-game ratio from the season.

The achievement of promotion is all the more impressive when you take into account how hard it has been for Bracken to build momentum at the club.

'You speak to some managers down the pyramid, county league level and lower, and they lose players to another club because they're offering an extra tenner a week! We're trying to keep players when they're being offered a lot more. Inevitably, people are going to move on, you accept that. But after we lost to Dorking in the play-off final, I lost quite a few players in the summer, which is a real challenge. It meant I almost had to build the side again.'

Despite the frustration this brings with it, Bracken thinks that adhering to the amateur model does bring some advantages.

'When I have got a player here, I know that they have come to play. They've not been lured by cash for a pay-day. They might move on at a later date and that's OK. We develop players at this club and we're always happy to see them go on to bigger and better things. But, when they come, we know they are here because they believe in what we are doing, for however long that is. From my experience, this makes for a great dressing room. We don't have prima donnas at the Casuals.'

There is also a tactical practicality about Bracken, a reactive simplicity born in part to the hand he has been dealt. The temptation to have some kind of playing 'philosophy' isn't available at King George's Field, and he sees that as a positive. 'You have to adapt to what you've got available and for us that's a limited pool of players. But I've found that this is what works best at this level. One week you can be playing on 3G, the next a decent grass pitch like ours and the one after that on a pitch that is barely playable. Coaches who think that one style can suit all those surfaces are going to come unstuck pretty quickly.'

The huge upheaval in personnel that has taken place at the club in recent years has obviously meant that recruiting and retaining players has been a significant part of managerial life for Bracken. The key throughout all of this for him has been the provision of the highest standards possible.

'We might be an amateur club but we are run like a professional one. The standards of coaching, the equipment, the facilities on offer, the whole environment is as close as we can be to a professional club. That's something that perhaps you don't often get at this level. And if you come here, not only are you going to be part of something unique, you are also going to develop. There is a reason so many of our players move on to better things, it's because we make them better players.'

Of course, none of the above comes easy. 'People I know look at my day and think I must be insane. I work as a builder nine to five, then I'm involved with the club, with either training or matches, three times per week. Some days I'm up at 6am, work all day, then down to the club for time with the players and I'm home around 11 at night. And all the work I am doing with the Casuals is done for free.'

Although Bracken's services come free of charge to the club, the coaching environment he's created does not. Offering a coaching experience for the players that tries to mirror the professional world has required investment; something that has been a struggle, as Stuart Tree explains:

'Like every other club at this level, we face financial challenges every year. We get money from the gate [which doubled after promotion], from sponsorship, pies and pints on matchday and also money from the government for our academy. But each year, to create the kind of club we want here, puts us in the red and we are constantly reliant on donations just to keep afloat.'

In the last few years, following that sojourn to Brazil, the club has become active in developing its 'brand' as a source of income, using this to generate better levels of revenue.

'We *are* something different,' explains Tree. 'We have a history that few clubs share, we have had a disproportionate influence on the game internationally and we are amateurs, which at this level is unusual. When you roll that together, you have a story to tell that engages people and sets you apart from other clubs. So, in recent years we have been more aggressive in promoting our brand, in pushing our story, in getting the Corinthian-Casuals name out there.'

And, it's been a success. Globally and online people now know who Corinthian-Casuals are. On Twitter the club boasts 25,000 followers, levels greater than many Step 1 clubs. On Facebook, it is the most followed non-league club in the country. And in traditional media outlets, its story has been covered by the likes of ESPN, *The Independent* and *The Guardian*.

'A short film about our trip to Brazil was even made by BT Sport, which gave a huge boost to our profile. And, on the back of that, *Tifo Football,* who make short videos on YouTube about all aspects of the game, and who have well over half a million subscribers, created a video about the club's history. All of this represents a huge opportunity for us, a potential reach that we are now trying to exploit.'

Through this greater promotion, attendances have risen, the club's online shop is doing better business and Corinthian-Casuals now sells its kits in the Paulista club shop too. It has also forged stronger links with London's 5,000-strong Brazilian community, positioning it as its club of choice.

'Turning brand recognition into income is a challenge. But at this level of the game I think we are one of the few clubs doing it well. It's interesting because a generation ago, a club like ours wouldn't have done anything like this. But we've found that nowadays there is much more interest out there in football stories that are a bit different. I suppose it has something to do with the sterile nature of the top flight and is linked with how I came to follow this club. There are football fans who want something beyond the norm and it's clubs like ours who offer that.'

Most clubs down at this level don't have 'brand' recognition, they don't have fascinating histories to draw upon and they don't have an international fanbase. And so, they have to look at other ways to remain competitive.

'And they are up against it,' explains Cornelius Nwadialor, joint-manager of Tooting and Mitcham United, who play at Step 4 in London. 'At this level, a lot of clubs are paying players decent money, which is costly. And it's getting more expensive every season. I think the higher wages that you are seeing in somewhere like the National League are starting to trickle down to our level, so clubs that want to compete are having to pay out more and more. And the growing influence of agents doesn't help either. There was a time, not that long ago, when you didn't really get agents at this level. But that's no longer the case. And bit by bit they are playing their role in pushing up wages.'

The need to generate money exists at every club in the pyramid. But when players start getting paid, rather than paying to play, which becomes more common the higher you go, and is near ubiquitous at Steps 3 and 4, the need becomes more pressing if you hope to remain competitive.

'You have to keep track of the value of every football activity in terms of its costs and its direct and indirect contribution to revenues,' says Tony Cox, vice-chairman of

Tooting and Mitcham. 'For example, an elite academy gets some government funding, but it also plays an important role in attracting talent and in developing those players to the point where a few of them can be sold on to professional clubs, generating future revenues. The playing style and tactics should be modern and the pitch quality first class, because those factors will help draw in the scouts. Your stadium has to work for you all week long, which in our case means renting our space to other businesses. And how you conduct yourself in the community and interact with local people matters, as this can affect crowd numbers, levels of sponsorship and the commercial arrangements you can make. If you don't think in these terms then the chances of being a sustainable business at our level are slim. And, unless you have some generous and inexhaustible benefactor, that's just going to mean financial problems.'

The biggest constant resource available for any non-league club is its fans. Clubs might benefit from a cup run or a player sale, but these are often sporadic and unreliable. Fans are always there, not just a source of gate receipts and drinkers of pints and consumers of pies, but also potential sponsors, those more likely to attend club events and those willing to put their hand in their pockets when the club calls for donations.

Fortunately for clubs, interest in the non-league game, specifically from around Step 4 and above, is on the rise.

'A lot of people are disillusioned with top-flight football and that's what is driving them to watch non-league sides,' says Tom Cullen, current managing director of National League South side Dulwich Hamlet.

Until a few years ago, Cullen, as he had been since he was a young boy, was still a West Ham fan, a supporter who had followed the club fervently home and away. 'I'd loved West Ham but, as time went on, I found myself enjoying the experience of supporting them less and less enjoyable. Part of this was just the whole "Premier League" thing, the stupidly expensive ticket prices, the terrible atmosphere, the growing commercialisation of the game. But there was also the sense that I was stuck in a crowd made up of middle-class, middle-aged, white men, with all the opinions and prejudices that image conjures up. I was so sick of hearing homophobic, misogynistic and racist language. Although the picture had improved on the past, it was still there, which I found hard to be around.'

Despite slowly falling out of love with top-flight football, Cullen still loved the game, something that frustrated him. Fortunately, an answer to his problem arose following a move to south London.

'I was an east London boy and so nobody I knew understood why I'd moved there. It's the whole, "no trains, no trees" thing. But it ended up being a great decision. The move sort of pushed me to try something different and part of that was something different with football. I googled local clubs to watch and Dulwich Hamlet, who back then were playing in the Isthmian League, popped up. I thought I'd give them a go and I went down with a mate of mine to watch them. To be honest, I fell in love right away. It was like Dulwich were the answer to everything I had been looking for from football.'

It was an answer that comprised a mixture of different elements. 'There was the price, which was significantly less. There was the ease of going, just deciding to go to the game on the spur of the moment. There was the atmosphere, which was so much more authentic, probably the best I had ever experienced. And then there was the demographics of the crowd. At Dulwich, it is a much broader church: women, kids, people of different ethnicities, gay, straight, a true representation of what London is.'

That first visit to Champion Hill, home of the Hamlet, started a love affair with the club that has only deepened since. 'At first I was asking mates to go all the time. And they did. But not everyone shared my enthusiasm. So, in the end I began just going when I felt like it, home and away. Dulwich is the kind of club where you can go and just meet people. I remember going to an away game against Tonbridge Angels on my own. I saw a few Dulwich fans on the train, got chatting and we ended up getting a taxi together to the ground. There we met even more fans, stood together and ended up, after the match, drinking in a Wetherspoons in Tonbridge until all hours.'

Cullen is just one of many fans who have made a similar journey. Not all abandon their first love in the same way that he did. The old adage that 'you can change your wife, change your politics, change your religion. But never, never can you change your favourite football team', still holds true for many. But dividing loyalties, opening yourself up to the idea of supporting your first love, but watching another has become more common.

'I think the football in the top flight, or the "product" as the Premier League terms it, isn't the problem,' explains Bill Biss, editor of *Stand Against Modern Football* fanzine. 'The quality of what people watch is unquestionably very impressive the higher up you go. But it's everything else that people have an issue with. The experience of going to a Premier League match is a bit crap. It's expensive, you can't afford to go with your kids, you can't sit with your mates, the food and drink costs a fortune, the atmosphere is lacking, the list continues. It's unsurprising that more and more people are turning away from that and looking for a football environment where the opposite of the above exists.'

One club that has worked tirelessly to try and capture a slice of this growing audience is Lewes FC, who play near Brighton, in the Isthmian League Premier Division.

'We've found that getting people involved with the club, getting them excited about what you are doing, is one way to expand your reach and improve what a club can generate in terms of income. And that doesn't just mean more people through the turnstiles, although that is part of it. When you're doing something exciting, something people want to buy into, it also means sponsors are more willing to get involved and partners are more willing to invest. Generating a narrative that appeals to people can transform a club, helping it navigate the choppy waters of football at this level,' says Stuart Fuller, chairman of Lewes FC.

For much of its history, the club had rarely set the non-league world alight. Its highlight had been a single season in the National League, back in 2008/09, during which it had ended the campaign rock bottom and on the verge of financial ruin.

And it was this financial crisis that precipitated the radical change of direction at the club, as current Lewes director Charlie Dobres explains:

'For a time, back then, it looked possible that the club would be wound up. And that would have been it, over a hundred years of history gone in the blink of an eye. Luckily for Lewes, the fans would not let that happen. A group of supporters known as Rooks125 [a fusion of the club's nickname and its age at the time] worked to transfer Lewes out of private ownership into a mass ownership, Community Benefit Society, called Lewes Community Football Club.'

Supporter, or community, ownership has been catching on within non-league football in the last few decades. The model has its roots in the early 1990s, an innovation created by supporters of Northampton Town. Back then, the fans invested to save the club from liquidation but in return demanded a share in the business. The vehicle to manage this share was the Northampton Town Supporters' Trust.

The trust was organised as an Industrial and Provident Society. Legally, these organisations fall into two broad categories, a co-operative (run for the benefit of its members) or a community benefit society (run for the benefit of the wider community). Both categories enjoy limited liability, which means the personal liability of the society's members is limited to the amount of their unpaid share capital.

This share capital is usually not made up of equity shares like those in a joint-stock company (the model adhered to by most professional football clubs), which appreciate or fall in value with the success of the enterprise that issues them. Rather they are par value shares, which can only be redeemed (if at all) at face value. The share typically acts as a 'membership ticket'. And voting is on a 'one member one vote' basis.

'Since supporters' trusts first emerged, they have grown across the sport. Some fully own clubs, others have a part-ownership and others act more like supporter pressure groups. What tends to happen with ownership is that the members elect a board to run the club. The board will then have a mandate to run the club in a certain way. It's democratic and accountable in a manner that private ownership can never be,' says Dave Boyle, director of The Community Shares Company and a former chief executive of Supporters Direct, the government-created quango, which since 2000 has been supporting the growth of supporters' trusts within sport.

At Lewes, when Rooks125 took control, the members elected a board who then addressed the dire state the club found itself in.

'We were in desperate need of working capital,' says Dobres. 'To achieve this, we appealed to the fanbase. In year one, we limited the ownership offer to Life Shareholders who could give £1,000 or more. Through this we raised well over £100,000. After that, we opened ownership out to anyone who wanted it, with prospective owners initially buying a share in the trust for £30 per year.'

After a few bumpy years of transition, the club is in a stronger position today. Organisationally, the elected board is now split into two halves, with one side looking after the short-term issues of team affairs and the other half considering the long-term developments for the entire club, including future budgets.

At the moment, Lewes has around 1,400 owners. Standard membership comes in at £40 a year (although there are more expensive packages for the more committed). Irrespective of how much you pay, that share gives the holder a single vote in club matters and the right to stand for the board.

Despite the healthy number of investors, not bad for a club that is only averaging around 600 through the gate, according to Stuart Fuller, being competitive with this model remains a daily challenge.

'So many clubs at this level have a benefactor to turn to. And what that often means is that they don't have to think that much about the bottom line. We don't have that, there are no bottomless pockets. We have the income we generate from members and the income we can make from the club. And that's it. And against that we have the same costs everyone else faces: wages, travel, stadium maintenance. So, we endeavour to make sure everything is run as efficiently as it can be.'

Getting a club like Lewes into the National League, a stated aim of the board, under this model will be difficult. The absence of an external cash injection means that the club has to do things differently, to innovate. And this is an area where Lewes has excelled in recent years, specifically in creating a unique 'brand' at the Dripping Pan, one that the club is trying to leverage to broaden both those choosing to support Lewes and those willing to become shareholders.

According to Charlie Dobres, being fan-owned forms part of this. 'When you're competing for the attention of fans, and here I'm not just talking local non-league clubs but also clubs in the Football League and the Premier League, being community-owned sets you apart. There are lots of fans out there who are feeling disenfranchised from football, especially in the Premier League. Our progressive style of ownership speaks to them, bringing Lewes a level of attention that would be perhaps denied to a more conventionally owned club at this level.'

Although this helps the club position itself favourably in a crowded marketplace, alone it is not enough. Partly because, as a 'USP', it's not as unique as it once was. There are currently several clubs in England where supporters have some form of control (a number of which are completely owned by the fans). Indeed, just a few miles from Lewes, in places like Eastbourne, Tonbridge and Peacehaven, there are non-league clubs run this way.

'And so, you have to do more,' explains Dobres. 'You have to build your brand, build on what separates us from other clubs and what makes us special.'

There are several adjectives that have become associated with the club since the fans took over: quirky, progressive, inventive. What they all add up to is the sense that Lewes do things differently. The 'sell' for fans is that by following or investing in the club you are getting the chance to be part of something beyond the norm.

This unique 'brand' comes at you, the prospective fan/owner, from a few different angles. Lewes's matchday posters are the stuff of non-league legend, some of the best of which adapt film publicity posters, tailoring them to their opponents, such as *Halloween* becoming Harloween (Harlow Town), *Eraserhead* becoming Leatherhead, and *Stargate* for Margate.

Then there's the 'corporate' hospitality. 'This started as an April Fool's idea but in the end turned out to be one of the best things we've done. We have a few beach huts at the home end that now function as our corporate boxes. For £40 punters get food, a minibar, free wifi and a match programme, along with the best view in the house,' says Dobres.

The 'corporate' hospitality at the Dripping Pan forms one part of a matchday experience that has seen it name-checked alongside the likes of Signal Iduna Park, Camp

Nou and the San Siro when it comes to rating the best grounds to visit in Europe. And you can see why. Aside from its setting, gloriously nestled amidst the South Downs, the Dripping Pan offers everything you would want from a non-league game – the friendliness, the sense of community, but with a twist. Whether it's the beach huts, the broad and eclectic playlist broadcast over the tanoy (The Fall, Aphex Twin and CAN anyone?) or the tea bar that sells the best pie and mash you've ever eaten, you're getting to experience something that is worth the trip, something that you might not get somewhere else.

But as important as the above is, perhaps the move that has truly set Lewes apart from the crowd, a move that cemented its reputation as one of the most progressive clubs in the country, was the decision back in the summer of 2017 to remove the funding disparity that existed between its men's and women's sides.

The plan forms part of Equality FC, the club's wider campaign that aims to raise awareness about gender inequality in the sport and encourage more support for women's football across the UK.

'Although the picture has improved in recent years, there is still a sense in football that the women's game is somehow lesser. We wanted to change that,' says Fuller. 'At this club we believe that there should be a level playing field for women in football. And that's why we made the decision to commit to pay our women's and men's teams equally, providing budget parity. By doing this we hope to spark a change across the UK that will help put an end to the excuses for why such a deep pay disparity has persisted in football.'

When Lewes announced its new approach, the club made headlines, with features appearing in the likes of *The Guardian*, *The Times* and on the BBC. And the story's reach did not stop with the UK. What Lewes has done brought an international focus, a rare degree of media attention for a club of this size.

'Despite making the decision because we think it is the right thing to do, the move has also really pushed our brand to a wider audience. We have seen an upturn in membership, more people coming to our men's and women's games, and a broader range of partners want to be associated with the club since the decision was made public. People want to be part of what we are doing here, and Equality FC is a big part of that,' says Dobres.

Although interest in non-league football is growing, it is not uniform. For every Lewes there are other clubs who continue to struggle to get punters through the gate. And although there are signs that people are more willing to consider going to watch a side at this level, the real upturn in interest is geared towards non-league tiers higher up, the divisions of the National League.

'For a lot of clubs, it remains a yearly challenge to get people in to watch non-league games,' explains Gary Keyzor, current chairman of Suffolk's Lowestoft Town, who play in the Southern League Premier Division Central at Step 3.

'You're competing against Premier League sides for their attention, sides who produce better football, have bigger name players and whose "product" is delivered in a more attractive way. We might have a price advantage over them, in terms of what it costs to get in, but our grounds are not as comfortable, our players are not famous and the quality of football cannot match what they produce. It's particularly hard to get young people to the game. They, perhaps more than any other group, seem to be drawn to the glamour of the top flight. It's not hard to see why what we offer, from their perspective, pales by comparison.'

Despite it being a challenge, that's not to say that clubs don't at least try to expand their fanbases.

'And part of this is about improving the facilities, making the matchday experience better. The popular image of a non-league ground being some semi-derelict, windswept throwback to a different age doesn't hold as much truth as perhaps it once did,' says Ian Townshend. 'While there is still a rough and ready element to a lot of non-league football, plenty of clubs have realised that you can't just compete with League football on price alone. They have invested in their stadiums and improved the matchday experience. Going to watch the non-league game nowadays can be a comfortable experience.'

Many stadiums have benefitted from investment provided by the Football Stadia Improvement Fund (FSIF). Funded by the Premier League with an annual budget of £6.5m, the FSIF provides capital grants to clubs from the Football League down to the lower levels of the National League system to improve safety at their stadia. Although the amounts provided only cover a proportion of any costs, with the rest being found by the respective club, the investment can be transformative.

'We recently received a grant from the FSIF and it has helped enormously in our efforts to build for the future,' says Trevor Bull, chairman of Step 3's Scarborough Athletic.

The club was only formed back in 2007, a supporter owned, phoenix club that rose from the ashes of the now defunct Scarborough FC.

'For a decade we had groundshared with Bridlington Town. But our aim was always to get back into the town. Luckily, the local authority worked with us to build a new stadium for the club.'

The stadium formed part of a £50m development built on the town's former Weaponness Park and Ride site. But, as welcome as the new ground was for the club, it turned out that it needed a bit of fine-tuning, as Bull explains:

'Once we had got in there and played a few games, it was clear that it needed further development. It held 2,000 but as soon as we got more than 900 for a game, a lot of the fans had a restricted view. There was also not enough covering. Only around 500 spectators stayed dry when it rained, which meant a bit of bad weather could hit our numbers.'

A development was planned: the creation of a new stand, part seated, part terraced, that would provide the extra seats and covered raised standing that the ground needed.

'The local council sold the naming rights to the new stand, which raised £100,000. We thought we could raise £50,000 ourselves, through the usual methods clubs can use, crowdfunding, sponsored fun runs, quiz nights, etc. And so that meant applying to the FSIF for the remainder, which was £150,000. It is a complicated process, and your bid has to be pretty comprehensive. But the FSIF were extremely helpful, taking the time to guide us through the process,' says Bull.

The new stand was opened in the summer of 2019, boosting the stadium's capacity to nearly 3,000 and forming a vital part of the club's long-term plan to create a ground, and club, capable of reaching the National League.

'If you want to grow as a club and expand your fanbase, you have to have a ground that is welcoming,' says Bull. 'For us, part of that meant making sure that people aren't getting soaked through. But it also means listening to supporters to give them what they want. We could've made our new stand all-seater; however, a proportion of our fans wanted terraces. For them, that's part of the appeal of coming to watch a club like Scarborough. The FSIF has made that possible. Yes, we have played our part, as has the local authority, but without the money provided by the FSIF, getting to the position that we are at now, where we are regularly pulling in good numbers through the gate, would've been a lot harder.'

A better infrastructure represents just one part of efforts to improve growth and retention of fanbases. Many clubs let kids come in for free, some undertake fantastic work in the community, and others try to broaden the matchday experience, putting on events at the ground to make the afternoon more than just about football.

'Non-League Day, which takes place during the international break in early October, is also a great way for us to tap into a wider audience,' says Gary Keyzor.

Set up as a social media experiment by QPR fan James Doe in 2010, Non-League Day has now grown to become an annual part of the football calendar. It is regularly backed by Premier League and Football League clubs, many of whom promote the idea of visiting a local non-league game, and some even offer discounts for entry.

'It's the one time in the calendar when the big clubs and the media are actively promoting our side of the game. And in return, it's a chance for us to put on a bit of a show, to really make a day of it. You're often getting people coming who don't regularly go to non-league games, so it makes sense to put our best foot forward,' says Keyzor.

As is the case throughout the pyramid, so much of the above – the creation of better grounds, the ability to get out into the community, the capacity to offer discounted prices – is all much easier if a club has a benefactor. Whether this is somebody investing heavily to power the club up the pyramid, like David Haythornthwaite, or just somebody spending their money to ensure that a club remains competitive at a certain level, having that investment available means that the club has the breathing space to develop.

But, as Matt Badcock explains, some benefactors are beginning to question whether endlessly writing cheques is good for the clubs they are involved with.

'The pyramid is littered with examples of clubs who rely upon benefactors. But for a lot of these clubs it's quickly an over-reliance. This is especially true of clubs who have rapidly powered up the pyramid due to a benefactor's spending. Often, when the transition is so quick, the club's infrastructure can't keep pace. And so, were that benefactor to get hit by a bus, for example, the club in question would be plunged into crisis.'

Although many examples still exist of owners who appear to care little about the long-term impact of their investment or what would happen to the club were they to no longer be involved, there are those, increasingly, who think the opposite.

'The word sustainability is now being talked about more,' says Badcock. 'Although we still have people getting involved with clubs and just throwing money at them, there are owners who are much more considered in what they are doing. You're beginning to see owners thinking about the bigger picture, trying to ensure that the infrastructure of their club is developed hand-in-hand with improvements on the playing side. The idea is to create clubs that ultimately pay their own way – that are essentially sustainable.'

Geoff Thompson, chairman of Step 3's South Shields, is one such owner. Thompson, a successful entrepreneur in the North East, made his money through the establishment of the energy-broking company Utilitywise back in 2006.

In 2015, he was approached by his local club about the possibility of providing some sponsorship.

'When Bob Wray from the South Shields committee first came to me, I thought my involvement would just be to provide a few quid of sponsorship and that would be that,' he says. 'Although I'd watched the club growing up,' he continues, 'I have to be honest and say that my interest had waned as I'd got older and so I had no idea just how bad a position they were in. I didn't even know that they weren't playing at Filtrona Park anymore.'

Filtrona had been home to the club since 1992, a new ground provided for it by the owner at the time, John Rundle. The move was the culmination of a near two-decade search for a stadium.

Although Rundle's generosity was welcome, there were limits to his benevolence. After some good times in the late 1990s, boosted by Rundle's investment and the financial benefits provided by the new ground, the wheels had gradually come off the club's surge. With his interest in the struggling club waning, in 2006 Rundle pulled the plug.

In response, a consortium was formed with new chairman Gary Crutwell stepping in to run Shields. The consortium, however, could only afford to keep things just about ticking over, a challenge made considerably more difficult in 2013 when the club found itself homeless. Filtrona Park had remained owned by Rundle and his family, and a failure to agree an extension to the lease that year meant that South Shields had to start playing its home games 20 miles away in Peterlee. Inevitably, because of the distance involved in travelling to the snazzily titled Eden Lane Community Sports Facility, attendances dipped, dropping from triple to double figures (and the low end of double).

'When I learned more about the predicament that the club was in, I felt I should get involved and do more,' explains Thompson. 'I'd watched the club as a boy, having fond memories of being taken there by my dad and late uncle. I'm also still really connected to the community, and Utilitywise was a big employer locally. But you know, ultimately, I'd been lucky in life, in business and in my personal life, and as a Shields lad it just made sense to do something, to put a bit back into the community.'

To begin with, Thompson had no desire to do anything more than simply get the club back home to South Shields. At this stage there was no plan to take control or invest heavily.

'I tried various options with the council and none of them came through. Then I looked at other sites but nothing seemed right. In the end the best avenue possible was going to John Rundle, who still owned the old ground, and seeing if he would sell me the stadium, which, after some negotiations, he did for £350,000.'

But Thompson's involvement with the club would not end there.

'Through the work undertaken to get the club home, I became more emotionally connected to what was going on there. That, and my investment in the stadium, meant I wanted to make the connection more formal, so I became chairman and set about financially assisting a rebuilding process at the club and the ground.'

On the pitch, a raft of new signings arrived at the now renamed Mariners Park; an expanding wage budget bringing a better quality of player to the club. Personnel changes also occurred at a managerial level, with Lee Picton and Graham Fenton arriving as full-time co-managers.

'Beyond the playing staff and setting up the academy, I've also spent over £2m on improvements elsewhere in the club. We've invested in proper drainage to the pitch, proper irrigation, and that doesn't come cheap. We've improved the bar facilities, making the matchday experience for the fans as good as it can be with our current stadium limitations. We've got a 250-seat marquee now, which is also available for non-matchday events, and we've improved the stands too. But, perhaps most important of all, has been the installation of a 3G pitch nearby, which cost around £500,000.'

It is important because it has been a key element in Thompson's drive towards making the club more profitable.

'Something like a 3G pitch, which can be hired out to the community, can provide significant income for the club for years to come. That, alongside what we have done with better matchday hospitality, greater capacity and using the stadium to generate income beyond Saturday afternoons, will provide the club with the ability to enjoy better levels of income in the future.'

All of this chimes in with Thompson's pet theme of 'sustainability', which he mentions several times during the interview, stressing its importance in the club's future plans. Thompson does not fit the mould of the traditional benefactor. He is not here to simply bankroll the club indefinitely, building a monument to his own financial power. Instead, he genuinely appears to want to create something that has the capacity to grow and thrive on its own terms. This is not an ego trip by a wealthy man with too much time on his hands but rather an example of a local businessman putting something back into the community simply for the sake of civic pride.

'Although I have invested a lot in the short term, in the long term I don't want to be endlessly underwriting the club. I see myself as a custodian, if you like, and therefore what I'm trying to do is build the club to a point where it's got a commercial model and an infrastructure that will allow it to survive without me. My drivers are a little bit different to what you might expect from a lot of benefactors. This isn't about me, it's about creating a sustainable football club. I desperately want to get the club to that position. I think we're kind of halfway there. The club's not making money, we are a loss-making club. But that's not a shock. However, we have a three-year plan, we know what we're doing, and it requires investment to get it to a certain point before the profits will follow.'

None of this will be achievable without the engagement of the local community, through higher attendances, better levels of sponsorship and improved commercial partnerships.

'And a big part of how we achieve this is through community engagement,' says Thompson. 'The South Shields foundation, which was founded in 2017, is the medium through which we do this. We are particularly invested in helping local children and now have a wide-ranging schools programme and also an array of other programmes on offer at the ground and at other venues locally that seek to use sport to improve the lives of local people. When you invest in the community, you're not just helping people, although that is important, you're also building relationships, cementing the bond that people will have with the club.'

Of course, both the club and Thompson realise that without improvement on the pitch, they're unlikely to see community support expand enough. Fortunately, investment in the playing side has yielded a dramatic turnaround in the club's fortunes.

Promotion has followed promotion and today the club stand in the Northern Premier League Premier Division. There have been plenty of highs along the way, including a 32-game winning streak, an historic quadruple in the 2016/17 season and, the jewel in the crown, a successful trip down to Wembley, the first time in the club's history that it had been there.

'We got to the final of the FA Vase in 2017,' says Thompson, 'taking on Cleethorpes Town. We took around 14,000 of our fans down there, which was amazing. The whole town had a buzz about it. I can remember looking out at the fans at Wembley and feeling such pride. Just a few years earlier our side were playing in front of 30-odd people in Peterlee and now here they were in front of thousands. To win it was the icing on the cake.'

When it comes to support from the wider community, the success that South Shields has had on the pitch, combined with the work that the club has undertaken off it, has begun to yield results.

'I think we've built a bit of momentum here. In financial terms, it's cost a lot personally, but we're starting to see the community get engaged. Last season our average attendance was around 1,500, which massively outstrips the league we are in. That's up there with what a lot of Step 1 clubs are getting. And, as long as what we offer on the pitch continues to improve, I think we can get better. 80,000 people live in South Shields and about 160,000 in South Tyneside, so we've got quite a big conurbation. There's every potential for us to get better and better attendance numbers.'

Here is a benefactor, you feel, who sees himself more as a catalyst, the medium through which a different kind of South Shields can emerge, bigger and more successful unquestionably, but also capable of standing on its own two feet.

'In football, there are too many examples of clubs that have done well on the pitch simply because somebody has thrown some money around. And then once that money is gone, everything falls apart. I don't want that here. I want a club that makes a profit, that is fully engaged with the local community, that can be successful without the need of somebody constantly pouring money into it. In the long term, that's what South Shields needs to be.'

The danger of not thinking about the long term, of simply pouring cash into the playing side without considering the wider infrastructure, can be potentially devastating.

'Beyond the top two tiers of the National League system, there is relatively little financial oversight. At steps 3 and 4 the FA's "fit and proper" persons test stops those with recent criminal convictions and a recent history of insolvency, particularly with regard to football clubs, from becoming owners, directors or significant shareholders. But once someone is in control of a club, there's very little to stop them doing whatever they want, whether that be loading it with debt, massively overstretching it or just running it badly,' says Matt Badcock.

And because of this, at this level of the game, clubs can still go under. That notion of permanence, the idea of a club that can see out the slings and arrows thrown against it, is not as sturdy as it is higher up the pyramid.

'Clubs do still disappear at Steps 3 and 4. It doesn't happen as often as it does much lower down the National League system, often because these are relatively important community ventures, which means there has tended to be someone on hand, a local businessman, the local authority or the fans to step in and help. But it does still occur. And the benefactor model, which remains common, is often to blame. Benefactors can lose interest, can lose their money or can pass away. And if a club has overstretched itself, by, for example, inflating its wage bill, it can very quickly find itself in a lot of trouble financially, especially if investment in the playing budget has not gone hand-in-hand with investment in the club's infrastructure,' says Badcock.

North Ferriby United represent one recent cautionary tale, an example of how the benefactor model can go horribly wrong.

There had been a football club in North Ferriby, a parish just outside of Hull, since the early 1930s. And for the first 80 years of its existence, things were relatively low-key, a solitary appearance in the FA Vase Final in 1997, which they lost, being the club's highlight.

But that all changed between 2014 and 2019, a period when North Ferriby United experienced pretty much everything that football can throw at a club: cup triumphs, promotion, more promotion, relegation, more relegation, even more relegation, new owners, new managers, threatened relocation, threatened name changes and closure.

It was a club for whom the phrase 'Football ... bloody hell' almost seems inadequate.

After a decade of comfortably competing in the Northern Premier League, the little club from East Yorkshire started creating waves back in 2013, under the guiding hand of its manager, Billy Heath. From nowhere, the club found itself gaining an unlikely promotion to the National League North, the success bringing media attention and the focus of investors looking to jump aboard a local underdog story.

Towards the end of 2013, it was bought by Steve Forster, owner of EON Visual Media, and his wife Eman, the daughter of Hull City's much disliked chairman Assem Allam. The Forsters promised support and were as good as their word (to begin with at least). It was investment that supported further success but which also left Ferriby reliant on the owners.

In 2015, the Villagers made it to Wembley, lifting the FA Trophy after beating the favourites Wrexham on penalties. In 2016, the good times continued as Ferriby gained promotion to the National League, the highest level it had ever competed at.

Although the club was riding the crest of a footballing wave, goings on behind the scenes were less harmonious. There were rumours that, despite the success, the Forsters were preparing to pull the plug on funding for the club, rumours not helped by the apparent restriction on Ferriby's budget for its inaugural season at Step 1.

Pre-season also presented further challenges, with Heath and his assistant Mark Carroll leaving for Halifax Town.

'A few players left the club too, because they couldn't accommodate the extra travelling that competing in the National League required. Despite the excitement of being in a higher division, there was some trepidation, I recall. You felt like the club was in for a tough year,' says Darren Norton, long-time fan and the man behind North Ferriby's fanzine *View from the Allotment End*.

Concerns were not helped by the club's finance director, Richard Watts, issuing a frank assessment of that season's chances on the eve of the new campaign, saying, 'we will have the smallest budget of all 24 clubs in the league by a country mile. It would be absolutely remarkable if we stayed up.'

And it's easy to see why. After all, this was a club that hailed from a village of just under 4,000 people and which was only getting around 300 through the gate on a Saturday afternoon. For all intents and purposes, this was a Step 3 or 4 club that had been rapidly financed beyond its comfort zone. If that financing dried up completely, life was going to be very tough.

With a limited budget, the Villagers' spell in the fifth tier of English football lasted a solitary season.

'We made a good fist of it, losing half a dozen games in the last five minutes, but we were very much second best most of the time,' Norton admits. 'We didn't really stand much of a chance at that level to be honest. The owners trimmed the budget and the necessary infrastructure improvements were never going to be done, regardless of the time constraints.'

When Richard Watts had offered his bleak assessment of the club's chances that season, he had softened the blow slightly by saying that 'if we go down, we'll be fine. This is not a boom or bust club, like many at this level.' But he couldn't have been more wrong. The club was far from 'fine', entering a death spiral that, when contrasted to its recent happier seasons, became the very definition of 'boom and bust'.

The Forsters jumped ship midway through the following season, selling the club to former player Jamie Waltham.

'I didn't have the kind of money to bankroll the club in the same way that the Forsters did,' Waltham explains. 'But what I could do is try to build some sustainability. In recent years, the previous owners had essentially been underwriting losses. Nothing had been put in place to improve what the club could earn. It was a classic case of just throwing money around. So, the wage bill, for example, was untenable. I was faced with the daunting task of trying to restructure the club, which really meant cutting costs.'

Except that wasn't all that Waltham concentrated on. Along with the club's attempted financial restructuring, the new owner also made a number of other proposals that immediately set him against the fans.

One was the unusual decision to try and repurpose the ground as a Travellers' site. Under the plan, which never ultimately came to fruition, it was envisioned that the ground would accommodate 46 caravans at around £50 a week. This would've given the club an additional £2,500 of weekly income. The idea was that the Travellers would temporarily relocate before matches, giving the club the run of the place for a few hours. Understandably, many fans were horrified at the idea of their home being used in this way, appalled at the idea of the pitch being churned up by the caravans and cars.

But their anger towards that plan was nothing compared to what would follow when Waltham revealed his next big idea.

'Waltham owned a stadium in Hull called Dunswell Park,' explains Norton, 'where a number of clubs had tried and failed to take off. What he wanted to do was take our club to that ground and change our name to East Hull FC. The plan was to effectively get a ready-made Step 2 club there, with an existing fanbase and structure, rather than build something up himself. As soon as that was proposed, alarm bells were ringing. We began to suspect that he was a bit of a "Del Boy" character, a wheeler-dealer who was only interested in exploiting our troubles for his own ends.'

In his defence, Waltham made a compelling case to the FA. He highlighted the lack of development opportunities at the current stadium, due to its landlocked status, the potential attendance growth that a relocation to east Hull represented (because of the area's significantly larger population), and the financial savings that could be achieved if, as he promised, the new club were able to reside at the new ground rent free.

In response, the fans launched the Save North Ferriby United campaign, their attempt to stop Waltham in his tracks. Support flocked in from across football, with national organisations such as Supporters Direct and the Football Supporters' Federation, along with supporters' groups and trusts from across the country, rallying for the cause.

'The wider football world really put the campaign on the map and secured lots of local and national media attention. We are only a small fanbase but we were able to make a national impact, and throw the spotlight on what was happening. I think the plight we were facing touched a nerve amongst football fans. It fed into fears about franchise football and commercialisation of the game. In particular, there is something sacred about a club's name. And so, the idea of someone taking it away from the fans and changing it really seemed to anger a lot of people,' says Matthew Kempson of Save North Ferriby United.

While turmoil surrounded the club off the pitch, on it Ferriby appeared to be giving everything to ensure that the 'bust' element of its 'boom and bust' story was fully embraced. After a dismal campaign, the club finished rock bottom during its first season back in the National League North, ensuring back-to-back relegations.

At the end of that lamentable campaign, the club changed hands again, with Waltham citing work commitments as the reason why he could no longer dedicate sufficient time to the club.

'In reality,' Norton explains, 'he kept a connection as the new owners Carl and Terry Chadwick were mates of his. Plus, the plans that he had proposed, the move and the name change, remained in place. The whole reason for Waltham's involvement with North Ferriby, the acquisition of a club for his ground, had not gone away.'

That it eventually did, came courtesy of the league authorities and the FA, both of whom rejected the proposals in January 2019. That should have been a moment to celebrate for the fans, and indeed, briefly, it was. But any joy was also fleeting.

'Not long after, it became clear that although the battle to save the name of the club had been successful, the victory could prove to be an empty one because the club itself might soon cease to exist,' says Norton.

In February 2019, the club were served with a winding-up petition, issued by Chappelow Sports Turf Limited over an unpaid debt regarding maintenance of the pitch at the newly named Chadwick Joinery & Builders Stadium.

'But we believe there was significantly more debt in the club,' Matthew Kempson told *That's Liquid Football* in 2019. 'It just so happened that it was the £8,000 to the turf management company that was called in. We estimate the total debt as being closer to £70,000. On top of this, we think there were further debts to utility companies and other suppliers.'

From the fans' perspective, it looked like Waltham and the Chadwicks had just let the club drift, ignoring debts that were partly accrued under the Forsters, gathering new ones of their own, all the while waiting to see what would happen with the relocation and the name change.

'Maybe if it had gone through they might have put their hands in their pockets. But while it was uncertain, very little was done and the problems just mounted,' says Norton.

In March 2019, with it clear that the club could not pay the debt, North Ferriby United was liquidated by Hull County Court. Soon after, the Northern Premier League, in accordance with FA guidelines, expunged its record for that season. Not that the campaign had been a memorable one: the Villagers were already doomed to another relegation.

'For Ferriby, the problems came with the lack of exit planning when, undoubtedly, the funding would be withdrawn. When the money is withdrawn, careful financial planning is required to restructure the club. It's not just the playing budget that is affected, the whole business model needs to change. Perhaps, the sensible thing, as we have seen with other clubs, is to take voluntarily relegation to a more sustainable level, where our budget would have made us competitive,' Kempson told *That's Liquid Football*.

North Ferriby United's story illustrates how precarious life can be at this level. Although the club's unravelling took a few seasons, and was in many ways avoidable, it shows what can happen in the wake of a benefactor's relationship with a club turning sour. Ferriby, in essence a Step 3 or 4 club, was thrust to a level it could not compete at without continued support or a broader infrastructure. It was then left to pick up the pieces when that support evaporated, with disastrous consequences.

Not every club that suffers a sudden reversal of fortune goes under, but the potential is always there if the wrong people take over and poor decisions are made. Clubs, irrespective of their long histories, are not immune to collapse.

In the case of North Ferriby United, not long after its demise, enough goodwill remained locally for the club to return, albeit in a different incarnation and at a lower level. A phoenix club, North Ferriby (without the 'United'), emerged in the spring of 2019, put together by former United chairman Les Hare, with the backing of a number of local residents and businessmen. The club is currently enjoying life in the second tier of the Northern Counties East League.

'It's great to see clubs bounce back. But not every club does,' says Matthew Badcock. 'And the ordeal that fans go through when clubs are spiralling out of control is tough. I think at Steps 3 and 4 life is hard. There's more money around than there used to be, more attention from the media, and, in some parts of the country, more people coming to games. But despite this, navigating through it all is not easy. And it doesn't really get any easier for those lucky enough to move up to the tiers above.'

Chapter Five

The National League

F OR much of its history, the National League (or the
Conference as those of a more mature vintage will
always know it as) was very much seen as the poor
relation to the Football League. It might have represented
the apex of the non-league system, but in the popular
consciousness it still belonged to the world of part-time
football, a world of dire pitches, meagre crowds and long
balls.

It had been formed back in 1979, an amalgamation of
the two strongest non-league divisions in England at the
time, the Northern Premier League and Southern League.
A key motivation for the restructuring was to create a single
champion who could then apply for election to the tier above.

Prior to 1979, clubs across the highest reaches of non-
league football could apply to join the Football League
by standing in an annual election, in which the bottom
four teams in Division Four were also obliged to take
part. Until 1977 it hadn't been necessary for a non-league
team wishing to stand for election to have even won its
respective division.

But whether champions or not, what tended to happen was the maintenance of the status quo. Most non-league clubs never got close to getting the necessary number of votes. The Football League was a bit of a closed shop, with its members understandably rarely voting to eject one of its own.

Through the restructuring, so the reasoning went, one single champion would have a better chance at gaining votes. The reasoning was flawed. Until the mid-1980s, when the 'election' element was finally removed, that single champion still had a hard time breaking the glass ceiling, the 'closed shop' remaining brutally effective for the established order.

It took nearly a decade of lobbying by the non-league world before the Football League relented, finally introducing automatic promotion and relegation in 1987 (part of a wider reorganisation of the Football League).

Something about the continuance of election early on, combined with the fact that once automatic promotion did come in it tended to be a recently relegated side that yo-yoed its way back into the Football League during the system's early years, only added to the sense of the fifth tier being a near-parallel footballing world, one with unglamorously named clubs and unfashionable sponsors.

Any division that could enter into a naming partnership with Gola, manufacturer of the kind of perennially un-hip trainers that your ma would buy you off the market when you'd specifically asked for Adidas, was never going to possess any degree of allure.

Inevitably, it was a division that would routinely lose your attention as the scores came in on the vidiprinter during a Saturday afternoon.

But that sense of disconnect could not be said to characterise the National League today. 'It is, in many ways, the fourth tier of the Football League, albeit not in name,' says Lee Clark, manager of National League North side Blyth Spartans. 'Full-time clubs are increasingly the norm in the National League, and are becoming more common in its two feeder divisions too. Wages and transfer fees are on the up, attendance figures are much higher than they used to be, and games are televised more often. The divide that there used to be between the Football League and the non-league world is far less clear than was once the case.'

The two 'feeder divisions' that Clark mentions are the National League North and the National League South. The pair were created back in 2004, following another reorganisation. There are two promotion places to the National League's top division from each regional division – the champions are promoted automatically, while the remaining place is decided via the play-offs. The four teams relegated from the National League are then allocated to one or the other of the regional divisions, depending on their geographical location.

'Even in the regional divisions, things have changed,' Clark continues. 'We've felt the expanding popularity of the non-league game, the growing professionalisation of football at this level and more interest from the wider football world. Although in both the National League North and South you still get the sense that some of the clubs competing share more in common with the divisions below than those higher up, the gap between the Football League and football where we are is not as large as it used to be.'

A growing interest in non-league football, as mentioned in the previous chapter, has been a contributing factor to the new environment, the associated rise in income enabling clubs to invest in players, coaching and infrastructure, making the division more closely resemble the Football League above.

As is the case in much of the pyramid, clubs that compete at this level remain hugely reliant on matchday income. The familiar need to get bodies through the gates is as pressing for Dover Athletic in the National League as it is for Whitchurch Alport back in the North West Counties League.

Fortunately for clubs playing at this level, attendances are on the up. Although this trend has affected many parts of the non-league world, it has been more keenly felt at Steps 2 and 3. In 2018/19, the National League was watched by over two million spectators for the first time in the competition's history, with clubs such as Harrogate Town, Braintree and Havant & Waterlooville seeing attendances rise by more than 50 per cent in recent years.

'Part of this trend is the fact that you've got some pretty big clubs that have been relegated from the Football League. In recent years, clubs like Tranmere Rovers, Leyton Orient and Wrexham have brought thousands of supporters to our game. Although some bounce back to the Football League quickly, others, like Chester, York City and Stockport County, have hung around longer,' says Neil Smith, current manager of National League side Bromley.

There has also been the emergence of clubs who, via the external investment of owners, have grown quickly, powering through the pyramid, amassing large fanbases on the way. These include the likes of AFC Fylde, Forest

Green Rovers and Salford City (the momentum of the latter two has already carried them out into the Football League).

The recent history of Salford City illustrates how quickly the attendances of a club can change when it is being jet-financed by new investors. Back in 2014, when the Singaporean entrepreneur Peter Lim and former members of Manchester United's Class of 92 – Gary Neville, Phil Neville, Ryan Giggs, Nicky Butt and Paul Scholes – bought Salford City, the club's average attendances were just a few hundred. By the time the Ammies were playing in the Football League in 2019, that figure had jumped to around 3,000.

But these clubs don't account for all of the rise in the National League, and nor can they account for the rise elsewhere in the non-league game.

'You've got a lot of factors at play here,' says Daniel Magner. 'People looking for a more "authentic" form of the game, people looking for affordable football, football hipsters on the lookout for the next "hip" club to get behind. Inevitably, because of how good the stadiums are, how good the football is and how much recognition some of these clubs now have, the higher levels of the National League system have seen the most growth.'

Interest in and exposure of the National League has risen to such an extent that broadcasters have got in on the act. BT now have a deal with the league and during the 2019/20 season broadcast 30 live games, plus a highlights programme featuring every goal from the weekly fixtures.

Alongside this, many National League clubs have begun to broadcast their own channels, often via YouTube. The days of witnessing a goal in the National League and never seeing it again are increasingly a thing of the past. Now, with varying degrees of quality, games are filmed and then broadcast as a highlights reel, expanding the reach of clubs for whom support was once restricted to going to the match.

Although the upsurge in interest in the National League has meant more people coming through the gate and therefore an increase in revenues, inevitably costs have not remained quiescent.

'With more money chasing what remains a relatively fixed stock of players, wages and transfer costs have increased,' says Matt Badcock. 'It's a trend that has been exacerbated by other factors affecting the National League, such as the arrival of a number of clubs with significant spending power and the parachute payments that are handed down to relegated clubs by the Football League.'

In recent seasons, several big, professional clubs, often armed with larger-than-average non-league budgets, such as Bristol Rovers, Leyton Orient and Tranmere Rovers, have spent time at Step 1. And they have been joined here by those fast-rising clubs, heavily backed in financial terms, like Salford City and Forest Green Rovers.

'As a result, more and more money has flooded into the playing side, which has inevitably further pushed up wages and transfer costs. For smaller clubs like ours, and we only have a playing budget that is about a quarter of the big boys, this is a real problem,' says Neil Smith.

Salford City came in for particular criticism as it climbed up the pyramid. When the takeover took place at the club back in 2014, Salford were a part-time member of the Northern Premier League Division One North, Step 4 of the pyramid. Since then, the owners have invested heavily, and successfully, powering the now full-time club to Football League status in just five years.

In its final season in the non-league world, the club made headlines when it signed the striker Adam Rooney from Aberdeen, paying him around £4,000 per week in wages (considerably more than the National League average). The move led to a brief Twitter spat between Gary Neville and Accrington Stanley owner Andy Holt, with the latter accusing the former of trying to 'steal' a place in the Football League, calling the situation a 'piss take'.

'You've always had Football League players drop down to our level,' explains Neil Smith. 'But in the past, you tended to get young players who might have been released, players who were looking for game time or older players who couldn't make the grade in the higher leagues. But the change with Salford, and other clubs, is that you're getting experienced pros, who are playing regularly for good sides, choosing to drop down. And part of why they'll do this is because clubs can pay Football League wages and Football League transfer costs.'

Although Salford is often held up as the poster boy for a new, moneyed approach to non-league football, it is not the only club to spend heavily at Steps 1 and 2. Other current members of the National League, such as AFC Fylde and Ebbsfleet United, have invested significantly in their squads in recent years.

As too have clubs further down, such as National League South's Billericay Town. While the Essex businessman Glenn Tamplin was involved with the club, a spell that roughly lasted from late 2016 to early 2019, Billericay underwent a period of dramatic transformation. During his brief tenure as owner, Tamplin pumped around

£2m into the club, luring a raft of former Premier League players (admittedly long past their prime) to New Lodge, including Jermaine Pennant, Kevin Foley, Jamie O'Hara and Paul Konchesky. With a rumoured weekly wage bill of around £20,000 during Taplin's first season in charge, Billericay were massively outspending rival clubs. While it lasted, the spending was enough to see the club win the Isthmian League Cup, reach the first round of the FA Cup and gain promotion to Step 2.

When clubs drop down to non-league football, they also come with parachute payments from the Football League.

'As of 2016/17, clubs relegated from the Football League receive 100 per cent of the League Two TV money in the first year following relegation and 50 per cent in the second year. At the moment, you're looking at about £750,000. That's a huge amount of money to be entering the league, a lot of which, based on recent experience, gets blown on transfers and wages,' says Matt Badcock.

This changing financial environment has made it increasingly difficult for smaller clubs to compete. For all the former Football League clubs there are at Step 1, and new, well-funded clubs emerging, there are still many members of the National League whose DNA has more in common with the clubs below them in the pyramid than those above.

'We're still quite a small, simple club, largely dependent on volunteers,' says Sutton United chairman Dave Farebrother. 'We don't have the money to employ many professionals at the club in the same way that others do. I know of one club who employ ten times as many people in their hospitality section as we do in total. We're obviously, in terms of our facilities, our playing budget and our crowds, more developed than most clubs you might see in something like the Isthmian League, but we're not that far away. If our fantastic fans stopped giving their time as volunteers tomorrow, for example, then it would be much harder for us to continue at this level.'

Back in the days of the Conference, when the division was the less-fancied, uglier sibling of the Football League, the DNA of the pyramid below haunted the league, best exemplified by the fact that so many of its member clubs were semi-pro. It was a fact that the media would always revel in when a Conference club came up against a giant in the FA Cup, contrasting the professionals of the Football League and the Premier League with the mechanics, postmen and butchers lining up to face them.

But, in the top tier at least, that is demonstrably no longer the case. 'In the last few years, as more and more money has come into the league, and bigger clubs have dropped down into it, the division has become tougher for those who are not full-time. And so, clubs have had to transition, becoming full-time or close to full-time, with playing budgets that are representative of that shift,' says Matt Badcock.

For those not blessed with huge crowds, a financial benefactor or the ability to generate significant sums of revenue from the football business, competing is a struggle.

'Right now, our budget, compared to what it has been in the past, is frighteningly large. Despite that, none of the players are employed for 52 weeks per year. And although we have raised the budget, ours is probably in the lower quintile for this league. I can think of at least two clubs with annual playing budgets reputed to be at least three

Rotherfield FC: everything a community club should be (Grassroots groundswell)

Dave Horocks coaches the next generation at Fletcher Moss Rangers

Brighton and Hove Walking Football Club: pensioner power in action (Andrew Finch)

The Palace for Life Foundation, offering a true definition of football for all

Corinthian Casuals v Corinthians Paulista (January 2015)

Geoff Thompson: The man bringing success and sustainability to South Shields (Kev Wilson and Peter Talbot)

The beach huts at Lewes FC, corporate hospitality with a twist

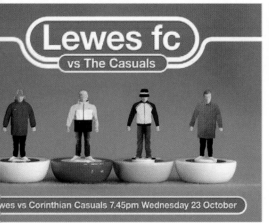

Lewes FC's much-loved match day posters

The North Ferriby United fanzine trying to find humour in the bleakest of times

Lowestoft Town in happier times, clinching promotion to Step 2 (Steven Gardiner)

AFC Unity: Feminist, socialist, community minded

Lewes Women in action against Crystal Palace: a club with gender equality at its heart

Everton's Simone Magill in action

Neil Pinkerton and Trevor Clark, the men who rescued Gateshead

Hartlepool's CEO, Mark Maguire, the man tasked with rebuilding the club (Shutter Press)

Exeter City's chairman Julian Tagg, the man behind the club's successful academy

Andy Holt: A very different kind of football club owner

Tranmere Rovers owner Mark Palios celebrates the club's return to the Football League (Richard Ault)

The Brentford B Team: the club's innovative experiment in player development

The long-awaited move back to Plough Lane for AFC Wimbledon

Hashtag United: A very different kind of football club

Hashtag United's young fans: the future of the game?

times ours! For clubs that aren't completely full-time in this league, it's a challenge, because in practice it means that coaches have less time with the players, and when it comes to signing players, those kind of clubs obviously have less freedom of movement in the market compared to a club who has a benefactor behind them writing off debts, access to parachute payments or large crowds coming through the turnstiles,' says Farebrother.

Lower down, in the regional divisions of the National League, the problem continues. Since inauguration, Step 2 has traditionally been a semi-professional tier, one not always blessed with the largest of playing budgets. But this has begun to change.

'You've had some big clubs down here in recent seasons, the likes of York City, Stockport County and Torquay United, professional clubs with big budgets. Then you have the likes of Billericay and Salford City moving up and, with their big budgets, unsettling the competitive balance of the division. What this means for smaller clubs, like us here at Blyth Spartans, is that competing becomes a lot harder. We've tried to get around it by putting more faith in youth and trying to bring on players from the pyramid below. It's not easy though. It means you have to work a lot harder just to keep up,' says Lee Clark.

For those clubs who don't have the financial ability to turn full-time, the reality of putting together sides that have to compete against better funded, increasingly professional rivals, is a tough one, as former Oxford City manager Mark Jones explains:

'I don't think people in the professional game appreciate how hard part-time players work. They are normally holding down another job and then coming to training of an evening and playing at the weekend. There are times when players turn up to train and they are absolutely knackered from work. A lot of people think that the limited time you spend with players is the biggest challenge for semi-pro clubs, but fatigue is just as important. If a part-time side is playing a club who have professional players, or even a semi-pro set-up, where you can afford things like professional conditioning coaches or nutritional experts, they're always going to be at a competitive disadvantage.'

The costs involved in competing at Steps 1 and 2 can sometimes simply be too much for many clubs. And there are occasions when the margins involved, the difference between being able to compete and not, can come down to something as apparently simple as how much it costs to get to a game.

Back in 2014, Lowestoft FC were riding high. The Trawlerboys had just beaten AFC Hornchurch in the Isthmian League play-off final, guaranteeing the club a place in the National League South for the following season. It was the club's fourth attempt to get there, the previous three occasions ending in heartbreaking play-off final defeats.

'That was a great occasion,' remembers club chairman Gary Keyzor. 'The club had never reached such heights. And, after the frustration of the previous three attempts, you can appreciate how happy everyone was. It was the culmination of several years of hard work by lots of people and several years of investment by me. We'd earned our right to be at that level and we were all looking forward to what would happen next.'

Keyzor, managing director of both a graphic design company in Lowestoft and an oilfield electrical supply company in Great Yarmouth, had always been involved in football locally.

'I watched Lowestoft when I was younger with my grandad, I'd played and I'd been involved in coaching with various local sides, so football was in my blood. When the club approached me to see if I could help out, I just thought I'd give that a go, although I have to admit that I probably didn't fully appreciate what a commitment it would be. I had no idea how often I would have to dip into my own pocket to help the club out either. That's the thing about football clubs, no matter how much you spend, it never seems enough.'

With Keyzor's financial input and a talented managerial team, which consisted of joint first-team managers Ady Gallagher and Micky Chapman and director of football Craig Fleming, Lowestoft had thrived.

'We thought we had everything in place,' says Gallagher. 'Micky and I got on really well and knew the club inside out. Craig had fantastic contacts in the game. And Gary's investment had helped propel our rise from county football to Step 2. But despite all of that, we didn't have enough to cope with a bit of bad luck. And when that came, it hit us really hard.'

Lowestoft's position, geographically not quite south but also not quite north, was a tough one for the league. In the end, the club was placed in the National League North, a decision that spelled disaster.

'To put it starkly, we went from playing teams like Margate, Maidstone and Billericay, sides that were in the home counties, to playing clubs like Barrow, Stockport County and Harrogate Town, sides that were hundreds of miles away,' says Gallagher.

The problems this created were twofold. First, the financial implications were severe, as Keyzor explains:

'Right away the playing budget was hit because the club's transport costs escalated. When playing far-flung clubs, for example like Barrow, we had to pay for hotel costs, because getting there and back in one day was too much to ask. The jump from what we had been doing to this was too much for us to cope with. It might not sound much to people used to following a Premier League club, but down at our level being put in the northern section overwhelmed us financially.'

And then there's the implications for the playing side. The thinning of the playing budget made it harder for the club to bring in the players required to compete at this higher level, placing it at a competitive disadvantage.

'And for those who remained, away games were a challenge,' Gallagher explains. 'You're asking some part-time players, people who have been working all week, to travel to Colwyn Bay and back, for example, in one day. The odds on them turning up fresh for that game are slim.'

Lowestoft managed just two seasons in the higher league before being relegated. 'We faced a bit of bad luck, but that's part of the game,' says Keyzor. 'Had the club been more commercially successful, had it been pulling in a lot more fans than it was, or had it been backed by somebody with greater resources than me, then it would probably have overcome the setback of being put in the National League North. But none of those things were the case. I certainly didn't have endless amounts of cash to spend.'

Although having an increasing number of 'big' clubs, combined with well-funded newer clubs at Steps 1 and 2 has changed the financial profile of life in the higher reaches of the non-league system, there is also a feeling that the relationship that exists between the National League and the Football League is also exerting a strong influence too.

'There is a palpable desire for Football League clubs that have been relegated to get back up as soon as possible,' says Mark Palios, chairman of Tranmere Rovers, a club that recently spent three seasons in the National League. 'That's not just for prestige or because the fans demand it, although those aspects really matter, but it's also because, financially, being down in the National League is costly.'

One of the areas most commonly affected by relegation is attendances, as Palios outlines:

'The longer you're down in there, the greater the chance that people will begin to walk away. Your figures will likely drop to begin with anyway, because smaller clubs will bring fewer away fans. But early on, if you're doing well, the novelty of simply winning games, which you obviously hadn't done the season before, might offset that. But that can only go on for so long. Getting mired in non-league football, or, worse, dropping further, can run the risk of permanently alienating some supporters. Not all clubs suffer the same fate, but there is a fear that stagnation in the National League could permanently remove part of your fanbase.'

Average attendances at Step 1 are about half of those in League Two, and those of the regional leagues at Step 2 are about a third of the size. So, for a club like York City, who were relegated from League Two back in 2016, and then relegated to the National League North in 2017, the sustained spell in non-league football has cost the club around 1,000 fans on matchday.

'And that matters,' says Mike Brown, chairman of the York City Supporters' Trust and a supporter-elected member of the club's board. 'Clubs at this level live and die by the numbers they can get through the gate on matchday. This isn't the Premier League, where TV money and all manner of commercial partnership power clubs forward. In the National League and below, losing a quarter of your fanbase then makes the job of getting back into the Football League so much harder. In the absence of some huge injection of cash from an owner, the longer you stay down at this level, the greater the chances that you're going to become a fixture.'

Of course, that relegation means a decline in attendances and income is nothing new in football. When a club drops down to a lower league it's not uncommon for a variety of income streams to suffer. Gate receipts often decline, for example, not just because of lower numbers coming to a match but also because ticket prices are reduced to reflect the calibre of the league.

'Lower numbers also means less money from "food and drink" on the day,' says Danny Macklin, CEO of Leyton Orient, a club that recently spent two seasons in the National League. 'Then you might find that sponsors are less willing to invest if fewer people are coming to matches too. And corporate hospitality also becomes a tougher sell, depending on the level that you are being relegated to.'

Although the above is just a reality of relegation at any level, the transition from the Football League to non-league football exaggerates the effect. The National League might be League Three in all but name, but psychologically, in the mindset of people, it still carries with it the whiff of inferiority.

'Leaving the Football League is still considered a huge blow to the fans,' says Tom Davies, vice-chair of the Leyton Orient Fans' Trust. 'Although on one level you are crushed by the drop because you know there will be financial implications, on a deeper level you just don't want your club to be playing non-league football. We all know that the fifth tier is much better than it once was. But there are plenty of people for whom that won't matter. Moving between League One and League Two is, for a lot of fans, sponsors and those in the business community who clubs seek to work with, not the same as moving from League Two to the National League.'

It's a situation that is then further exacerbated by both the funding relationship that exists between the National League and the Football League above and the system of promotion and relegation that currently governs this part of the game.

Each season, teams in League Two get about £450,000 per year from the Premier League broadcast deal in the form of a 'solidarity payment'. Added to this, from the English Football League's (EFL) broadcast deal with Sky, League Two clubs also get a figure close to £500,000 in the form of the 'basic award'.

'So, what that means in practice is that relegation is costly. And on the other side, promotion represents a decent financial prize. For clubs going down, even with parachute payments, after a couple of seasons they are well over a million pounds worse off. For clubs going up, promotion alone can mean millions more over that same time period. For many clubs at this level that is a large amount of money to be in the balance,' says Danny Macklin.

'And then there is the issues of academies,' says Mark Palios. Under the Elite Player Performance Plan (EPPP), the youth development scheme initiated by the Premier League back in 2011, which has sought to raise standards and to improve the quality and quantity of home-grown players, academies within the highest four divisions receive central funding in relation to what category they are (ranging from one to four).

'When we were relegated, despite being one of the best performing category three academies in the country, we lost our EPPP status due to the first team being outside the Football League. And that meant that not only did we lose around £400,000 per year in central funding, we also lost registration rights for players aged 16 and under, meaning young players who had been coached at our academy for many years could leave without notice and without the club receiving any compensation.'

Because of the current set-up above, there is a huge financial imperative for relegated clubs to bounce back as soon as possible, as there equally is for ambitious clubs to access the financial benefits that exist in the Football League and beyond. But achieving this is exceptionally challenging.

The system that exists in the National League today, one automatic promotion for the champions and one more for the play-off winners, was established back in 2002, a time when the Conference, as it was still known, was widely seen as the poor relation of the Football League, that parallel universe of inferior clubs.

The current set-up, according to Danny Macklin, creates a distorting effect on what clubs spend. 'It's an incredibly tough league to get out of. I would say that it's probably the toughest league in the country. It's 46 games a season to try and win one of two places to gain promotion, one of which requires a further three games to get there because of the play-offs. The chances are so slim that inevitably clubs are going to do everything they can to get there, which sometimes means spending huge amounts of money, undertaking something of a financial gamble to get into the promised land of the Football League.'

Alongside the heightened competition two promotion spots encourage, the lack of comprehensive or consistent financial regulation at this level means there is little to stop teams spending all they have (and more) in pursuit of those golden tickets. The thousands per week that Salford were supposedly paying Rooney might be beyond the norm in the National League but, with such thin margins, Salford clearly felt the need to go for broke to ensure promotion, a decision that was ultimately vindicated.

Calls for change *have* emerged in recent years, with The National League Board stating their commitment to achieving three promotion places, something that the EFL has refused to consider.

'The National League have been keen to expand the number of promotion places for some time,' says Matt Badcock. 'But they've probably been reticent to push too hard because it is within the power of the Football League, should they wish, to go back to the old system and just have one promotion place. And so, the changes that have occurred, the increase in the number of play-off places in May 2017, from four to six, have been undertaken by the lower tier.'

According to Badcock, with the relationship very much weighted in the Football League's favour, what's required is some leadership from those above.

'We need the Football League to take ownership of the issue and bring in three relegation places in League Two. But realistically will that happen? Probably not. The Football League is aware that its members are not overly keen on the promotion places, and by extension the relegation spots being extended. What's in it for them, after all? Why would clubs vote for a system that is going to increase their chances of being relegated to non-league football?'

One totemic issue that seems to illustrate the disconnect that exists between the non-league world and the Football League above concerns artificial pitches. For a number of non-league clubs, like Sutton United, Sevenoaks Town and Oxford City, one solution to the problem of postponed matches has been the installation of 3G surfaces.

'I think people forget how much of non-league football is a cashflow business,' says Dave Farebrother. 'A lot of clubs live one week to the next and so something like a postponement can be a significant financial challenge. In the winter, if you have a succession of postponed home games, it can mean a month without money from gate receipts. And that can spell problems for clubs.'

Although the installation of a 3G pitch can provide greater certainty when it comes to fixtures, they represent a problem for any club that finds themselves chasing promotion to the Football League. And that's because, at the moment, the EFL does not allow member clubs to play on artificial pitches.

'And so,' says Matt Badcock, 'if a club like Sutton United, for example, did get promoted, it would have to dig the pitch up and lay a new grass one. For Sutton that would be hugely expensive. It's not an issue that affects a lot of clubs, but it is one that perhaps reveals the EFL's lack of understanding with regard to what life is like in non-league football.'

Alongside calls for there to be a change in the relationship that exists between the Football League and the National League, there have also been calls for a change to the financial environment that exists at this level of the game.

Back in 2011, the then president of the Conference, Bill King, outlined the board's plan to introduce a salary cap to the assembled owners at the League's AGM. It was regarded as the best way to stop the growing number of clubs who were threatened with going under.

The proposal did not go down well. Led by the then owner of Kettering Town, Imraan Ladak, a strong resistance movement to the change was mounted, and by the following summer the measure had bitten the dust. Ironically, two years later, Kettering, still with Ladak at the helm, would be in administration.

Since then, calls for a salary cap have never gone away. Just last season, Maidstone United co-owner Oliver Ash was the latest to call for its introduction, labelling the current set of financial controls as a 'joke'.

This 'joke' of a system is the Budget Monitoring Scheme. It requires clubs to submit a projected budget ahead of each season to an Independent Financial Review Panel. If that panel has concerns about any club, they may also ask for a mid-season budget. Although this sounds good in theory, and a number of clubs, such as Hartlepool United, Hereford United and Notts County, have been placed under a transfer embargo for budgetary violations, in practice it hasn't stopped several clubs, such as Chester,

Dagenham & Redbridge and Gateshead, from nearly going out of business.

There is also a concern that the FA 'Owners and Directors Test', which is meant to prevent unscrupulous or criminal individuals from gaining control or influence at clubs, is not always up to the job, the murky recent history of Gateshead providing an illuminating insight into both the test's limitations and the failings of the league's current financial controls.

The north-east club was once a non-league success story. First under the ownership of Graham Wood, and later under Richard and Julie Bennett, who owned the club between 2015 and 2018, 'The Heed' transitioned to full-time status, rose through the pyramid and nearly made it to the Football League, narrowly losing the 2014 play-off final.

'After around a decade in the Northern Premier League, the club became a mainstay of the National League. And often within that period having a shot at promotion. The owners had invested in the squad, which they had promised to do, and transformed the club into one that was able to compete at a higher level than it had for some time,' says current club chairman Neil Pinkerton.

When the Bennetts announced that they were looking to sell the club towards the end of the 2017/18 season, it was in good shape. As Richard Bennett said at the time:

'We are leaving the club debt-free and in a healthy position, which presents a fantastic opportunity for potential new owners or a consortium who share the same aspirations of securing a return to the Football League.'

New owners arrived fairly swiftly in the guise of the Hong Kong-based businessman Rangjan Varghese, who was assisted by his associate Joseph Cala, the latter acting as the club's chief financial advisor.

Cala had form when it came to takeovers, having unsuccessfully tried to buy both Portsmouth and Morecambe in the past. Supporters of both clubs sounded warning bells regarding his association with Gateshead, pointing to a CV riddled with holes and one that included a brief stint as owner of Italian club Salerno Calcio, which was cut extremely short due to a 'non-compliance' violation, with Cala failing to pay the bills despite promising €40m of investment.

There were rumours at the time, later supported by outgoing Gateshead general manager Mike Coulson, that Cala had been the original proposed buyer, with his associate Varghese only stepping in once he had failed the 'Owners and Directors Test'.

But even Varghese was not considered risk free by the League. So concerned were they about the new owner and the budget he submitted, that he was requested to put up a bond of £200,000 as an insurance against financial issues.

'It wasn't the most auspicious of starts to the new regime. But it was probably quite fitting because what would unfold behind the scenes over the next season was disastrous,' says Pinkerton.

Ironically, despite what would happen, on the pitch Gateshead didn't have that bad a campaign. Under Steve Watson, the club started brightly and remained in the top half of the table, only narrowly missing out on a place in the play-offs.

But off the pitch it was a different matter. Payments were being missed, rent defaulted on, trust with businesses in the community worn thin. By December

2018, it was revealed that the club was under a transfer embargo, the League baring its teeth in response to the playing budget surpassing the initial estimate submitted in the summer.

Soon after, Watson left to manage York City, taking the unusual step of dropping down to the National League North to do so. The new boss, player/manager Ben Clark, then found himself immediately on the back foot when he discovered that two key players had been sold without his consent. That was followed by general manager Mike Coulson departing, leaving something of a vacuum in the club's leadership.

On his departure, Coulson, who had been at the club for 30 years, gave a stinging interview to the *Sunderland Echo* in which he described Cala and Varghese as 'working to a very different moral compass to the one I have,' adding, 'I think there has been so much damage done to the club over the past few months and some of it is irreparable. The reputation of the club has been slaughtered by this whole situation.'

In the interview he also stressed his belief that Cala owned the club, and that Varghese was just a 'front' for it, saying, 'I have never dealt with Ranjan, with the club, it has always just been polite conversation. Cala is making every single decision with regards to players, transport, day-to-day decisions.'

More difficulties arose not long after when Gateshead Council evicted the club from the International Stadium, the athletics ground that Gateshead leased, but for which it had been neglecting to make payment. Although it was allowed to see out the season, it looked like the club was going to be homeless the following campaign.

The players were the next to suffer when their March wages went unpaid, leading to a strike threat which was only avoided following a late emergency payment. By this point, things were so bad that the club were becoming reliant on a fans' group, Gateshead Soul, for assistance with costs, even including the provision of pre-match meals for the players.

And there was also the small matter of a winding-up order, issued in response to a £20,000 debt to the HMRC. The club manged to pay it in the March of 2019, thereby surviving to fight another day. But its existence was more evidence of a club that appeared to be careering out of control.

As the season came to a close, this image of a club in crisis was fuelled further by a number of redundancies, which saw players, management and other staff leaving the club. What remained by the campaign's end was a club spiralling, with only one registered player, no management, no stadium, and a complete absence of direction.

With Gateshead facing oblivion, suspended from the league and refused a licence for the following season, the owner(s) put the club up for sale for £1.

'And that is where we came in,' says Pinkerton, who, with Trevor Clark, fronted a consortium that took the club over in May 2019. 'By the time our takeover was completed, I think the club was around 72 hours away from being wound up. I honestly don't think the previous owners cared about what happened to the club. In my short time in football, I have realised there are two types of people in the game. There are those who want to do something and want to help. Then there are those who are in it to try and make money for themselves, and, unfortunately, the previous owners are in the latter group.'

The tale of Gateshead, Varghese and Cala reveals the potential impotency of the current financial regulations covering this level of the game. All the tools available to both the League and the FA were brought against the owners and the club. Improper candidates for ownership were repelled, bonds were required for questionable individuals before taking control, and punishments were meted out for financial transgressions. But none of it stopped the club from undergoing a season of hell, one that ended with it very nearly disappearing.

And one that has left Pinkerton, and the rest of the consortium, with an unenviable task. Rebuilding the club will not be easy. On the footballing side, Gateshead are now facing life in the National League North, having been demoted at the end of the previous season.

'We appealed but because of what had gone on at the club the League felt compelled to act. It's a blow for us. Obviously, when you're trying to build something new at the club, it would've been better had we been in a higher division, which would've made it easier to attract fans, sponsors and players. But, on the plus side, it gives us a bit of breathing space to try and get this project off the ground.'

On the financial side, the brief reign of Varghese/Cala has savaged the reputation of the club locally. When clubs get into financial trouble, for those taking over the mess it's not just a case of clearing the debts and then everything is OK, as Pinkerton explains:

'Through our investment we have put the club on a sounder financial footing. And we also worked with the council to get us back to the International Stadium. But from there we have to make it a sound business during this season, next season and beyond. And to do that you have to work with the community through things like commercial partnerships, sponsorship and ticket sales on the revenue side, and, on the cost side, the services we use. The problem with the club at the moment is that the previous owners have tarnished our reputation, which means we have had to spend a lot of time trying to rebuild those vital community relationships.'

If those involved with Gateshead need any inspiration, a story of how a struggling club can be turned around in the National League, then they need only look a few miles down the A19.

Back in 2018 there was a time when it looked as though Hartlepool United were close to going out of business. The disastrous tenure of owner Gary Coxhall, combined with the club's relegation from the Football League, had left the 'Pools facing a bleak future.

'The club was a mess,' says current chief executive Mark Maguire. 'The crisis was a mixture of poor management, poor commercial development, relegation and overspending on contracts and transfers. At one point the club was in the National League while still having contracts in place that were a hangover from its days in League One. All of the above would've ultimately spelled disaster in the end but was probably hastened by the fact that the club consistently thought it could spend its way out of trouble [a mindset that carried on after relegation to the National League]. There was no contingency in place if that didn't work out, which is why everything went wrong so quickly.'

The club was saved from administration when Teesside businessman Raj Singh took over in the spring of 2018, appointing Maguire in the process, someone who, as chief executive of Chester FC, had recently spent time navigating that club through its own particular financial difficulties.

'Just to keep going we have needed a donation by the owner to sustain losses,' say Maguire. 'And added to that we have had to restructure the staff, cut back the youth side of the club [having lost central funding for the academy] and renegotiate a lot of contracts. For example, we were paying £1,000 per week for our refuse collection, which we have cut to £300. Doesn't seem much, but that could be the cost of a player's wages.'

Alongside these cost saving measures, Maguire has also overseen an improvement in the club's revenue generating potential.

'So, for example,' he explains, 'we have revolutionised the retail side of the business. Previously, we only really sold kits and merchandise in the summer and at Christmas. Now, we have broadened our lines, digging deep into the club's heritage, and created business all year round, with total sales up by a third.'

The club has also been keen to develop and expand its fanbase, particularly with the younger members of the community. 'Under 12s now come free to the match if accompanied by an adult, which has seen their numbers swell. And we have forged stronger connections with local junior teams. The idea is to grab their attention while they are young, try to get them as fans for life.'

Maguire is a big believer in the community role that clubs play, regarding community work as not only necessary but also something that in the long term can pay dividends for a club.

'I remember while I was working at Stockport County that the charity work the club did was quite sporadic. We did good things but it often lacked coherence and was a bit ad hoc. I recall posing for a photo at some charitable event and feeling a little bit like a fraud. Community work should be all year round, not just bits here and there to provide a good photo opportunity. And that's what we are doing here, really investing in our community work and making sure that the club is a presence all year round. Clubs need to put something back. And if we support the community then it's more likely that in return the community will support us.'

Although it's still early days, according to Maguire, the seeds of recovery at Hartlepool are evident. 'The club's finances are in much better shape than they once were, the crowds are nearing the levels that the club enjoyed in League Two, which is not bad for our second season down here, and the club's recruitment has reoriented towards younger players. In the past we would've just splurged on established pros, with no thought to development or sell-on fees. That's not the case anymore. Recruitment, like any other part of the business, is focussed on value for money.'

Hartlepool and Gateshead, along with many other clubs at Steps 1 and 2, have still benefitted from external investment. It might not always reach the levels enjoyed by clubs like Salford City or AFC Fylde, but it represents a way for clubs to deal with the reality that profitability at this level is a rarity.

'The game will take any money you throw at it and I'm sure that at almost every level apart from the very top, where TV money makes all the difference, getting by season to season without piling up debt is a constant struggle,' says Gary Keyzor.

Every club at this level, like many of those below, has recourse to the same tools when it comes to generating money, gate receipts, hospitality, broadcasting, sponsorship, commercial partnerships and player sales.

'But being able to maximise those depends on a lot of factors,' says Dave Farebrother. 'Take us as an example. We don't own our own ground, which limits what we can make on matchday. When it comes to the gate, we need about 1,500 to break even. This season we are doing that regularly. But in the past that wasn't always the case. Sponsorship is getting harder and the TV money from BT, although welcome, doesn't go very far. So, we've had to put a lot of effort into our academy, because this not only attracts funding but also potentially produces players for the future, which can mean sell-on fees or savings on transfer costs.'

The example of Sutton also reveals just how beneficial a bit of good luck can be. Nowadays, it's fashionable in some quarters to denigrate the FA Cup, with fans, players and managers from the 'elite' devaluing its importance when compared to the Premier League or the Champions League.

Perhaps the most high-profile illustration of this in recent years was the decision by Liverpool to field significantly understrength sides during the 2019/20 FA Cup. So dismissive of the competition was Jürgen Klopp, that in the club's fourth-round replay against Shrewsbury Town he was not even present at Anfield, allowing U23 coach Neil Critchley to take charge. Klopp instead watched the game via a laptop.

But the competition still has tremendous value, particularly for smaller clubs. The prize money that is given out from the preliminary rounds right up to the final is one way that the FA attempts to redistribute funds across the game. And through a combination of other factors, including TV money, additional home gate revenues and advantageous away draws against bigger sides (where visiting teams really benefit from the cup's sharing of gate receipts), progress in the competition can prove hugely lucrative. A decent cup run is still a big deal for lots of clubs, which is exactly what happened with Sutton.

Back in 2017, the club made it to the fifth round of the FA Cup, beating Leeds United and AFC Wimbledon along the way to set up a home tie against Arsenal. Although Sutton got knocked out, losing 2-0, according to Dave Farebrother the run transformed the club.

'We earned £1m from that cup run, which for a club like ours is a massive sum of money. That enabled us to make lots of improvements to the ground.'

But the impact didn't end there. 'The Arsenal game was watched by around 200 million people worldwide. So, suddenly we had a bit of brand recognition and now we are selling shirts all over the world. We also got a bump in our attendance figures. You'd expect this to go away after the excitement of the cup run had ended, but it mostly hasn't. It seems like people have come here, enjoyed what we offer and stayed.'

Sutton got something of a short-cut when it came to cultivating a larger fanbase, capitalising on the interest that the cup run generated. But for a lot of clubs at this level, building a large enough fanbase to hopefully achieve a degree of financial sustainability is a challenge. The interest in non-league football might be growing, but that doesn't mean that all clubs have capitalised upon it equally or that it is always sufficient to cover costs.

Some clubs are much better than others at harnessing this growing interest. In recent years, relative to its size, and in the absence of an external benefactor or significant footballing success, perhaps none in the entire non-league world, or possibly the entirety of English football, has been better at this than National League South member Dulwich Hamlet.

There was a time, not too long ago, when this south London stalwart were pulling in around 150 people through the gate. Today, that figure stands at a staggering 1,600. It's a success story that stands out within the non-league game and one that other similar-sized clubs must look on with wonder (and a hint of jealousy).

Gentrification has played a big part in what has happened. As south London has shed its rough and ready image, young professionals have swept in, accompanied by a tsunami of coffee shops, delis and pop-up Iberian cheese markets. And it is from the ranks of these young professionals, the weekend curious, the hipsters of south-east London, that those seeking out a more 'authentic' form of football have often come.

'There are lots of people who have similar stories to mine,' says Tom Cullen, whose journey with the Hamlet has seen him transition from newbie supporter to managing director.

'People who have moved to south London and are looking for something different. Sometimes they are football fans who are disillusioned with big clubs and are actively looking for a "less commercialised" form of the game, a throwback to the football they remember as kids. And other times it is the experience of actually coming to Champion Hill that changes their outlook. They see what we have here, the atmosphere, the inclusivity, the feel of the place, and they realise that this is what football should be about. Suddenly, the sterile, commercialised, money-obsessed world of the Premier League loses its appeal.'

To the original fans, the self-described club 'dinosaurs', the 'nouveaux', as these new arrivals have become known, brought a new sensibility to the terraces at Champion Hill. Their outlook – liberal, open, tolerant – began to feed into the terraces, in the process ridding it of lingering football ills of racism, homophobia and misogyny, which in turn has encouraged more attendees. It's acted like something of a virtuous circle. As the crowd has become incrementally more liberal in its feel, more people in tune with that aesthetic have been encouraged to come, which has then made the atmosphere increasingly liberal and so on, until a critical mass of sorts has been established wherein the club itself has become indelibly progressive in its outlook.

The left-wing vibe at Champion Hill is perhaps best expressed amongst 'The Rabble', the collective of superfans who congregate behind whichever end of their team is attacking and who are responsible for much of the singing (which is near constant) that characterises the crowd. They might still verbally abuse an opposition goalkeeper but unlike fans of old who would have done so by questioning his parentage or drawn from their unsavoury, un-PC arsenal, The Rabble will pour scorn on the fact that the keeper in question votes Liberal Democrat.

They are particularly evident on the road. When the club played at Step 3 a few seasons ago, Dulwich Hamlet would regularly bring hundreds to away games, sometimes coming close to eclipsing the turnout of the home supporters. And in the stadiums they attended, the ever-present sound of The Rabble, with their endlessly inventive songs and chants, would dominate, a near-constant accompaniment to the play.

The club itself seems keenly aware of how important this growing element of the crowd is, gradually harmonising with the political and social composition of its expanding fanbase. There have been fundraising drives for food banks and refugee centres and a Trade Union Day (offering members of any union £4 tickets). One game against Bognor Regis Town raised funds for the International Brigades Memorial Trust to remember and honour the men and women who volunteered to fight fascism in Spain from 1936 to 1939. Brigadista Ale, an anti-fascist tribute beer, was the guest brew at the bar that day.

'This "liberal" element to the crowd is something that the club has become aware of and it makes sense to cultivate it. Not that it's a particularly difficult thing to do. It chimes with how I and many others involved in running the club want Dulwich Hamlet to be. We want our club to be open and inclusive, to be progressive, to make a difference to our community,' says Cullen.

But although welcome to it, the club is not defined by 'The Rabble', or the political sensibilities of the 'nouveaux'.

'Fundamentally, we are just a great non-league club,' explains Cullen. 'We are good at getting out into the community to bring local people to the game and we have worked hard to ensure that families feel welcome here too. We have endeavoured to create a fantastic matchday experience, and that is a big part of the reason why so many people come to watch us.'

And it's fortunate for the club that it has proven so adept at tapping into a local appetite for non-league football. During the past few years Dulwich Hamlet has been embroiled in a dispute with the owners of Champion Hill, Meadow Partners. It's a dispute rooted in Meadow's continued inability to develop the site for housing. At one point, so frustrated were they at the local authority's perceived unwillingness to green light their plans that Meadow took it out on the club, evicting them from the ground and threatening legal action over the 'Dulwich Hamlet' name, over which they claimed to hold the copyright.

'While we groundshared in nearby Tooting and attempted to fight our case, both legally and in the media, we were hugely indebted to our thousands of fans,' says Cullen. 'They kept coming to see us, volunteered their time to the campaign and made sure that our cause was constantly mentioned across social media. When we finally got back to Champion Hill towards the end of 2018, they were there again in numbers, volunteering to give the ground some much needed care and attention.'

At most levels in the pyramid, the growth and retention of fans remains a vital part of how clubs survive and compete. It's not the only thing that matters, but it is important. And that is particularly the case for non-league clubs, who are often very reliant on matchday income. But the reality, as the case of Dulwich illustrates, is that good fortune plays a role in what happens. There are lots of non-league clubs in south London, and any one of them could've benefitted from the trend that has impacted on

Dulwich. Yes, the club has made the most of it, adapting accordingly and cannily capitalising on this 'hipster' incursion. But being in the right place at the right time also helped enormously.

'It's interesting,' says Cullen, 'how something as intangible as "fan culture" can have such an impact on a club. It's completely changed life at Dulwich. We are, in so many ways, a different club to the one that existed here a decade ago. And through the changes it has brought, the club, which doesn't have a benefactor to turn to, has been able to thrive, to weather tough times and actually compete at a higher level. It's quite remarkable when you think about it.'

Dulwich's fan culture has been aped elsewhere in the non-league game, notably at clubs like Clapton, Whitehawk and Eastbourne Town. At these places, the inspiration is both Dulwich and the 'Ultra' culture of Europe, the uber-passionate sections of various fanbases that populate continental football. Think of images and video clips that you might have seen of the European game in the media, depicting a sea of flags, explosions of flares, of fans in near constant voice, and it's likely that instigating much of this are ultra groups, such as the *Delije* groups at Red Star Belgrade, the *Torcida* at Hajduk Split and the *Banda Noantri* at Lazio.

Although the groups operating in the non-league world clearly lack the numbers and spectacle of their European counterparts (and also tend to come from a left-leaning political direction as opposed to the far-right tendencies that often characterise many ultra groups in Europe), they do reflect a resurgent fan culture clearly evident in the non-league game.

But capturing a wider interest in non-league football as a way to push a club forward does have its limitations. As least it does if the cautionary tale of MyFootballClub and Ebbsfleet United is anything to go by.

The idea was a bold one, to bring together around 50,000 football enthusiasts from across the world to purchase an English club. MyFootballClub's paid members would then control the club through a democratic voting process conducted online. Member voting would include matters both on the pitch, such as team selection and player transfers, and off the field, like what type of food to serve at the stadium.

The concept came from the journalist, copywriter and Fulham fan Will Brooks. He was inspired by the success of the *Football Manager* franchise, the management simulation game that devours your time, enveloping you in a fantasy world from which players can often take months to emerge.

Brooks felt there was a desire out there from supporters who wanted to simulate the experience of running a club. And so, he wondered, why not do it for real?

Initially, Brooks discussed his idea with a number of club owners and potential sponsors. Despite plenty of enthusiasm, no real progress was made. And so, in 2007, he took it upon himself to just make it happen, creating a simple, one-page website.

'I launched that website just completely speculatively and that was pretty much ten years ago,' Brooks told *The Blizzard* in 2017. 'Those were the days when you'd email your friends links to stuff. You wouldn't do it on WhatsApp or Facebook. I just started it like that. I sent it to about ten friends, who in theory sent it to ten friends.

Luckily, what made it really mushroom was that the BBC Football website picked it up as a sort of curiosity story. From that moment, I never looked back.'

The media interest in Brooks's idea was palpable. MyFootballClub was everywhere and within three months the project had 53,000 people registered. And along with the members came the money, with membership costing £35. On the opening day of payments, which turned out to be PayPal's fastest ever launch in Europe, £250,000 was raised. By day ten, that figure had reached half a million.

'The day we started taking money, we launched the forums. They were just awash with threads from different countries and people were meeting up in different areas and setting up little sub-groups. It was a lovely, organic, happy kind of thing. In those early days of MyFootballClub the forums were very friendly. There was none of the nasty stuff that you can quite often get with social media. It had a lovely innocence to it and a real kind of hopefulness,' said Brooks.

In response to the site's evident early success, a number of clubs around England, most of whom were in poor financial shape and desperate for a sudden injection of cash, started to get in contact with Brooks. There were even rumours that Leeds United was at the front of the queue.

Ultimately, because of the gap that existed between registering an interest and actually paying to become a member, the amount raised could only cast MyFootballClub's net so far, meaning it was limited to League Two and below. From the clubs that came forward, Ebbsfleet United, then playing in the Conference, emerged as the favourite, and in February 2008 MyFootballClub's takeover was completed.

The manager of Ebbsfleet at the time was Liam Daish. 'My first impressions were fine,' he later told *The Blizzard*. 'They were good lads and they obviously wanted me to buy into what it was all about. It was definitely new – no one had done it before. It was quite exciting, they had big plans. They were very professional, they showed me the website they'd built and that they had more than 30,000 members. It was a new concept that I had never come across. It was something that I didn't dismiss. I went along with it and tried to make it work.'

Theoretically, the takeover should've challenged Daish's role. After all, the idea that members could pick the side was one of MyFootballClub's big selling points. But in reality, it never happened. Each week members voted on who should pick the team, themselves or the manager, and they plumped for Daish on every occasion.

Along with the manager's support, despite some wariness on their part, the fans of the club were also willing to give this new experiment in ownership a go, their accommodating nature no doubt sweetened by the fact that not only had the takeover improved the club's dire balance sheet, but it had also strengthened its competitive position in the league.

A victory in the FA Trophy over Torquay United at Wembley just months after the takeover made acceptance that bit easier.

But the good times were not to last. Waning interest set in quickly, with many investors disillusioned by the limited extent of their influence (restricted to things like setting the weekly playing budget and potential kit designs). Five thousand members alone never returned to the website after paying their £35.

And the club's form didn't help. When a fifth-tier club had been chosen to be taken over, talk had been about a push into the Football League. Instead, during the second full season of MyFootballClub's ownership, Ebbsfleet got relegated. Although the club made an immediate return via the play-offs, yo-yoing in the wrong direction hardly set the pulse racing.

By the beginning of the 2012/13 season, there were just 1,300 members left and the club was rapidly losing money. Winning matches became a secondary concern for Daish, who was preoccupied instead with trying to keep the club afloat.

'It just wasn't sustainable,' he told *The Blizzard*. 'In the end I had a budget of £4,500 to £5,000 a week to run a team in the Conference National that was full of ex-league sides and it just sort of fell apart really ... In the last year the club was basically on the brink of folding. We were trying to organise events to bring money in.'

Despite the bright start, what began as an innovative attempt to own a National League club ultimately fizzled out. Brooks, who had been employing six people to help run MyFootballClub, walked away, frustrated at how the project had unravelled. A pared-back website was given over to existing members. The dream began to wither.

In April 2013, the remaining members voted in favour of handing two thirds of their shares to the supporters' trust (the Fleet Trust). KEH Sports Ltd, a group of Kuwaiti investors, arrived to take over not long after and are still in charge today.

'One of my biggest conclusions is that perhaps the idea was more exciting than the reality. I think people loved the idea of it, and the media loved the idea of it, but then when you announce that you've bought a Conference club and nobody's heard of the players, then people began to potentially switch off a bit,' Brooks told *The Blizzard*.

For all its innovative nature, MyFootballClub still represented a version of the benefactor model. These were not, largely, Ebbsfleet fans taking over a club they were emotionally connected too. They were investors, providing capital in return for a share and a say in what was going on. A multitude of investors, yes, but investors nonetheless.

And it's easy to see why Ebbsfleet let itself get taken over in this way. Competing at this level is not easy. Even back in 2007, the cost of competing was often more than many clubs could afford. That was part of the reason why Ebbsfleet was in debt prior to the arrival of its internet 'saviours'.

Climbing up the National League system can be a frustrating journey. As much as you are heartened by the stories of those giving their time to keep the game alive, there is an inescapable feeling that they are fighting against the odds when doing so. And so, it's worth having a pit stop to take the opportunity to look at a part of the game that is, in most areas, on the up, filled with hope and bursting with potential. And it's a pit stop that starts with a simple video.

Chapter Six

Give Her the Ball
and a Yard of Space

THE video was a short one, but to eight-year-old Katie Owens it meant the world. Simone Magill, the Northern Ireland and Everton forward, had taken the time to record a message of support to Katie and her friends who turn out every Saturday for Hull-based girls' side Costello Vixens.

'Like me, Katie is a big Evertonian. But whereas I would probably be made up if I got a personal message from Richarlison or Jordan Pickford, for Katie it's players like Simone who are her heroes. It's the players from the Everton women's side that she looks up to. Seeing her face when we got that video was amazing. I think it might have been the highlight of her season,' says Paul Owens, Katie's dad and one of the coaches of the Vixens.

Women and girls' football is riding high. According to the FA's recent State of the Game report, there are now nearly three million women and girls playing some form of the game, unprecedented levels of participation.

And more people are choosing to watch the sport too. At the recent World Cup in France, almost 12 million people in this country tuned in to watch the England Lionesses' dramatic semi-final against the USA, making it the most viewed TV programme of 2019.

The Women's World Cup has acted as a huge boost to the game in England. In its wake, participation at FA 'Wildcat' centres, where 5- to 11-year-old girls can get involved in football, rose by nearly 50 per cent. 605 new girls' youth teams were registered to play and the amount of adult teams has risen too.

For women's football in England, the boost from the World Cup was timely. The game is in the midst of a period of transformation, from grassroots to the elite level. The headline aspect of this change has been the creation of a professional tier for the first time in this country.

'Making the top tier of the game, the Women's Super League, professional is a momentous moment for women's football,' says Kelly Simmons, FA director for the women's professional game. 'I really believe that women's football can be the first female team sport to break through into the mainstream. What I mean by that is that there are a lot of women's sports that have peaks of interest at the Olympics or major tournaments, but they then disappear. But with the clubs we have and the investment that is taking place, we can be that breakthrough sport where the players are household names, playing in front of large crowds.'

What's happening with the Women's Super League (WSL) marks the current highpoint of a trend that has been building within English football for a couple of generations, a trend that has seen the women's game begin to recapture some of the energy that once characterised the sport.

In the 1880s, as millions of men were being swept up in the late-Victorian football boom, women were not inured to the game's charms. The highest profile of the women's teams set up was the British Ladies' Football Club (BLFC), established by Nettie Honeyball in 1885.

The BLFC arranged fixtures between teams representing the north and the south of England, where money would be raised for charitable concerns. Although crowds were healthy to begin with, they eventually dropped off as the growing popularity of men's football came to dominate public interest. In a world where women were still very much seen as second-class citizens, denied the vote and socially barred from many professions, it would take something extraordinary for their footballing endeavours to eclipse those of men. That something 'extraordinary' arrived in 1914.

As men signed up in their millions to fight in the First World War, many women did their bit for the war effort by entering the workforce. Around 700,000 women took up work as 'munitionettes', producing most of the weaponry used by the British Army during the war.

And just as men had done before them, women working in factories began to play informal games of football during their lunch breaks. After some initial trepidation, their superiors came to see these games as a means of boosting morale and productivity. Teams soon formed and friendly matches were arranged.

With men's professional football suspended, women's football began to fill the void. Teams grew in popularity and matches between these various sides started to pull in big crowds. Perhaps the most popular of these teams came from Dick, Kerr & Co, a Preston-based locomotive and tramcar manufacturer. Known as Dick, Kerr's Ladies, by the end of the war they were capable of drawing over 10,000 punters to a game.

Though the war ended in 1918, Dick, Kerr's and other women's teams continued to draw large crowds. By 1920 there were around 150 women's sides in England, with more still in Wales and Scotland. That same year, a game between Dick, Kerr's and St Helens Ladies on Boxing Day brought 53,000 fans through the Goodison Park turnstiles, a world record for a women's club fixture that lasted for nearly a century.

As far as the FA was concerned, such high levels of popularity were considered unwelcome. The men of Lancaster Gate, the handlebar-moustached, high-collared purveyors of misogyny, had always taken a dim view of women's football, considering it an unladylike pursuit for the 'fairer sex'. While it had been tolerated in wartime, acting as a morale booster for workers and a form of entertainment for a war-weary populace, there was a fear that, if left unchecked, this 'unfitting' sport for women might actually be entertaining enough to draw attendances away from men's football.

Its solution was brutal. Citing that football was 'quite unsuitable for females' on 5 December 1921, the FA forbade its members from allowing women's football to be played at their grounds. The FA also ruled that its members could no longer act as referees or linesmen at women's fixtures. For an organisation that has long possessed a reputation for moving at a glacial pace, it's frustrating and saddening that the one occasion the FA acted quickly and decisively, it was to do something so reactionary.

Forbidden to use football facilities and with fewer officials available, the women's game went into decline. Those who still wanted to play could, but found themselves shunted on to rugby pitches, scrubland, school fields – whatever they could find. It meant that the FA edict effectively marginalised women's football.

By the 1950s, a generation later, although teams such as Fodens in Cheshire, Manchester Corinthians and the still existing Dick, Kerr's (now renamed Preston Ladies FC) did offer opportunities for some women to compete, the FA's efforts to extinguish the game had been largely successful. Playing opportunities for women in England were thin on the ground, with any that existed hugely reliant on localised, informal pockets of organisation.

But the story of women's football in England would not end there. An upturn in interest after England's victory in the 1966 World Cup dovetailed with the growing confidence of the women's movement, which sought to challenge male dominance in society.

For the latter, such an overtly patriarchal sport as football, one in which an exclusively male governing body had wilfully acted to supress the opportunities of women, was something of an open goal. A new generation of women, not content to allow themselves to be effectively bullied out of the sport, began to take up football. As, incrementally, more and more women were drawn to the game, the number of grassroots women's sides began to expand across the country. In this, they were helped by the establishment of the Women's Football Association (WFA) (entirely independent from the FA) in 1969, a body established to better organise and promote the sport.

But what of the FA? Under gentle pressure from UEFA to relent, and frustrated by the reality of a sport growing in popularity and participation in spite of its edict, the FA gradually started to soften its hostility. Not long after the WFA was created, female clubs were allowed to affiliate to their local County FA. Then in 1971 the FA decided to rescind its ban, finally giving women's football a better foundation on which to build.

For the following few decades, despite the game enjoying a freedom denied it for a generation, its expansion was best defined as slow. Although the WFA was instrumental in establishing competitive women's leagues, helping increase the number of affiliated clubs and promoting the number of female coaches and officials, low levels of funding and a reputation for poor administration meant that by the early 1990s, women's football remained a minority sport.

Although the FA had softened its stance, that didn't mean it actively sought to promote the sport. During the 1980s, funding and support were limited. The FA remained a reluctant participant in the gradual reintroduction of women's football to England, one whose support often only arose after the organisation was prodded and poked by higher bodies.

This happened again in the early 1990s when UEFA, FIFA and the UK Sports Council collectively applied sufficient pressure on the FA for it to eventually step in and take over the administration of the game from the struggling WFA, which it did in 1993.

Having taken control, the FA assumed responsibility for the league system and embarked on the installation of a pyramid structure, linking the grassroots level of the sport with the elite leagues higher up.

Although progress since then has not always been smooth, there is little doubt that coming under the aegis of the FA has been of significant benefit for women's football. As Carrie Dunn writes in *The Roar of the Lionesses: Women's Football in England*:

'It has allowed women's clubs to draw fully on the development opportunities by the FA; it gave clubs an incentive to improve their standards and gain the FA Charter Standard status, which signifies that a club has achieved a quality benchmark and which demonstrates to the public, club members and parents that the club is well organised; it has assisted – albeit with limited success – in promoting women's football to the wider public; and it has enabled links to be built with professional men's clubs [although not all links have prospered].'

The FA is currently nearing the end of its most recent strategy for women's football, 'Gameplan for Growth', which covered 2017–2020.

'Our current strategy is an ambitious one,' says Kelly Simmons. 'The aim is to drive participation and awareness, change perceptions surrounding women's football, increase the number of women coaching, refereeing and administering the sport, develop a world-class talent pipeline, improve the commercial prospects in women's football and enhance the profile of the England team and players.'

To support the strategy, the FA has created four new roles: a head of women's performance, a head of women's coach development, a women's refereeing manager and a head of marketing and commercial for women's football.

'The idea is to create the right environment to attract new players into the game, to help new clubs build and also to improve the football experience for the players and clubs already playing. We think that women's and girl's football has enormous potential. It's now down to us to help realise that potential,' Simmons continues.

A key element in this has been investment in the youth side of the game. From modest beginnings, over the past 20 years girls' junior football has steadily grown, the number of participants and girls' teams greatly proliferating in the process, particularly in recent years.

'We are starting to get to the point where young girls are beginning to see football as something that is open to both genders, and not, as has often been the case, a sport more geared towards boys. One great aspect of current participation levels is that although a lot of girls are opting to play in single-gender sides, there are also increasing numbers playing in mixed-gender teams too,' says Simmons.

The FA raised the mixed football age limit a few years ago so that girls are allowed to play in boys' teams up until the age of 18. This brought the English grassroots game in line with a number of other European countries.

'We have three girls in our sides who have been with us since around age five,' says Rob Selby of Rotherfield FC. 'And I think it's great that we've been able to keep them. This is the club they first joined, they have mates here, so why shouldn't they keep playing with us? And I personally love the fact that our girls, who are fantastic players, constantly defy the expectations of some opposition coaches. I remember one coach laughing and saying he'd go easy on us because we had a couple of girls in the team. He wasn't laughing at the end of the game when one of our girls had scored the winner against them.'

The barriers between the genders has been further blurred in recent years following the FA's decision to alter the 'career pathway' for girls, allowing elite junior teams to compete in boys' leagues. The theory behind this being that the standard and physicality of boys' leagues would provide more of a challenge. Although, if you looked at the recent form of U12 girls' team SB Frankfort, you'd question whether boys' leagues *did* offer that much of a challenge after all. The Plymouth-based side stormed the Devon Junior and Minor league, going unbeaten during the 2018/19 campaign, winning the title with two games to spare.

'Compared to a generation ago the picture is a lot better today. For a young girl, playing football is much more of an option than it was in the past and the football world is more open to them playing than it previously was. The FA gets a bit of criticism from some quarters with how it interacts with the grassroots game and sometimes that is warranted. But it has done some great work with regards to women's football in recent years, specifically when it comes to young girls. One of the most effective examples of this is the Wildcat programme,' says Jen O'Neill, editor of *She Kicks*.

This programme gives each county support and investment to help clubs who are setting up new girls' sections.

'At a county level we have driven Wildcats and have seen the growth of this particular programme grow from seven centres to 53 in just three seasons,' says Emma Burden, football development officer at the Essex County FA. 'This in turn has seen an appetite to affiliate more girls' teams and we have seen a huge growth in our mini soccer figures. We now also have a greater number of leagues who are offering a product for girls to play football from age six to seven years old, including the Brentwood Community Football Alliance and the Essex County Girls League.'

Nationwide, there are now over 1,250 Wildcats centres across England that offer thousands of girls (aged 5 to 11) regular opportunities to play football on a weekly basis.

'With Wildcats, the FA are putting their hand in their pockets and providing organisers with the funds, and also the equipment and the support, to target girls and get them involved in football at a young age. There are many girls out there who might not have tried football before, perhaps because there are no nearby girls' clubs, maybe because they didn't have the confidence to go along to a boys' club, or perhaps they just assumed it was something that boys did. But through something like Wildcats, the FA are bringing football to them, letting them know that it's a game anyone can play and delivering fun, regular coaching that previously might not have been available,' says O'Neill.

When it comes to expanding the game at a junior level, programmes like Wildcats work hand-in-hand with the FA's wider efforts to raise the profile of women's football. These attempts to improve 'brand awareness' are essentially efforts to normalise the idea of playing the game for a new generation of prospective players.

And there have been tangible improvements. In recent years, annual social media interactions for the Lionesses and the WSL have trebled to 2.5 million. During the current season (2019/20), BT Sport and BBC will continue their regular coverage, screening live games in the case of the former, and in the case of the latter, a weekly highlights package. Complementing this, the FA will also be televising all 132 WSL matches via the FA Player, widening access through its free-to-watch format.

The recent Women's World Cup in France has been the apex of this trend, both at home and internationally. Domestically, even before the Lionesses had reached the semi-final, three of the side's matches ranked in the top ten most watched football games of 2019 – something that would have been unthinkable barely a decade ago.

The success of the England Lionesses has boosted the profile of players like Jill Scott, Lucy Bronze and Ellen White, players who, although big names in their own sport, were nevertheless hardly, in media terms, household names.

'There is still a long way to go, but for young girls you have people they can now look up to in the same way that boys do. Stars of the game, who are competing at the highest level. And the more that women's football is broadcast, and the greater its impact on social media, the more the brand will grow, drawing in more viewers, higher attendances at live matches and hopefully more and more girls playing the game,' says O'Neill.

As welcome as these changes are, girls playing at grassroots clubs, whether mixed-gender or all-female, still encounter the same problems that boys do. They still play on poor quality pitches, still face escalating costs and still face periods of the season where fixtures are repeatedly cancelled.

'You're trying to convince girls, many of whom have never played the sport before, to come and play football. And what you're offering them, in many cases, is an environment that is almost hostile to the game. So, where we are in Hull, loads of teams have emerged out of the Wildcats set-up, which is fantastic. But how many of these players are going to keep with the game if the reality is shocking pitches, games being called off week-in, week-out and costs that keep going up and up?' says Paul Owens.

To compound this, there is also the problem of sexism. At the recent Women's World Cup, a competition that displays female footballing talent at its best and which boasts a level of technical ability that the overwhelming majority of men could only dream of, a foul throw taken by Japan's Aya Sameshima drew derision across social media as a legion of men used it as proof that women's football was not to be taken seriously.

Never mind that there are plenty of examples of male footballers messing up any number of throw-ins, free kicks or corners. Never mind that it was one mistake in an otherwise accomplished performance by Sameshima, a player who has already been a World Cup winner and Asian Games gold medallist. Never mind that such bovine attitudes belong in the dark ages. She made an error; therefore, all women's football should be measured against that error.

The reality is that for all the progress that has been made within women's and girls' football, when it comes to the issues of sexism and gender inequality, there is still considerable room for improvement. According to a recent survey by Women in Football, in the past year nearly two-thirds of female players have endured sexist jokes or so-called 'banter', half have experienced sexism, and four in ten have received derogatory comments about their ability based on gender. Although these are issues that affect women and girls in almost every part of society, there is a feeling that they are perhaps more pronounced within football because the sport has spent so long being thought of as a 'male' activity.

Katee Hui's club, Hackney Laces, along with sister clubs South London Laces and Limehouse Laces, has been providing the opportunity to play football for hundreds of girls and women across parts of the capital since 2011. For Hui, who has been running the club since it was founded, these issues are a depressing reality in the life of female grassroots players.

'We constantly encounter sexism from male teams. We can be waiting to go on to a pitch that we have booked, for example, and the men's team who have it before will eat into our time and say things like "shouldn't you be at home doing your makeup?" And when our girls play, you sometimes get boys' sides, who might be on after, simply wandering on to the pitch to start their game early, because they think they have more of a right to be there than the girls.'

According to Hui, there are three little words which, for her, sum up the problem that her players face.

'I hear these words all the time and they never fail to annoy me. And they are "for a girl". I have lost count how many times I have had a male coach come up to us and say so-and-so is "a good player ... for a girl". Those three words show that we are not seen as equals. Because you would never say "he's good ... for a boy". The people saying them probably think they're being nice. But to me they are just revealing how much work there is still to do in football to bring in gender equality. And until we start addressing this problem, some girls are going to be put off trying football, some girls are going to walk away from the game and clubs are going to suffer as a result.'

The problem of gender inequality is particularly noticeable in education, where it remains perfectly acceptable for a school to offer different sports to boys and girls. Although the government and sports governing bodies increasingly champion mixed sport sessions, gender-segregated sport remains legal.

A recent *BBC Sport* article, which told the story of a 13-year-old girl in Wales who had complained to her teachers about not being allowed to play football as a PE option in school, produced a flurry of replies on social media from parents of girls across the UK who had a similar experience. It seems that there remain many schools where archaic and gender-specific ideas about physical activity – football and rugby are best suited to boys; netball and dance are best for girls – still hold sway.

'Some of our girls put together a documentary called *This is What a Footballer Looks Like* that outlined their experiences of football outside of our club,' says Hui. 'And it's telling,' she continues, 'how different some of their experiences were at school compared to boys. Although they might get exposed to it at primary school, you pretty much see girls' football disappear at lots of secondary schools. Or, it is provided, then it's secondary to boys' football in terms of resources. One of our girls played in a team at secondary school where the coach was the minibus driver, someone who didn't really know what he was doing. By contrast, the boys got a qualified PE teacher.'

The FA and the Youth Sport Trust have recently worked together to try and change this problem in secondary schools via Game of Our Own. The programme, which provided support and resources to expand the provision of girl's football within a number of schools, targeted specifically at years seven, eight and nine, managed to support just over 5,000 girls, over half of whom had never played the sport before at all.

But although many girls face social barriers when it comes to playing football, at least the picture is better today than it was in the past, as Faye Barker, who plays in goal for Lewes Women, recalls:

'Playing football as a girl was tough when I was younger. For a start, you had no chance of making a career out of it. Then the infrastructure wasn't really there for you to make the best of yourself, there wasn't the same pathway that there is today. You also tended to be the only girl in a team, or even the only girl in an entire league in my case, which was hard. Although there were always great coaches around, all along the way, you battled to have the same opportunities as boys. By contrast, when I look at the girls we have in the junior section at Lewes today, it seems so much better. There's a lot more investment and attention given to them, by the FA, by clubs, by coaches. It's not perfect, and there is still a way to go, but it is a whole lot better.'

But what about those outside the youth and schools system? The 'Gameplan for Growth' was not just about getting more girls to play the game, it was also about bringing more women to football and ensuring that those who already play enjoy a better football experience.

If you wanted to pick a club that embodies the vibrancy of women's football in England today, then you could do worse than take a trip up to Sheffield and have a look at what AFC Unity is doing. The club is the brainchild of

Jane Watkinson and Jay Baker, who founded AFC Unity back in 2014.

This is a club that has the empowerment of women at its very heart, as Watkinson explains:

'When I set up the club back in 2014, with Jay [Baker], the idea was to make this a football club that embraced feminism. So, giving women power is central to everything we do. With the coaching, the running of the club and so on, the aim is to create an environment where women take on key roles, feel comfortable having a voice and having a say in how the club is run.'

AFC Unity represent everything that the FA want women's football to be. It's a club run (largely) by women for women. Historically, many women's teams in England have tended to be attached to an established men's club – at grassroots, and in professional football. This can mean that women are sometimes an afterthought or, occasionally, simply utilised to bring in funding from governing bodies.

'AFC Unity is different,' says Watkinson. 'We are entirely focussed on, and dedicated to, women's football, reflecting its feminist values, commitment to female empowerment, and passion for equality. Although this makes us almost always the underdog, we prefer it that way.'

The club's badge, an imposing red star, gives you an inkling as to AFC Unity's political leanings. If it was Bill Shankly who first saw the parallel between the collective unity of a football team and the collective unity evident in socialism, it's clubs like AFC Unity who are making the connection more concrete. But although founded on feminist and left-wing principles, being a card-carrying socialist is no benchmark for participation.

'Our approach is to engage women in the football club due to its appeal based on empowerment, ownership, and community engagement, and through inclusion we hope that dots are connected and that these principles are tied to democratic socialism. And I think that's worked. If you ask someone if they're a socialist, they might not self-identify that way ... but if you ask that same person if they believe in fairness, equality, public ownership of key services, greater democracy, more tolerance and respect, and so forth, almost all will tell you they're all for it,' says Jay Baker.

This sense of inclusivity is probably best expressed in AFC Unity's award-winning Solidarity Soccer sessions, an initiative that engages women (16+) of any experience and ability in non-competitive football.

'We welcome women who have never kicked a ball before, women wanting to return after an injury or to regain fitness, and women who are wanting to get more football practice. It's part of our efforts to illustrate that football can be a force for good, increasing confidence in life and interpersonal skills and body image, improving health and fitness whilst breaking down barriers and divisions that exist in society,' says Watkinson.

This desire to use football as a 'force for good' is evident in the work that AFC Unity has done off the pitch too. The club's Football for Food campaign, for example, encourages players, management and supporters from both teams, alongside the general public, to come to home fixtures not only to watch a good game of grassroots football but also to bring donations of food that are then passed on to local food banks. While another campaign, #UNITYFORALL, has seen the club partner with Sheffield Trades Council to promote the benefits of belonging to a workplace trade union and to highlight the positive work that trade unions do.

For many of the players who make up their 25-woman first-team squad, this is what sets AFC Unity apart from other women's teams and gives the club its unique appeal. Sarah Choonara, a member of the first team who's been involved with its trade union initiative, talks passionately about the attraction of the club's social and political side.

'I am so proud that, through football, we can give another arm to organisations like the Sheffield Trades Council, like Stop and Scrap Universal Credit to promote their causes – our causes – in a unique and imaginative way. It's important that clubs like Unity, and others, such as Republica Internationale and the St Pauli community teams, are safe and welcoming spaces for players who may not feel that a club without a political profile would prioritise inclusion. If we are outward with our politics we are making a statement about how we will treat each other. No one owns football. No one owns grassroots football. Networks of clubs with a political message support each other to shape the world of grassroots football into something we believe is better, a world we want to play in and have ownership of.'

Although important, AFC Unity's political orientation is not the only appeal of the club to the women who have flocked to join. Of equal attraction is its playing philosophy. In contrast to many adult sides, of both genders, where the end result is all that matters, the club has adopted a more holistic approach, one that has more in common with what the FA are trying to do with youth football. Player development and positivity are the themes that run through the club. Players are encouraged to be brave on the ball, to see mistakes as part of the learning process and to take joy in everything that they do.

'If we wanted to, like a lot of other teams, we could set things up so that all that mattered was the win. But we want our players to build their confidence, to develop as footballers and to enjoy what they do. Positivity is a huge part of that. It creates a supportive environment, where people feel they have the confidence to try new things. We have lots of players here who have said that they wouldn't have played football, wouldn't have stayed involved if we had not been here. And a big part of that appeal is our philosophy,' says Watkinson.

AFC Unity is just one of the hundreds of new football clubs that have emerged in the senior women's game in recent years. Under the Gameplan for Growth, the number of affiliated sides and participants is growing every year.

'It's been really pleasing to see more women come to the game,' says Kelly Simmons. 'In some ways it's harder for them, because they might have grown up with preconceptions about football being a "male" activity. So, for so many to come to football, it shows that the changes we have introduced into the game are really having an effect. And I think that, for a lot of people, old and young, the new professional WSL will be a big part of that in the future.'

The WSL, women's football's top tier, has been in existence since 2011, back then running as a summer league for eight teams. Over the following years it was expanded to two divisions, WSL1 and WSL2, and its closed-league status was scrapped via the introduction of relegation and promotion into the structure.

'Today, we now have the FA WSL, a fully professional domestic women's winter football league, and below that the FA Women's Championship. We are hoping that the new structure, with a dedicated professional tier, and semi-pro tier below, will drive women's football forward, raising the standards in the game, bringing it to a wider audience and establishing it as part of the football conversation,' says Kelly Simmons.

The problem with the previous system, at least from the FA's perspective, was a clash between two very different perceptions of women's football.

Traditionally, when it came to funding provided and resources given, the women's game at the majority of clubs has often been seen as a low priority. This has specifically been the case in the Football League, where finances tend to be stretched.

But exceptions did exist within the game. At a number of clubs, usually those with deeper pockets in the top flight, women's football has grown in importance in recent years. This has seen an increase in investment, the sharing of facilities with the men's section and bigger transfer and wage budgets. The end result was widening levels of disparity within the top levels of women's football, which on the pitch translated to an uneven playing field and the emergence of a quasi-permanent elite.

'The FA,' says Jen O'Neill, 'felt that this was creating a product that struggled to attract sponsors, fans and television cameras, and which did not equip England players to face elite opposition.

'So, their solution was to effectively introduce a set of minimum standards, compelling members to provide funding and resources that should, in theory, mean that any member of the WSL could compete against the top clubs.'

The new structure works on a licensing system for clubs, meaning all teams had to re-apply for their places in the top two tiers of the game. Although what is required of clubs differs between the WSL and the Championship, with the former requiring greater levels of investment, professional amounts of contact time with the players and the introduction of academies, the entire system is aimed at raising standards across the two tiers by demanding greater commitment from clubs. In return, the clubs allocated licences receive partnership funding from the FA, which amounts to £92,500 in the top tier and £62,500 in the second tier.

Although the new system is widely seen as essential for raising standards at the top levels of the game, the changes that have taken place were not universally welcomed. A number of clubs, such as Doncaster Belles, Sunderland and Sheffield FC, lost their place in the second tier because of the financial implications of the licensing system, effectively being relegated despite performing well on the field.

The pervading sense that money rather than on-the-field performance was increasingly governing the game was not helped when Manchester United, whose re-established women's senior side had only been in existence since 2018 (having been scrapped back in 2005), gained one of the places vacated by Doncaster Belles and Sheffield FC, simply by virtue of the fact that the club had the financial heft to obtain a licence in the second tier.

And despite the supposed raising of standards, there remained a fear that the bigger clubs will still be in the strongest position.

'Those attached to big clubs, like Manchester City, Chelsea and Arsenal, are going to have access to better facilities. They also have exceptionally wealthy parent clubs to back them and underwrite what they're doing. Smaller clubs that for years have been competing in the women's game, clubs like Yeovil, Barnet and Bristol City, are going to be at a disadvantage,' says Lee Burch, former manager of former WSL club Yeovil and current manager of Championship side London Bees.

These fears have not been helped by the fact that the bigger clubs have already benefitted from a recent change to wage regulation that has been introduced by the FA. Back when the WSL was first founded, the eight teams involved were only allowed to pay a maximum of four players over £20,000 per year. The thinking behind this idea was that limiting 'star' players to four per club would help spread talent across the division, thereby creating a more competitive league.

But since 2014 the cap has been softened. In place of the previous regulation, player salaries are now merely capped at 40 per cent of a club's turnover. The switch has made the rule pretty meaningless. Deep pocketed parent clubs are able to provide extra overall investment and thus increase the percentage they can spend on wages as needed, something that the likes of Chelsea, Manchester City and Manchester United are better able to do than clubs such as Bristol City, Birmingham City and Reading. In reality, the salary cap is now more about accountancy slight-of-hand than it is about regulating sustainable salaries and club finances.

'The big clubs are spending massively to get a competitive edge. A lot of clubs can't do that. And, in fact, sometimes just adhering to the FA's minimum standards under the licensing system is too much. All that's going to happen in the end is that the WSL is going to be made up of big, rich clubs. And smaller clubs, some of whom have been championing the women's game long before the likes of Man United got in on the act, are going to be cut adrift of the elite,' says Lee Burch.

Burch is well placed to comment on the issue of money in the game, having previously managed at Yeovil, where financial problems nearly caused the club to go into administration in 2019.

'If you look at Yeovil, my last job, the situation there was tough from the very start. Our budget was a fraction compared to many of our rivals in that league. That made it a challenge to afford the calibre of players necessary to compete at that level. We were also competing against clubs like Man City, Arsenal and Chelsea, whose facilities are Premier League standard. Despite the changes that the FA introduced to raise minimum standards, you can't look at the current WSL and think that it represents a level playing field.'

Although Yeovil worked with the FA to avoid going into administration, the club still received a ten-point deduction and were relegated from the top tier. Following this, it was also denied a licence to compete in the Championship and so has had to rebuild in the third tier, the National League South.

It is not the only club in recent years to have faced such hardship. Millwall Lionesses narrowly avoided administration in April 2018, only surviving at the time through a crowdfunding page that raised over £17,000. Crystal Palace Ladies nearly folded back in September

2018, surviving because of a substantial donation by Wilfried Zaha. And Notts County Ladies were wound up in 2017 by the club's owner, who refused to cover its losses (although the side did return a year later).

When it comes to finance, the hope of those restructuring women's football is that as it develops and grows in profile, rising attendances, more generous broadcasting deals and better commercial relationships will broaden the sport's income generating power, meaning less reliance on parent clubs and, in theory, more opportunities for all clubs to compete.

And they can point to signs that some of these changes are taking place. Midway through the 2019/20 campaign, average attendances in the WSL are more than four times higher than the previous season. Brand awareness of the WSL is up by ten per cent, helped by clubs like Manchester City merging the men's and the women's social media channels. And commercially, the WSL has recently gained several new partners including Head & Shoulders, Mars, PayPal, Lucozade Sport and Budweiser.

Most headline-grabbing of all, the WSL also secured a three-year partnership with Barclays, a deal which is believed to be closer to £18m than the £10m widely reported. The deal, which runs until July 2022, represents the biggest-ever investment in UK women's sport by a brand. Under it, the top tier of women's football will be renamed as the 'Barclays FA Women's Super League'.

'The game is definitely changing and more money is coming into it. Whether smaller clubs thrive in this changing environment, only time will tell. I suspect that what will likely happen is what's happened with the men's game, where focus and the money tends to go to the elite.

Yeovil had a taste of what that's like last season when not a single one of our games was chosen to be broadcast. That big club bias is already evident. I don't see it getting any better just because Barclays are sponsoring the league,' feels Lee Burch.

One way for smaller clubs to compete against better-funded rivals is through budget parity. The disparity between men's and women's football, not just in terms of finance but also in terms of the value placed on each by clubs, has long been a characteristic of our national game, with men's football receiving far more support than its female equivalent. Since the re-emergence of women's football in the 1970s, clubs have often viewed this part of the game as an add-on, something significantly down the list of priorities.

Perhaps the most high-profile example of how low a priority women's football was seen to be by some in football occurred back in 2007 at Charlton Athletic. After the men's senior team was relegated from the Premier League, the club's hierarchy made the controversial decision to axe the women's section, citing a need to control costs as justification.

What this meant in practice was management staff and 140 female players from senior teams down to centre of excellence level being forced to find new clubs or employment. The cost saving to the club was £250,000. At the time Charlton were set to receive parachute payments of £11m a year for the following two seasons, while the impending sale of Darren Bent to Tottenham was set to bring in £16m.

To add insult to injury, Charlton WFC *was* a successful side. In contrast to its male equivalent, it had, in recent years, finished runners-up in the top tier and won both the FA Cup and the League Cup. Not that it mattered to the club.

Ultimately, in the summer of 2007, sponsorship was found to save the side from being fully disbanded and it was able to continue, at that point under the control of the Charlton Community Trust. But the damage had been done. Due to the exodus of players after the original closure announcement, only two members from the previous squad remained by the time the club's rescue was in place. The reconstituted team finished bottom of the league at the end of the 2007/08 season.

'Although the picture has improved in recent years, there is still a sense in football that the women's game is somehow lesser. We wanted to change that,' says Stuart Fuller, chairman at Lewes FC. 'At this club we believe that there should be a level playing field for women in football, hence our introduction of budget parity.'

When it comes to the women's game, Lewes FC has form, as club director Charlie Dobres explains: 'A few years ago, we led a campaign to reform the league structure within the sport, to allow promotion to the higher reaches. We've always regarded women's football at Lewes as being important. I think one point that starkly illustrates this is our decision to have the women's team play at our home ground, which is rare in the game.'

Under the club's current funding arrangements, playing budgets for the women's and men's first teams are set at an equal level, providing matched resources for coaching staff and equitable levels of investment in local youth grassroots outreach efforts.

From a wider perspective, what Lewes has done forms part of Equality FC, the club's campaign that aims to raise awareness about gender inequality in the sport. This campaigning dimension to what Lewes is doing was evident back in 2019, when the club publicly called out the FA for the disparity that exists between the men's FA Cup and the women's equivalent.

'In the 2018/19 season the total FA Cup prize fund for men's teams was £30.25m. The total FA Cup prize fund for women's teams was £250,000, which means that the total prize money for women is less than one per cent of the total prize money for men. From our perspective, this is just wrong and so we said so via an open letter to the FA board,' says Dobres.

It's a level of disparity that, in gender terms, marks the FA Cup as one of the most unequal playing fields for prize money in world sport. In 2017, a study commissioned by Women in Sport revealed that 83 per cent of sports now rewarded men and women equally. And this included high-profile sporting events such as Wimbledon, where the £38m prize pot has been shared equally between the genders since 2007.

'Obviously, nobody at the FA has consciously engineered the difference between the genders; they are the result of many people making many decisions with various desired outcomes over many years. But look at where we've inadvertently ended up. It's an outcome that is unfair and an issue that we felt needed raising,' says Dobres.

What Lewes are trying to do, both with Equality FC and with its own changes to the club, is revolutionary. It's an attempt that, for the first time, challenges the primacy of men's football within the sport. Inevitably, as with any change, not everyone has been on board, as Stuart Fuller explains:

'You inevitably get a handful of supporters who would rather as much money as possible go to the men's first team. We expected that. What we are doing is challenging something that has been the norm for decades. And it was always going to be the case that when the men's side form dipped, questions would be raised regarding how our resources are allocated. But, overall, I think most people are behind us and understand what we are trying to do. We have certainly attracted more supporter investors because of it. People appear to be buying into what we are doing.'

By increasing the budget that was allocated to the women's side, Lewes, as a club, has been able to punch well above its weight within the game. When the licences were being allocated for the WSL and the Championship, the club was accepted into the second tier, joining the likes of Manchester United, Spurs and Aston Villa.

'Club wise, we're surrounded by other teams whose men's sides are drawn mostly from the Championship and the Premier League,' says Fuller. 'So, for us to be competing at that level has been a huge boost for the profile of the club. It's got us a lot more media attention and we've also had big names come down to the Dripping Pan to play us, which has helped attendances too.'

The hope for those who run the club is that everything that is currently being done, the improved budget, rising attendances, more media attention, will be enough to bridge the gap that exists between Lewes and the other clubs at this level.

'Our aim is to get this club to be promoted to the top tier of the game,' says Dobres. 'Not only would this give us access to greater FA funding, it would also potentially increase everything, from sponsorship to attendances.

We've survived our first season in the Championship and we think we have the foundations in place to succeed in this league. And it is our hope that if we can prove to others in the game that success can come through greater equality then perhaps more and more clubs will start to copy what we have done.'

Despite widespread agreement that the changes that have taken place in elite football are both welcome and overdue, for many of those who play their football just beyond its reaches there remains a degree of frustration.

Caz Henry Evans believes she has done every job possible at Chichester City Ladies: 'I spent one year as a player, six years as reserve-team coach, then on the admin side I think I've done everything, treasurer, fixtures secretary, secretary [for 11 years] and now chairman, which I've been doing for the last three. Like a lot of football clubs, men's or women's, you always struggle for volunteers so that means I've had to plug a lot of gaps!'

Chichester ply their trade in the FA Women's National League Southern Premier Division, one level below the Championship. When you talk to people involved in women's football at this level and below there is a sense that two varieties of the sport are developing. One, centred on the higher reaches, and specifically the WSL, that is better funded and which is challenging the gender inequality that has long characterised the game. The other, played at the levels below the top two tiers, is one where money remains a constant issue.

'The money is geared towards the top and towards youth football. In-between the FA are virtually non-existent. We would love some help from the FA for our senior side, and I know from talking to other clubs that we are not alone in this. But it's not forthcoming. When the FA has extended help, it's only ever for junior football. Although, even then, it's for specific uses, like new equipment, not for what we actually need it for. It's great that there is more investment in the game, and we don't begrudge elite and youth football getting more money, it's long overdue. But what about the rest of us?' Henry Evans says.

For clubs beyond the elite, life is tough. Although Chichester City Ladies have a relationship with the men's club (Chichester City), it is a separate legal entity, responsible for its own funding.

'Finances in particular are a constant problem,' says Henry Evans. 'We don't make a great deal from matchday, as we are not that well attended, despite technically being in a higher division than the men. So, pretty much everything for the £50,000 we need comes through sponsorship. And we are all responsible for that. For example, just the other day I was in a local tattooist and got chatting about the club. The owner was interested in what we do and I asked him about sponsoring. It's just like that. Even the players are at it.'

Along with a lack of funding for those just outside the elite, there is also the sense that through the changes that have taken place, the FA has created a glass ceiling within the pyramid, separating the higher two divisions from the remainder. Although the Championship has a lower bar to entry than the WSL, letting clubs operate as part-time entities, requiring less investment and commitment of resources, the barriers still exist. For Henry Evans, these barriers are making the game more about a club's bank account and less about what it does on the pitch.

'We are probably good enough in football terms to play in the Championship if we were to win the league. But there is absolutely no chance of us being able to take up that place because of the financial restrictions of the licensing system that the FA have brought in. There are stipulations in the licensing agreement, like having tens of thousands in the bank and employing full-time staff, that are ridiculous for a club that is entirely dependent on volunteers. By having them in place, what you are really saying is that for some teams, this is as good as it will ever get, so don't even bother trying to do any better.'

That frustrations remain in women's football is perhaps inevitable. No system was ever going to be perfect and it's probably no surprise that as the game comes to better resemble men's football in its organisation, the sense of inequality that exists between the elite and the grassroots that is endemic within that medium of the sport will also come to affect women's football too. It's doubtful that the rumoured takeover of the WSL by the Premier League in 2022 will do anything other than exacerbate this trend. While a formidable force for enriching its members, the Premier League has never been particularly interested in what happens beyond its borders.

But despite the problems that exist, women's and girls' football today has still, according to Jen O'Neill, come a long way:

'Young girls now have the opportunity to play with a mixed team or an all-girls' side. They can follow a club and can look up to stars like Lucy Bronze, Ellen White and Nikita Parris. And that same girl, if she wants, can also try and follow a pathway that could see her have a career in the game. A generation ago, so much of that would not have been part of her football world. Is the game perfect? The answer is no. But it's got better and you have to have faith that the improvements will continue. You feel like football is finally getting its head around the idea that women and girls matter just as much as men and boys. And long may that continue.'

Women's and girls' football today is in better shape than it has ever been. Participation is riding high, the number of teams has blossomed and for the first time the sport boasts a professional division, an end point for those with talent to look towards.

But evidently, some of the ills of the modern men's game – such as inequality and a propensity for attention, both within the media and within the game's governing body, to focus excessively on the 'elite' – are beginning to make themselves felt. You feel that, despite the manifold improvements, the sport is potentially making the first tentative steps on a path that will see it encounter many of the problems that currently exist in the professional realm of the men's game. And, as we start to once again climb the men's pyramid in the following few chapters, it is apparent how devastating to clubs these ills can be.

Chapter Seven

Crisis Clubs

I N the end, the challenges facing the club were simply too great. After weeks of uncertainty, with rumours circulating in the media, the EFL finally acted. On 27 August 2019, Bury FC was expelled from the Football League, bringing to an end 125 years of continuous membership.

'No one wanted to be in this position, but following repeated missed deadlines, the suspension of five league fixtures, in addition to not receiving the evidence we required in regard to financial commitments and a possible takeover not materialising, the EFL Board has been forced to take the most difficult of decisions,' said Debbie Jevans, the EFL's executive chair.

The origins of Bury's sorry tale lie in the tenure of its penultimate owner, Stewart Day, who took ownership of the club in 2013. Day subsidised the loss-making club with loans from his property company, Mederco. But Day was no Abramovich, able to endlessly bankroll the club though bottomless pits of money. When his business collapsed, the cash dried up and Bury, unable to pay its players or anyone else, came close to bankruptcy.

A temporary patch-up of sorts arrived in the form of a loan from Capital Bridging Finance Solutions, which was rumoured to be costing around £1,500 a day to service.

With Bury on life support, it was then sold in December 2018 for £1 to Steve Dale, a man who at no point illustrated to the EFL that he had the financial resources to rescue the club. Despite this, his takeover went ahead.

Dale later claimed that he did not appreciate just how bad the problems were at Gigg Lane, an admission that did little to help the club. Although it survived a winding up order just a few months after he had taken over, the writing appeared to be on the wall. As the season wound to a close, the list of creditors and the amount owed swelled, with the latter standing at around £8m according to *The Guardian*. The players and coaching staff had also not been paid since February, something that made the club's surprise promotion to League One that season all the more remarkable.

During the summer, Bury's plight became more acute. Before a ball had even been kicked, the club were already facing a 12-point deduction for enduring an 'insolvency event', following its decision to enter into a company voluntary arrangement (CVA) in July.

But worse was to come. Bury never got to start their campaign, never got to kick a ball. The club's ongoing financial problems led to a series of suspended games, compelling the EFL board to meet a few weeks into the season to discuss the crisis.

The club was given a 5pm deadline to complete a sale. C&N Sporting Risk, a sports analytics firm, waited in the wings, poised to take over. But its offer never came. C&N withdrew around 90 minutes before the deadline, baulking at the scale of the financial problems facing the club. The failure to complete the sale would ultimately mean that Bury became the first team to be expelled from the Football League since Maidstone's liquidation in 1992.

On expulsion, the club's players had their contracts invalidated, making them free agents. It left Bury a club without players, without its coaching staff and without a league to compete in. All of this while also trying to grapple with a crippling level of debt, with limited means to generate the necessary income to pay it back.

Losing one club from a league might, at a push, be seen as an aberration. While never welcome, it has happened before in the Football League. But losing one and then potentially losing another the same week is less easily brushed off. And yet, that was very nearly the case during the summer of 2019 when League One's Bolton Wanderers, Bury's neighbour, almost went the same way.

Ken Anderson, the man that many blamed for the club's most recent crisis, came to Bolton in March 2016, part of a consortium led by former Wanderers striker Dean Holdsworth. The consortium bought the club from previous owner Eddie Davies.

Prior to the sale, Bolton hadn't been in the best financial shape. Years of overspending had left it debt-ridden, the money from several seasons in the top flight largely squandered. Although Davies did the club a favour by wiping around £185m worth of debt owed to him, Bolton had been in a parlous state, a club in hock to a number of creditors, hobbled by ongoing losses and which was also under a transfer embargo after failing to submit accounts to the EFL in 2015.

The insolvency practitioner Trevor Birch had struggled to find anyone prepared to take on the club. With HMRC about to wind Wanderers up for unpaid tax, Holdsworth and Anderson had stepped in at the last minute.

A year after the takeover, Anderson bought out Holdsworth and took sole control of Wanderers. His story is an interesting one. In September 2005 Anderson was disqualified from being a company director for eight years after his firm, Professional Sports International Ltd (PSI), went bust.

According to the Insolvency Service, Anderson had failed to ensure his companies paid VAT, then failed to cooperate with liquidators. A notice from the case outlined that at PSI, 'Mr Anderson diverted/sought to divert PSI's funds by depositing them into a personal bank account in his own name and invoicing in the name of another connected company.'

Although that disqualification order had concluded by the time he came to Bolton, his recent disbarring hardly made him a risk-free arrival.

Under the consortium, and then under Anderson, the problems that had characterised the latter days of the Davies regime continued. Debts grew, for periods of time players and coaching staff didn't receive wages and creditors went unpaid. The club flirted with administration and bit by bit tested the patience of the EFL.

What motivated Anderson to get involved in a club so systemically flawed as Bolton, outsiders can only guess. Maybe he possessed a genuine belief that he could turn it round or perhaps the lure of a potential profit on a club with Premier League infrastructure available at a knock-down price was too good to resist. Either way, the end result wasn't great for anyone connected to Bolton. The problems proved too significant to manage, even in the short term. Eventually, the club was placed in administration in May 2019.

By August, matters had gotten so bad that the club, who had been relegated to League One at the end of the previous campaign, was on the verge of liquidation. The EFL gave it a 14-day final deadline, with the administrator, Paul Appleton, being told to either sell Bolton or prove it could be funded for the rest of the season. If neither could be achieved then the club would face expulsion.

Fortunately for Bolton, who at one point in the summer only had five senior pros left at the club, a deal was eventually made. But it was a close-run thing. Just two days before the deadline, Appleton had revealed there was no money left to fund the club and a takeover bid by the Football Ventures consortium had stalled. As it was, through Appleton's hard work, undertaking what he described as 'one of the most complicated administrations I have been involved with', the deal eventually went though, with the club being saved just one day after Bury had been expelled.

Welcome to the world of crisis clubs. Bury and Bolton might represent the extreme end of the trend, clubs whose finances were so bad that expulsion from the league was put on the table, but they are far from the only transgressors. Over the course of the past few decades, the Football League has suffered a period of unrivalled financial instability, the only surprise being the fact that a 'Bury' has not occurred sooner.

That big, professional clubs suffer financial problems is nothing new in the game. In his exhaustive history of league football between 1888 and 1988, the writer Simon Inglis, at random, made the effort to flick through the 1981/82 season's *Rothmans Football Yearbook*, which provided an insight into the extent of the financial crisis hitting English football at the time. According to the book, many clubs were haemorrhaging money, with the likes of Bristol City and Chester City losing thousands per week. Others, such as Darlington and Rochdale, spent most of the campaign on the verge of collapse. And some, like Hull City, even went into receivership, so dire was the financial situation at the club.

Historically, professional football clubs have not been great at turning a profit and the sport's history is littered with examples of clubs scraping through due to the generosity of owners and fans. But they did mostly scrape through. Although financial problems became more common from the 1980s until the turn of the century, examples of catastrophic failure at clubs remained rare. Maidstone aside, so too was the idea that a club would be expelled and liquidated. Everything was just about manageable.

But that changed.

Since 2000, financially instability has become endemic, with multiple clubs enduring either formal insolvency proceedings or coming dangerously close to that unwelcome outcome. Within examples of formal insolvency that have occurred, some of the clubs affected have experienced repeat bouts, seeing the likes of Darlington and Portsmouth enduring more than one 'insolvency event' in the past 20 years. According to R3, the trade body for the insolvency profession, the rate of insolvencies in professional football is higher than almost any other sector of the economy.

For many of the clubs involved, so dramatic, and in some cases enduring, have been the problems faced that they become more famous for their financial issues than anything that takes place on the football pitch. Few people who follow the game would, for example, at the mention of Portsmouth not bring to mind that club's sorry descent into financial oblivion a few years ago, a period of turmoil that has eclipsed its more recent footballing achievements.

'Although there are plenty of good people out there involved in clubs because they genuinely want to make a difference to what is an important community asset, there are also people whose motivations are less wholesome and people who are simply incompetent. We as fans have experienced first-hand what can happen when there are people like that involved in your club, people who don't seem to care about the supporters and who seem content to wreak havoc. It can be devastating,' says Andy Higgins of the Blackpool Supporters' Trust (BST).

In Blackpool's case, the owners in question were the Oyston family. The club spent decades in the family's hands after initially being bought by local businessman Owen Oyston back in 1988.

Oyston is a controversial figure to say the least. Irrespective of what would later happen at Blackpool, his name will always be synonymous with a conviction for rape in the mid-1990s, for which he spent three and a half years in prison. While incarcerated, control passed first to his wife and then to his son Karl, the latter of whom served as chairman from 1999 until 2018.

The timing of his stepping down as chairman was largely forced upon Karl Oyston, a response to events which had seen both he and his father undermine Blackpool and rupture the relationship between the fans and the club.

Back in 2017, in a high court judgment, the pair were found guilty of the 'illegitimate stripping' of Blackpool's assets. It was found that the Oystons had bled the club during its solitary season in the Premier League back in 2010/11, paying £26.7m out to companies they owned. They did so, according to Justice Marcus Smith, in a manner which involved 'fundamental breaches' of their duties as directors.

'They'd taken the money from the Premier League, which should have been put to use improving the club's infrastructure and the squad, and given it to themselves instead. The financial and footballing problems we faced after relegation from the top flight, which saw us drop down to League Two at one point, all stem from the actions they took. The money should've been there to help the club build something. Instead, what they did meant that, once we were relegated, the club seemed to be in a state of near permanent crisis.'

Many fans spent several years in opposition to the Oyston regime, organising campaigns and boycotts with the aim of creating a hostile environment at the club. But as effective as they were, the nail in the coffin for the reign of the Oystons was the dogged pursuit of the regime in the courts by Valērijs Belokoņs, former club director and the man who had funded the club's surprise promotion to the Premier League. It was he who had brought the initial high court case against the Oystons, and he who continued to pursue them through the courts when payment was not forthcoming, an act that ultimately resulted in Blackpool being put in receivership in early 2019 and the Oystons finally removed from the club.

'Few clubs would welcome receivership. But for us it marked the point where we were at last free of an owner who was destroying the club. But should it really come to that? In fact, the possibility existed at one point that had the Oystons been able to raise the money to pay Belokoņs off, that they could very well still be in charge at the club. We were just lucky in the end that they couldn't,' says Higgins.

The case of Blackpool threw a spotlight on the existing regulation regarding who can and cannot become a director at a football club within the Football League: the Owners and Directors test, or the 'fit and proper persons test' as it is more commonly known. The test isn't really a 'test', but instead a list of conditions which must be met in order for the EFL to deem an individual or business 'fit and proper' to run a football club.

Anyone who takes over as a director in the Football League, becomes the owner of more than 30 per cent of a club's shares, has to pass the 'test'. The principal disqualifying conditions are: being involved in the administration or ownership of another Football League or Premier League club, being subject to disciplinary matters by a sporting or professional body, having been subject to insolvency proceedings, disqualification as a director of a company, and having certain unspent convictions (based on dishonest behaviour) in England and Wales.

'With Blackpool, this test didn't bar Owen Oyston from owning the club, a convicted rapist who will remain on the sex offenders' register for life. And it did nothing to stop the Oyston family remaining as directors despite the judgment that was handed down to them in 2017. Apparently, directors of football clubs can commit "fundamental breaches" of their basic duties as directors, but still be "fit and proper". At some point, those in charge finally have to realise that this no longer makes any sense,' says Higgins.

The Oyston family also had a history of intimidation and bullying towards fan groups opposed to them, most notably in their decision to sue fans for comments made on social media. Tim Fielding, the honorary vice-president of the BST, was one of those sued; an action that caused a great deal of personal stress and ended up costing him £20,000 (£10,000 to settle the action and £10,000 in legal costs). Again, while not an approach that disbarred the Oystons under the 'fit and proper' test, it raises questions as to how useful the test is if it still allows owners to pursue supporters through the courts in such a manner.

'The limitations of the current regulations have not just failed to prevent unfit people from taking control at clubs and staying in control. As the recent crisis at Bury illustrated, the stipulation that requires new owners to illustrate that they have proof of funds also seems to lack teeth. Steve Dale should never have been able to take control, because he clearly lacked the finance needed to save a club in as much trouble as Bury. And yet, that's exactly what happened,' says Sheffield Hallam University's football finance expert, Dr Rob Wilson.

The EFL has publicly stated that there have been times when it has blocked takeovers because a prospective bidder has not satisfied them that the money exists to run a club. But, importantly, there is wriggle room. Despite it being clear that the League can block a takeover where a person has engaged with the process in advance, if the takeover is concluded quickly, without going through the League's requirements first, which is what happened at Bury, then it can take place irrespective of the prospective owners financial limitations.

Although sanctions do exist for those who have failed to provide the necessary information related to a takeover, in the form of a player registration embargo, the takeover itself remains unaffected. It seems, when it comes to poorly funded takeovers, it's sometimes better to ask for forgiveness than permission.

At the time of writing, a new regulation that would allow the EFL to take 'direct action' for 'A very serious single act or persistent serious acts – where the individual's conduct is clearly damaging to the standing and reputation of the wider profession and the game of football' is being considered. But, to date, the detail of this rule and how it will work in practice has still not been thrashed out and passed by the clubs. And how the EFL defines 'a very serious single act or persistent serious acts' remains open to interpretation, an interpretation that might not tally with how a supporter views an owner's behaviour.

'There is little in the EFL's recent track record to suggest that it takes these problems seriously,' says Tom Davies, vice-chair of the Leyton Orient Fans' Trust. 'They have sat idly by for years and years and watched as clubs have struggled. When Orient were in trouble, a crisis that ended up with us being relegated out of the Football League and nearly going under, the EFL weren't interested in the slightest. The prospect of a club going out of business altogether has been on the cards for some time and the EFL have just turned a blind eye. It would mark quite a turnaround in outlook if they suddenly began caring a lot more about who takes over a club and how owners behave once in charge.'

The sense of a football authority indifferent to the problems within its divisions was not helped by the revelation, in the wake of Bury's expulsion, that the EFL had been warned that insolvency events were becoming more likely and had failed to act. Following research into the Football League back in 2017, the financial data firm Vysyble was so concerned by what it had found that it arranged a meeting with the EFL board to stress how precarious a position many clubs were in and to stress that unless action was taken then outcomes such as Bury and Bolton were likely to occur. The EFL responded to Vysyble's report by stating that its competition was in a 'strong financial position'. The EFL also said that such reports 'confuse the reality of the situation for supporters'.

'To be honest, I think the EFL will always tolerate a handful of crisis clubs if the overall product is OK,' argues Davies. 'From their perspective, if a club goes bust now and then, it's not a big deal. And that's because, as a whole, the product produced by the 72 Football League clubs is pretty good. I think you'll only ever see them truly act if that's threatened. The problems that we see with the likes of Bury and Bolton have been going on for years and the EFL haven't cared at all. There's nothing to suggest that all of a sudden they're going to change how they feel.'

That supporters feel a lack of faith in the EFL, specifically those like Davies whose club has gone through a crisis period, should probably not come as a surprise. But it's not just the fans who have a problem. It's owners too.

Andy Holt isn't like most football club owners. For a start, he had no desire to become one in the first place.

'I didn't want to own a football club, let alone Accrington Stanley,' he says. 'But a friend of mine, a big fan of the club, was constantly on at me to invest. I had no intention of agreeing but one Saturday, in pre-season, I was persuaded by him to go along to a friendly.'

Holt is a successful and popular local businessman, a man who made his money from the plastics industry, via his company What More UK (Wham).

'I think the idea with the friendly was for me to get a taste of the club and to become a sponsor. I have always been a big believer in putting something back into the community. I've done it throughout my business career. Wham is a big local employer and the company is always looking at what it can do to make sure that it remains community focussed. I was of a mind before I'd even gone that sponsoring the club would be a great thing for Wham to do.'

The game he went to see was against Burnley, during which Stanley found itself 3-0 up in no time.

'I was having a great time, specifically as I had mates there who support Burnley! Then Stanley ran out of beer. Can you believe that? Such a great match, everyone really enjoying themselves and the bar ran dry. I asked them why and was told that they hadn't paid the bills. It was soon made clear to me that the club was in trouble, that it wasn't paying players, staff, suppliers.'

Holt offered to 'have a look' over the books, thinking his years of experience might offer them some ideas.

'When they showed me, I was really shocked. The club needed an extortionate amount just to keep afloat. There were unpaid bills for everything like pies, wages and other suppliers. When I looked a little closer, I saw how there was money being put in from all kinds of non-business sources, from trustees, from fans, from people in the community, from their personal pockets. It was then I really got a sense of the importance of the place to the community. The people in the town were pouring money into this club just to keep it alive, money they were never going to get back. That's how much it mattered to them. I realised then that I had to get involved. I knew it definitely wasn't going to be an easy fix. But for such a treasured community asset to get back on its feet, it was going to be worth it.'

Holt took a controlling stake in the club in October 2015, taking on 75 per cent of the shares in a deal that saw £1.2m of old debt cleared and £600,000 of new working capital provided. In two separate deals, worth just over £200,000 in total to the club, the Crown Ground was renamed the Wham Stadium and Holt brought in a key partner, PlasticBoxShop – which retails Wham brand products online – to become Stanley's new shirt sponsor.

His arrival at the club has precipitated a significant change in fortunes for the 'Accy'. Off the pitch, the ground has been renovated, the playing surface dug up and re-laid (to reduce the number of postponed fixtures) and more investment has gone into the academy and the community trust. Attendances, commercial revenue and sponsorship are up and so too is the playing budget. And the increase in the latter is important as, on the pitch, in the spring of 2018 the club earned promotion to League One, the highest level that Stanley has ever played at.

'It's been a wonderful few years,' says Holt. 'Not only have I made great friends and had some fantastic times, it's also been a pleasure to see this community really get behind the club. You feel that our success has really created a buzz around Accrington and people are buying into what we are trying to do here. I think people might have been a bit wary at first, viewing with a bit of suspicion someone coming in and making so many changes. But I feel they can all see now that I have nothing but the best interests of the club and the community at heart. I'm not in this for some kind of ego trip. I'm here to help.'

Despite the happy memories, Holt admits that his tenure as an owner in Leagues One and Two has been something of an eye opener. Talk to him, follow him on Twitter, or take the time to read any of the many interviews he has given, and it becomes quickly evident that Holt has little affection for how football is run in England, specifically how the lower divisions in the Football League are regarded within the game.

'Part of the problem with the system as it currently stands it that, although someone who is a criminal or who has a recent history of serious financial problems should be unable to take control of a club, if someone later turns out to be financially incompetent or reckless, very little can be done. And unfortunately, the wider world of the Football League is one that seems to encourage recklessness. So, it's not just a case of needing reform of the "fit and proper" test, we also have to look at why we have allowed a system that encourages so much risk to be the norm within our game.'

For Holt, and a number of other owners, such as Mark Palios at Tranmere Rovers and Dale Vince at Forest Green Rovers, all of whom have publicly expressed concern at how English football is governed, the system as it exists today is in desperate need of some kind of reform.

'Every club wants to get promoted and play at the highest level they can. Football has always been about that,' says Holt. 'But there is so much money sloshing around the upper reaches of the game, in the Premier League and the Championship, that it has started to encourage some owners to take massive risks to try and get there. And it's this that is, in part, destabilising the game.'

Two factors that have been driving the increase of money in the Football League are the broadcast deals that the EFL negotiates on behalf of its member clubs and the payments that are handed down in solidarity from the Premier League's own broadcast arrangements.

When it comes to the former, unlike in the Premier League, where teams' prize money is partly awarded based on finishing position, each club in the EFL receives the same figure as the others in its respective division.

The basic award for the Championship is in the region of £2.3m and is a direct product of the television deal the league has with Sky Sports. This figure drops to £732,000 for League One clubs and around £500,000 for those in League Two.

Clubs also earn money every time a game is televised, with the financial rewards dropping significantly in Leagues One and Two. So, in the Championship for instance, a club can earn £100,000 hosting a televised Saturday game. For League One, that figure drops to just £30,000.

In addition to the above, a 'solidarity payment' from the Premier League represents another source of income. The payment is designed, in theory, to ensure the gap between the top tier and the Football League doesn't become too large. In the Championship this amounts to

£4.5m per club, in League One, £675,000, and in League Two, £450,000.

'What this means in reality,' says Holt, 'is that getting into the Championship is hugely lucrative for clubs. You're talking about millions more in income just because you've gone up a tier. And if you get into that league then you've got a chance to keep going, to follow the likes of Leicester City, Wolves and Huddersfield who have managed to go from the third tier to the Premier League, where the real money is.'

According to Deloitte, the average League One club has a revenue of £6m each year and a League Two club just £4m. But these figures are often skewed upwards by a handful of larger clubs in each division, with the average for the majority being somewhat smaller. Set against that, it seems clear why the owners of lower league teams are often so willing to bet the farm on chasing promotion.

'And this is only going to get worse in the future,' argues Holt. Accrington Stanley recently undertook a ten-year future income projection that looked into how the current five-year television deal for the EFL, the deal to follow it, and solidarity payments provided by the Premier League to the rest of the Football League will be divided up between each of the 72 EFL clubs in the future. Although only an estimate, for those in Leagues One and Two it made grim reading.

According to the club's projections, in the absence of any meaningful change by 2027, each club in the Championship will be receiving an average of £13m per season. By contrast, clubs in League One and League Two will only receive modest increases.

'An idiot can see that the gap between Leagues One and Two and the Championship is only going to get bigger,' says Holt. 'But that won't stop some clubs from trying to breach it, spending way more than they can afford in an effort to do so. When you will be talking about sums that are transformative, it's not going to be a huge surprise if you see more and more owners having a gamble.'

Even before these changes kick in, under the system as it currently exists today risk is still encouraged, with some owners trying to do whatever it takes to get to the promised land of the Championship (and on to the Premier League). And one of the areas where this is most keenly evident is wages, as clubs splurge ever-escalating amounts on a finite resource, pushing up the price/cost in the process.

Theoretically, in Leagues One and Two, wages are meant to be controlled via the Salary Cost Management Protocol (SCMP) which was introduced back in 2004.

The SCMP was created to ensure clubs in the third and fourth tiers spend responsibly and don't get into financial trouble, while also trying to ensure something resembling a level playing field. At a very base level the rules state that clubs can't spend more than a certain percentage of their annual turnover on player wages (60 per cent in League One and 50 per cent in League Two).

'But there are ways that owners can get around the regulations,' says Kieran Maguire, author of the *Price of Football* blog.

'For example, the owner can inject equity into the club, this increases the SCMP total on a pound-for-pound basis. Stuart Day did this at Bury. The club could also employ a player's partner/mum, etc. for a non-playing job as it is only player employment costs that are used for SCMP. And the club owner could give the player a part-time job in another company owned by them. There are lots of loopholes available, ways that owners can pay to get the players they want. As an idea the SCMP is laudable, but as we have seen in recent years it's not preventing some clubs from significantly breaching the recommended limits.'

According to Deloitte, overall, 2017/18 saw League One's wages/revenue ratio increase from 84 per cent to 94 per cent, eclipsing the previous high of 93 per cent seen in 2011/12. In the same year, League Two's wages/revenue ratio rose to 78 per cent, the highest since the 2000/01 season.

'The idea that SCMP is somehow stopping clubs from overspending or making poor financial decisions is not borne out from the reality,' says Maguire.

The trend of overspending in the hope of reaching the promised land above has been made potentially more financially risky because the sums required to compete have inflated too. Parachute payments, large sums of cash given to Premier League clubs on relegation to ease transition, have played a role in this.

'Clubs are coming down into the Championship, and sometimes League One, as with Sunderland and Wigan recently, armed with millions. And that money is often splurged on new players. And all that does for the rest of the clubs is inflate prices. While the trend is most keenly felt in the Championship, inevitably it has begun to trickle down into the lower leagues too. And so, spending for "success" gets more and more expensive for those who want to do things that way,' says Rob Wilson.

The inevitable result is that clubs are making consistent losses. In League One, for instance, according to Deloitte, 24 clubs reported a collective loss of £81m in 2017/18, an average of around £3.4m per club.

'Although there is more money around the Football League than there ever has been, largely driven by TV revenue, it remains the case that clubs are exceptionally poor at making profits. Football is not a game that offers investors a great return. As recent years have illustrated, it's a sport that will take any money you are able to offer it,' says Maguire.

A recent report by professional services firm BDO found that only 11 per cent of League Two and 24 per cent of League One finance officers regard their clubs as being in a 'very healthy' position.

With spending set to consistently outstrip revenues, a huge number of football's smaller clubs could soon find themselves on the brink of becoming the next Bury. According to *Argyle Life,* the Alternative Plymouth Argyle Voice, from the most recent club accounts submitted (for the 2017/18 season), Coventry currently owes £42m to its owners, Colchester £22m, Fleetwood £13m, Bristol Rovers £13m, Southend £13m, MK Dons £10m and Chesterfield £10m.

And these represent just a handful of the many indebted clubs that populate the bottom two tiers of the Football League.

These clubs are run no differently to Bury. All that separates them from enduring the same fate is the fact that the owners haven't exhausted the ability or the will to bankroll losses.

The reality is that the majority of clubs within League's One and Two just don't make the kind of money necessary to fund what it takes to sustain upward progression. In fact, many clubs even lack what it takes just to simply remain competitive.

'We got into League One and, despite increasing our playing budget by about ten per cent, we still had one of the smallest in the division. The only way we could become more competitive would be to do something stupid, like spend way more than we can make. If, like us, you want to run a club sustainably and prudently, the chances of having a go at promotion are limited. That's the system we have now,' says Holt.

Part of the problem throughout the lower two tiers of the Football League concerns attendances. Last year, the EFL proudly released figures that showed attendances in its leagues had reached a 60-year high, with almost 18.4 million people attending the 1,655 matches in its divisions – the most in tiers two to four since the late 1950s.

But although welcome, the figures were boosted by the fact that a few 'giants' of the game were having a spell in the doldrums. Aston Villa was one such club, having been relegated from the Premier League for the first time at the end of the 2016/17 season. Villa, in fact, was responsible for eight of the ten biggest attendances in the Football League during that season.

Despite the EFL's boasts, the picture beyond the big clubs is a lot less rosy that the figures would suggest. As many as 31 of the 48 clubs in Leagues One and Two had average attendances for the last season that were less than half of their stadium capacities. Attendances might be marginally up for many of these clubs, but they are not up by nearly enough to make a significant difference.

There is a theory, one that is supported by the Football Supporters' Federation, which says clubs need regular gates of above 5,000 to be sustainable in League Two, and above 10,000 in League One. If this theory holds, then that would mean that 36 clubs (18 across both divisions) are in trouble.

When you talk to those involved in the running of clubs down at this level, the need to get people through the gate on a Saturday afternoon comes up constantly in conversation.

'If you want to move away from the patronage or benefactor model, then one of the things you have to do is expand the fanbase,' says Tranmere Rovers owner Mark Palios. 'Growth and retention is part of what we do here. Although we know that what happens on the pitch will always, to some extent, dictate whether people are willing to come and see you, it's not all that matters. Since I have come to the club we have worked hard to engage more with the fans, to promote the club within the local community and also begun to offer a better matchday experience.'

After years of drift and dwindling attendances, the work that Palios has undertaken since arrival at Prenton Park *has* reversed the trend. At one point, Tranmere was getting more through the gate to watch National League football than it had been to watch the club in the Football League a few seasons earlier, challenging the often-held assumption that supporter numbers tend to decline following relegation to the non-league world.

'The days of simply offering football and a few pints and hoping that people will come and watch you in good numbers are probably gone,' he thinks. 'Nowadays you have to have first-class facilities at the stadium, you have to work within the community to promote the club, especially amongst young people, and you have to make sure your brand is a positive one, one that people want to be associated with.'

Despite the improvement in numbers going to the game, Prenton Park remains at least half-empty on any given match day. Part of this is down to the fact that many clubs at this level are swimming against the tide, fighting against wider societal changes that they, and the sport's governing bodies, can do little about.

'Football is changing, especially amongst the young. The old-school, dad-and-lad approach regarding your induction into the game just doesn't exist in the way that it used to. And nor do gangs of schoolmates going to the match together. Football is being consumed differently by the young in the digital age and that's something that is making life hard for a lot of Football League clubs,' says Kieran Maguire.

Faced with a game that, even in the lower regions of the Football League, remains pretty expensive and with the digital revolution providing alternative ways to consume football, the attraction of spending Saturday afternoon shivering on the terraces is losing its appeal for many young people.

As *COPA90* recently found following research into how 16-to-24-year-olds interact with football, increasing numbers now follow games online at home for free (through 'illegal streaming'). And with no cost barriers to entry, they are choosing to follow clubs from the Premier League. These are the clubs who have the stars they recognise from social media and video games like *FIFA*. These are the clubs who are more adept at developing their social media side, a way of interacting with football that this age group values. And these are also the kind of clubs who younger people can chat about with friends during games, using social media and WhatsApp, an important part of how football is consumed by this age group. Set against all of this, it is easy to see why a drizzly Saturday afternoon fixture between Doncaster Rovers and Rochdale might not be the draw that it once was.

Not that clubs in Leagues One and Two are giving up without a fight. There *is* innovation out there, clubs who are thinking outside the box to try and build fanbases, not just amongst the young, but within the wider community. Clubs trying their best to fill their stadiums. And one of the most eye-catching of these is League Two's Forest Green Rovers.

Carbon neutrality and veganism are not things that you usually associate with the lower reaches of the Football League. There is a kind of small 'c' conservatism that haunts this part of the game, as it does much of the pyramid beneath it; a world of Bovril and crumbling terraces, one that for many seems frozen in time. Although the truth is more complex, as the previous chapters have shown, what the Gloucestershire club has done in recent years is still pretty revolutionary, a club that is run like no other in the country.

The catalyst for this revolution was the arrival at the club of green energy industrialist Dale Vince as owner back in 2010.

'I was approached by the club because they said they needed a little bit of help to get through the summer,' he says. 'I was happy to assist. I thought it would be a nice thing to do. My company Ecotricity was based nearby and we are always looking at ways to help the local community. But within a couple of months, after I'd got a bit more involved, it was clear that they needed much more than just a little bit of help.'

With Forest Green in danger of folding, Vince was asked if he could come on board as chairman, bringing both his business knowledge and investment to the club.

'It was a big commitment, and at first I was a bit wary as I wasn't sure that I had the time. But I then faced the choice, if I walked away they would probably go out of business. I recognised how important the club was to the community, so in the end I felt that I really had to do what I could to help.'

Although the move into football represented a new area for Vince, it was not the first time he had leapt into the unknown. Just two decades earlier, he had been living an off-grid life in the countryside when something caught his eye during a journey through Cornwall.

'It was England's first modern, proper wind farm,' Vince says. 'I was so impressed by these big machines. I'd been using little windmills to power my trailer and batteries from the scrap yard and stuff. This was a different level.'

The sight inspired him to build his own windmill farm in 1996, venturing out into the uncertain world of renewables.

'When I got started, green energy powered about two per cent of Britain. Last year, it was 30 per cent. And as it has grown, so have we. We have expanded to become a company of around 700 people supplying about 200,000 customers.'

Vince has always been fairly evangelical about his passion for sustainability and he saw his relationship with Forest Green as a great way to speak to a new audience.

'This will always be a football club, first and foremost. But from the beginning I felt that we should make sustainability a big part of what we do here. Aside from the fact that that is how I would choose to run a business, it's also true that football can touch so many people's lives and can have a huge influence. It made sense to me that by introducing ideas and practices centred around greater sustainability to the club, we can get the message out to so many more people.'

Ten years on, the club now plays on an organic pitch that is free from pesticides and which is irrigated with rainwater. The New Lawn stadium is powered with green energy, most of which is produced by its own solar panels, and the stadium's kitchens recycle cooking oil into biofuel. Even the kits are green, with those for the 2019/20 season made from 50 per cent bamboo mix, which significantly reduces the use of plastic. In fact, so complete has the green revolution been that in 2017 Forest Green was recognised by the UN as the world's first carbon-neutral club.

But perhaps the most headline-grabbing of the changes that have taken place since Vince's arrival has been the introduction of veganism at the club. The days of getting a pork pie and a cup of Bovril at the game are long gone at Forest Green.

'I'm a vegan, and have quite strong views on the environment, animal welfare and human health,' he explains. 'So, just days after I became chairman I took red meat off the menu. A while later I stopped the club serving white meat, then fish, followed by milk and cheese, and by the start of the 2014/15 season the whole club was fully vegan and has been ever since.'

The change in menu even applies to the players. 'Although they don't have to be vegans,' Vince explains, 'they do have to eat plant-based meals at matches and training. No animal products are on sale at the stadium.

For most of them, the change has been quite profound, making them completely rethink their diet, moving towards one that is more plant-based.'

Initially, a few fans were a bit disgruntled at the change, a lingering love of mashed pig and reconstituted meat engendering a degree of hostility towards the new menu. But it wasn't to last. The changes brought in have ultimately proven to be popular, largely because the traditional fare of the match-going fan (pies, burgers, pints) has remained intact.

'People are still getting the food they always got except we have changed, and improved, the ingredients. Our Q-pie is so good, in fact, that it's won awards,' says Vince.

According to him, in the tough world of Leagues One and Two, where the fight to build a fanbase is a constant struggle, the club's message of sustainability is setting it apart from the crowd:

'The work we do has helped us reach a wide audience. There are people interested in environmental issues who have been drawn to FGR because of our work. And then there are football fans who have never seen a club take a stance like this before, and as a result have got into us. It's a new combination that's getting traction everywhere. Ahead of our appearance in the National League play-off final at Wembley in 2017, we had messages of support from over 20 countries, and our Wembley story reached 300 million people globally on TV, radio, print and online. We're different and, increasingly, people like that about a football club.'

Using progressive issues, such as sustainability, to tap into a wider audience is particularly effective amongst the 16 to 24 demographic. Research by *COPA90* found that clubs taking an ethical stance, such as Forest Green and Lewes (the latter with its commitment to gender equality), are registering on fans' radars by embracing progressive values that they hold dear. In an increasingly fragmented football landscape, where previous determinants of fan loyalty, such as geography and family links, are not as strong as they used to be, striking out into uncharted territory might represent one way to focus people's attention on to the club.

In the absence of a unique selling point, that special something to set you apart from the herd, another option for clubs is to diversify, to become something more than just a football club.

'The business model of lower league clubs has to change,' says Mark Palios. 'If gates are your sole limit in terms of the potential of a club then you will struggle.'

A hard-grafting midfielder who played more than 400 games for Tranmere and Crewe Alexandra, Palios once had the honour of being the only part-time player in the Football League (Tranmere allowed him to pursue a career as an accountant whilst playing for them). And it was through a sense of gratitude for what the club had given him that he was lured back to Prenton Park when the opportunity to buy the club arose.

'The club gave me so much,' he explains. 'I didn't have a silver spoon upbringing so playing for Tranmere as a kid helped me move on. It gave me a bit of kudos and confidence. It made my life easier and I suppose it ignited me in a lot of ways. The success I have enjoyed in business since leaving football owes a lot to that club, so the chance to come back here and help them out seemed a great way for me to put something back.'

Since he took control of the club in the summer of 2014, Palios has worked hard to broaden Tranmere's income generating potential.

'When I arrived, the total turnover from non-matchday income had been £150,000 a year. Having invested in the club, to improve its facilities, that income has now risen to more than half a million a year. But we want to do more.'

The aim for Palios is to avoid the trap of developing a 'dependency culture': 'Too many clubs rely on central funding. And the danger there is that you create undue pressure. When a club is reliant on TV money, it makes relegation a potentially devastating event. And it also means that you don't put enough effort into the wider business. It can create a sense of inertia. At the moment, we use the income generated from our average gate of nearly 7,000 to fund the playing budget, which stands at around £2.5m. We then try to use corporate methods to cover the maintenance and development of Prenton Park and non-football staff costs.'

Locally, the club has become a leading education provider, using both the Tranmere Rovers Sports College (established in 2015 to offer BTEC and Higher National Diploma qualifications to school leavers on the Wirral) and Tranmere Rovers in the Community (which is a partner of the Wirral Lifelong Learning Service) to do this. Last year, for example, over 160 young people completed their BTECs in Coaching and Sports Nutrition – with 98 per cent of those students continuing on to complete their diploma at the College.

It has also begun to invest in and use its facilities better. A £120,000 investment in a futsal court outside the ground now produces an income in the evenings and at weekends.

'And we have sought to look beyond the local area in the search for growth too,' says Palios. 'For example, the club's International Soccer Academy [ISA] offers aspiring players the chance to develop their skills through the guidance and training provided by the club's experienced coaching staff. It is the only academy in the UK that is approved to deliver the FA International Coaching Award to aspiring coaches across the globe.'

Through the ISA, the club has also developed a memorandum of understanding with the Inner Mongolian Government to develop coaching standards in the region's capital, Hohhot.

'With much of what we are trying to do, the idea is to create revenue streams that are "football agnostic". And, by that, I mean income that is not affected by what happens on the pitch. Football, as a business, is riven with uncertainty. You cannot know how a season will go. And if everything you do is tied to what happens on the pitch in that season, then you are taking a huge risk. If you have any desire at all of trying to be financially sustainable then diversifying, creating less reliance on central funding [or a benefactor] and developing a "football agnostic" side to the business is paramount. We've made a great start in this area, but we can always do more.'

Sustainability is the holy grail that seems to course though the game, the desire to run a self-funding, debt-free club. Although many in the Football League struggle, there are a few exceptions, a handful of clubs who have managed to run their affairs in a prudent manner while remaining competitive.

One of best examples of this, a club who for some represent everything that is right in the game, is Exeter City. In the past few decades the Devon club has experienced its fair share of ups and downs; a period when it seemed as though it might go bust, relegation to the old Conference, promotion back to the Football League, Uri Gellar as a director, promotion to League One, relegation to League Two, the list goes on and on.

It was during a financial crisis in 2003, a time when it looked as though the club might go under, that the current owners, the Exeter City Supporters' Trust (ECST), took control, setting the club on a path that has seen it achieve that rarest of things in the Football League – sustainability.

Back then, Exeter had been taken to the brink of financial oblivion by its owners, John Russell and Mike Lewis, two men with dubious backgrounds and who it turned out did not possess the necessary funds to run the club. In fact, so shady were they that both men would later go on to be convicted for fraudulent trading during their time with Exeter.

The pair had left the club riddled with debt. With no potential buyers on the horizon, the ECST, which had been founded a few years earlier, was approached by the club with the idea that it could take on the day-to-day running. It was a move that revealed how bad things had got. No one involved with the Trust had any experience of running a football club and yet it seemed to be the only party available to step in and try and save the Grecians from ruin.

The Trust managed to negotiate a deal to buy a controlling stake (along with responsibility for the club's £4.2m worth of debt) for the price of £20,000.

'And from there, for the first few years, it was just a case of fire-fighting,' says Paul Farley, Trustee with the ECST. 'We were fortunate in being able to broker some favourable deals with players, managers and other clubs, clearing the football debts. These had to be tackled first under the football creditors rule, which dictates that "football creditors" are paid all that they are owed, at the expense of "unsecured creditors". After that, we then put the club into a CVA and painstakingly began to work with our creditors to clear the remaining debt. It was a tough process but we got there in the end.'

Under the ownership of the ECST, the Grecians were promoted back into the Football League in 2007/08 and have remained there since (even enjoying a few seasons in League One). The club's story since 2003 is one of hope, an illustration of what fan power can achieve and a template of how a football club can be run differently.

'As a club we are hugely reliant on our fans willing to go that extra yard,' says club chairman Julian Tagg. 'We have around 3,500 members in the ECST, from which we draw a proportion of our annual budget and which also provides so much of our volunteer workforce. Without these volunteers, who do many important jobs around the stadium, the financial picture would be more challenging.'

Another potent source of income for the club in recent years has been its academy. All clubs, to varying degrees, invest in youth, recognising it as a future provider of players who can be sold or used in the main squad. But Exeter has been more successful than most. In recent seasons, the Grecians have earned millions from selling home-grown graduates like Matt Grimes, Ollie Watkins and Ethan Ampadu.

'I could see from the beginning of this project, when the fans first took control, that the future was very much dependent on us bringing youth through. We were never going to have the kind of budget to just spend and spend on players, especially as there was never going to be a benefactor. And so, we've spent a lot, for a club of our size, in this area, investing heavily in the infrastructure we have here.'

When it came to the investment in youth, the club was fortunate in having someone like Tagg as its chairman. He had cut his teeth at Exeter, running the club's first-ever U12 team, which then evolved into the current Academy. Tagg, along with Eammon Dolan, played a key role in its development, building a team of 12 boys into an academy of 200.

'With academies, patience is vital,' Tagg says. 'It took ten years to get ours into a space where it's functioning to support the club. And then maybe another five or six years to make it how we want it. For us, it is a vital part of our model. We would be in a very different place if it wasn't for our academy.'

Despite this, there are limitations to how beneficial it can be, in part due to the inconsistencies of finding talent but also because of the power structure that exists within English football. 'Like a cup run, which is often welcome but unexpected, you can't rely on earnings from player sales,' says Tagg. 'You will have periods when the players you are producing are better than at other times. So, you can't plan on the assumption that every year we will produce an "Ethan Ampadu".'

And then there is the problem of the EPPP. While standards have unquestionably improved across the four categories of academy running in the Premier League and the EFL, the power structure within the EPPP, specifically between smaller clubs in the lower leagues and those much higher up, has come in for some criticism.

Under the previous system, when a player under the age of 24 moved between clubs and those clubs could not reach an agreement, the Professional Football Compensation scheme (better known as the Tribunal scheme) would set the fee, based upon the player's potential. Today, under the EPPP compensation scheme, if mutual agreement cannot be reached then the Professional Football Compensation Committee arrives at a fee based upon the cost to the selling club of developing that young player and nothing else. Potential no longer enters into the equation. Commonly, the PFCC figures are strikingly low, as Exeter found out to its cost when Chelsea bought the highly rated youngster Ethan Ampadu for a miserly £2.5m.

'And that can be very frustrating,' says Tagg. 'Under the EPPP, football clubs at the top, those with much bigger resources at their disposal, are able to take young players from successful academies like ours at a fraction of the cost of which they are valued. We don't feel as though we are being adequately rewarded for the hard work that we are putting in.'

Although the club invests heavily in the youth set-up, the way Exeter generates income differs little from many other League One and League Two clubs, reliant on a mixture of sponsorship, matchday income and commercial partnerships (with central funding supporting this). But the main difference between Exeter and the overwhelming majority of similar-sized clubs at this level is its aversion to debt.

According to Tagg, Exeter's fan-owned origin story has, to a large extent, shaped this approach: 'I think when you come close to losing your club, which we very nearly did, it makes you slightly risk averse. The ECST, as the owners, never want the club to end up in that position again. And as chairman, I am ultimately answerable to their wishes in a way that other owners and chairman might not be. At our club, the wishes of the fans, at least expressed via the medium of the ECST, can dictate how the club operates. So, not only has there been a desire to minimise risk, there has also been a medium to make sure that desire becomes a reality.'

Both Exeter and supporter-owned AFC Wimbledon in the division above are run along these lines, models of sustainability at odds with their surrounding environment.

'The crisis at Wimbledon was started because of the club's financial difficulty,' explains Ivor Heller, commercial director at AFC Wimbledon. 'The club was making huge losses and needed to redevelop Plough Lane or build a new stadium to satisfy the conditions of the Taylor Report [but lacked the finance to do either]. The buyout and the move to Milton Keynes, where a stadium already existed, was presented as the solution to the problem, one that the owners, in defiance of the fans wishes, opted to greedily accept.'

In both cases the fan groups who subsequently took control, by either taking over the existing club in Exeter's case or starting a new club of their own in AFC Wimbledon's, had learned the hard way how damaging debt could be to a club and how powerless supporters were under traditional models of ownership.

'We've gone from open trials on Wimbledon Common to county football, to the Conference and then to the

Football League, eventually ending up in the same division as MK Dons, the club who took up residence in Milton Keynes. Through it all, the club has been very careful. We've progressed steadily and conservatively, resistant to both debt and outside investment. Other clubs have done what we have done in a much quicker time span but done it by spending heavily and having a benefactor on hand to cover losses. Our progression might have been slower, but it was sustainable. And it's got us to a point where we have been able to compete while staying true to those principles of sustainability,' says Heller.

Despite the club's success, Heller admits that remaining competitive *is* a challenge. 'When you run a club the way we do, not going into debt and not allowing a benefactor to come in and call the shots, you are potentially restricting what you can do on the pitch. You can try all kinds of ways to increase the budget you have, and we do that through sponsorship and through our commercial partnerships. And you can hope that through the right scouting, the right youth policy and the right appointment, you get lucky, which is what I think happened when we got promoted into League One. But in the end, the reality is that you are competing every season against clubs with significantly larger playing budgets, a lot of which is underwritten by owners covering losses or by reckless borrowing.'

The above would seem to run counter-intuitive to the wishes of most football fans. If football is about anything, it is about upward progression, the desire for teams to finish as high as they can. But sustainability can militate against this. It might be something that the Football League values publicly, that clubs run themselves in a prudent and sensible manner, but the system that it and the Premier League has created, a world of escalating wages, spiralling transfer costs and tantalising riches as you edge up the pyramid, produces the opposite. It produces clubs and owners who gamble recklessly and makes debt endemic within the system.

And this means that those who choose to pursue sustainability, whether it be those who have achieved it like Exeter and Wimbledon or those who aspire to it, like Accrington Stanley under Andy Holt and Tranmere Rovers under Mark Palios, can be at a disadvantage, punished for doing the right thing.

'Clubs like ours have arguably had an advantage over others in this area,' thinks Ivor Heller. 'Because of our history our fans have tended to think slightly differently. So far, progression at all costs has been off the table because they know how damaging those costs can be. They have experienced the dark side of football. So, they have valued the model we have here and what it represents, appreciating that bringing in an external investor or taking on debt could weaken it. That doesn't mean they aren't ambitious, they're still football fans after all. It just means that, for them, what happens on the pitch hasn't been the be-all-and-end-all to what this club is about.'

And perhaps that's the problem with how things are in Leagues One and Two at the moment. It's an environment that is crying out for more clubs like Exeter and AFC Wimbledon, a much-needed antidote to the frontier-like, Wild West aesthetic that runs through the game at this level. But to have more clubs like that would mean a sea change in what it means to be a fan, an acceptance that, season by season, you run the risk of falling behind, that the possibility of one day playing in the glitz and glamour of the top two divisions is a glass ceiling you are unable to break through.

But even amongst those, like AFC Wimbledon, who have pursued a different way of running a football club, the realities of competing within the Football League constantly present challenges to their approach to the game.

Towards the end of 2019, members of the Dons Trust, the fan group that owns AFC Wimbledon, were informed that the new £31.5m, 9,000-seater stadium the club is building on the site of the former Wimbledon Greyhound Track, just 200 yards from the original Plough Lane stadium, had encountered a funding shortfall.

In a letter to members, the chairman, Mark Davis, said that borrowing the necessary money had proven difficult and so discussions had been held with a group of investors prepared to put in £7.5m. In return, they would want shares.

Although the Dons Trust would retain a veto over 'existential issues' such as selling the stadium, relocating the club or changing the club's name, colours or badge, the move, should it be voted for, would bring an end to the era of total fan ownership at the club.

The proposal prompted a mixed response from supporters, ranging from the cautiously receptive to outright hostility. It was a reaction that brought to mind a point that Ivor Heller made when I interviewed him just prior to the announcement of the proposed investment deal:

'We've never assumed that how our fans, and those who invest in the Dons Trust, view the club is fixed. There will probably always be those who want to remain true to the full fan ownership model. This would likely include people who have been with us from the early days and can remember the horror of the Milton Keynes move. But, for others, specifically younger supporters, those who have only really known us as a Conference or a Football League club, that emotional connection to fan ownership might not be as strong. For them, the sacrifice of total control in return for the chance to become more competitive might be more palatable.'

Whatever happens to AFC Wimbledon, at least it, and Exeter City, have illustrated that a modern club in the Football League can be accountable, responsive to the fans and sustainable. Such an approach might come with risk, the possibility of stagnation, but for the moment, at least, sustainability and membership of the Football League are not mutually exclusive.

And yet, when it comes to upward progression, it's a difficult path to take. Not only do clubs that make prudent choices flirt with the possibility of falling off the pace, they also have to possess the institutional strength to resist the lure of riches above. And these are considerable. As the following chapter illustrates, so considerable that it's easy to see why throwing caution to the wind and recklessly gambling on a tilt towards the highest reaches of the game is so tempting.

Chapter Eight

The Big Time

IT is, by all measures, the most financially lucrative game in world football. There was a time, back in the analogue days of the past, when promotion from the second tier to the first was just about the pride of playing amongst the brightest and best, the chance to perform on the biggest national stage. But that was before the TV money began rolling in. In the age of Sky, promotion now means something else. Yes, the pride is still there. But it's also about the bottom line too. Win the Championship play-off and untold riches await.

Back at the end of the 2018/19 season, the two clubs fighting for the right to claim this cash bonanza were Aston Villa and Derby County. Finishing fifth and sixth respectively, both had ended the campaign some way off second-placed Sheffield United on points. And yet, due to the peculiarities of the play-off system, here they were, one match away from glory.

How much 'glory' would largely depend upon how the winner would ultimately fare in the Premier League. But even if the following season was a disaster, resulting in immediate relegation back to the Championship, it would still mean an extra £170m to swell the coffers, £95m from the single season in the top flight and £75m in parachute payments to ease the transitional pain of relegation.

In the end it was Villa who would make it, edging Derby 2-1, meaning that they would join Sheffield United and Norwich City in the following season's top flight, to fight it out amongst the game's elite.

For as long as professional football has been played, the elite of the game have always enjoyed a financial advantage over the rest. The idea that some halcyon golden age existed when football was a level playing field, where money did not dictate who rose to the top and who lingered down below, is largely a fiction. The gap between the best and the rest might have been tighter, but once money started rolling in during the 1880s, as football professionalised and clubs grew accordingly, it was always the case that those who could build the biggest stadiums, who could bring in the biggest crowds, whose shareholders had the deepest pockets, were always going to have an advantage over the rest.

But the difference today is all about that gap. Inequality between the elite might have always existed but never has the level of inequality been so great. And the biggest contributor to the chasm, the principal reason why the top flight has incrementally pulled away from the rest of the pyramid over the past 30 years, is the staggering levels of income that the Premier League is able to provide its members. And underwriting much of this are the TV deals that the League has been able to strike with broadcasters such as Sky and BT.

The 2016 to 2019 TV deal negotiated between the Premier League and its various broadcasters, which has recently reached its conclusion, came in at £8.8bn. At the time of writing, it is thought that the next deal, covering 2019 to 2022, will hit the £9bn mark. It's all a long way from the £304m five-year deal that Sky signed with the Premier League back in 1992.

Under the 2016 to 2019 deal, the Premier League divvied up the money pretty evenly. Half the domestic deal and all the overseas and *Match of the Day* money was divided equally between all 20 members. The remainder (50 per cent of the domestic deal) was split, 25 per cent based on the number of times the clubs were shown live on TV and 25 per cent based on the final league position.

What this meant in practice was that the champions, Manchester City, received just over £150m and Huddersfield, who finished bottom of the league, got around £96m.

'This set-up changes slightly in the future,' says Rob Wilson. 'The "Big Six" (Manchester United and City, Liverpool, Arsenal, Chelsea and Spurs) have long claimed that overseas viewers are only interested in seeing their clubs on TV and so have been agitating for a bigger slice of the overseas money, which they have finally managed to achieve under the new deal.'

Overseas revenue has undergone something of a boom recently. Under the 2019 to 2022 deal, it stands at £4.35bn, representing just under half of the League's broadcasting revenue, the largest percentage share it has ever taken.

'It's little wonder that the "Big Six" have been pushing to get more of this growing revenue stream,' says Rob

Wilson. 'Under the new deal, the bigger clubs are set to receive up to £80m more in overseas broadcasting revenue compared to the League's bottom sides.'

And that's in addition to what those same clubs are already earning through European money. Because, for them, membership of the Premier League has also provided regular opportunities to enjoy the financial benefits of playing in European competitions.

These sums can be considerable. When prize money and TV money were added together during the 2018/19 competition, eventual winners Liverpool brought home around £65m from the Champions League. While winning the whole thing will always bring in more cash, just participating in the group stages of the Champions League can see millions added on to a club's balance sheet each season. It's thought that the £90–118m gap that exists between the 'Big Six' and the remainder of the league is predominately down to the lack of European adventures among those outside the elite.

When it comes to income in the top flight, it is of course not just about people sat at home watching on their TVs and European money. Gaining a place at the top table enables clubs to broaden what they can earn from the game right across the business. During the 2018/19 campaign, for example, Premier League clubs earned a record £349m from shirt sponsorship deals. While skewed toward the bigger clubs, with the yearly deals struck by the likes of Manchester United (£64m Chevrolet), Manchester City (£45m Etihad) and Liverpool (£40m Standard Chartered) dwarfing those enjoyed by the rest, even those at the lower end often enjoy more pulling power by right of playing in the big time.

'You also have kit deals that are pulling in millions for clubs, with the likes of Manchester United, Manchester City and Chelsea earning yearly figures of £60m or more with brands such as Puma, Adidas and Nike. And there is commercial revenue to consider too. Premier League clubs have, with varying degrees of success, become much more commercially savvy over the past few decades. What once might have been a few commercial partnerships has grown to become something far more expansive,' says Rob Wilson.

The Manchester clubs are particularly adept at this. In 2017/18 United's total revenues were £590m, with £280m coming from commercial activity. City, which for a long time has been playing catch up to its neighbour on the commercial front, looks to be finally closing the gap, posting total revenues of £500m, with commercial activity accounting for £232m of that.

But, although the leading lights, they are not alone in leveraging their brands to squeeze greater and greater amounts of revenue from commercial link-ups. It's increasingly become more common to see clubs in the top tier possess an array of commercial partners, from the relatively mundane (official drinks partner) to the more unusual (global lubricant oil and fuel retail partners).

Set against this explosion in revenue, you would think that Premier League clubs would have given their fans an easy ride, limiting how much they had to shell out to come and watch the game. But instead, tickets in the top flight have seen price rises that would make the inflation of the Weimar Republic look modest by comparison.

Back in 1990, if you wanted to go and watch a club like Arsenal or Liverpool at home then the cheapest ticket available would set you back £5 and £4 respectively. Fast forward to today and those same two tickets would cost ten times as much. If football had followed the rate of inflation across the rest of the economy over that same period those tickets should have cost around £10 and £9 today.

Fans tend to feel it most painfully after clubs come up from the Championship. When Villa and Sheffield United came up together in 2019, their fans saw season tickets rise by 15 per cent and 11 per cent respectively.

'Clubs have to do this because life at the top doesn't come cheap. Despite the enormous amounts of money generated by Premier League clubs, in keeping with the rest of the game, the costs that they face have escalated too,' says Rob Wilson.

The problem is essentially one of inflation, or, in the Premier League's case, hyper-inflation. According to estimates, one British pound in 1992 – the year the Premier League was born – is worth around £2 in today's money. In the world of top-flight football's transfers and wages, that very same pound increases its value 40-fold. To put it in context, according to TotallyMoney, if the price of day-to-day items increased in line with Premier League inflation, a loaf of bread would cost £18 today.

What the league has faced is something that economists call demand-pull inflation. This is when an increase in the supply of money (demand) is not met with a consummate increase in the supply of goods. In English football, despite the wider international markets now available, the increase in available transfer funds has not been matched by a similar expansion in the number of world-class players and so prices have not just increased, they have rocketed.

When it comes to transfers, spending by Premier League clubs has risen exponentially over the past few decades, and particularly in recent years, surging from the millions into the billions.

For a mid-table club like Everton, £25–30m fees are now routine, when five years ago figures such as those would've represented club records, figures only shelled out on an exceptional player and not regularly splashed around on such luminaries as Michael Keane, Theo Walcott and Cenk Tosun.

Along the way, the world of transfers has somehow come to saturate the game. A generation ago, transfer rumours might have accounted for a small column in the back pages. Today, they swarm all over our sports coverage, filling pages in newspapers, smothering social media and gobbling up hours on Sky. The satellite broadcaster even has its own countdown days when the summer and winter transfer windows close, a whole day of broadcasting just to see if Peter Odemwingie has moved to QPR.

'The perspective of fans had changed alongside this,' says Neil Atkinson of *The Anfield Wrap,* Liverpool's fan-run podcast and website. 'Supporters now seem to demand some kind of outlay in a way that was probably absent, or certainly less keenly felt, in the past. You almost get the feeling that not spending in the summer transfer window in particular is met with a kind of suspicion. A summer of inactivity can lower the mood, make a supporter base approach the season with trepidation. It's not helped that when clubs do this, and it can often be the case that it makes perfectly valid football sense to limit your transfer spending, you get articles in the media questioning inactivity, suggesting it might be bad for a club. And this, in turn, fuels fan unrest.'

The stratospheric rise in transfer costs has been accompanied by an equally dramatic rise in wages. In 2017/18, all Premier League clubs' combined wage expenditure stood at a record £2.9bn.

Although agents often get the blame for rising wage costs, and do play some part in exacerbating the trend, there is little doubt that, as with transfers, it is TV money that's driving much of the increase.

'A lot of that money has just poured into transfers and wages. Some Premier League annual average salaries are now exceeding £3m a year. Although definitely skewed towards big clubs, the median level is still £2.5m. When you compare that to "just" £80,000 in League Two, you get a measure of how much of an impact the TV money has had. In many ways, it's a different sport to that played in much of the pyramid below,' says Kieran Maguire.

Although clubs are spending an enormous amount on wages, as a percentage of turnover, the level shelled out each season remains relatively modest. The average in the Premier League was 63 per cent in 2018. Although this can, in part, be attributed to the fact that there is so much money given to clubs under the recent broadcast deal, that even ever-escalating wages have yet to fully absorb what is available, according to Rob Wilson, the various financial controls that cover the league are also playing a role.

'Both the Premier League's Financial Fair Play (FFP) rules and those imposed by UEFA, all of which, to differing degrees, try to limit the losses that clubs are permitted to make, have helped bring a degree of control to wages in the top flight. Although the former has more wriggle room for accountants than the latter, having two structures in place that can sanction clubs for enduring excessive losses has made a difference. Clubs, specifically those aiming to get into European competitions, have had to think more about what they spend.'

UEFA has on occasions bared its teeth over FFP and illustrated it will take action over transgressors. The most recent example being the decision to serve a one-year ban from European football on AC Milan for breaching its rules.

The various financial controls evident in the top flight, combined with the exceptionally generous broadcast deals available, has meant that profitability, that rarest of things in so much of the national game, has started to become more commonplace in the Premier League. According to Deloitte, during the 2017/18 season, Premier League clubs generated a collective total pre-tax profit of £426m. The average for the league was £21m, with the number of clubs being in the black standing at 13.

But, despite the bumper TV deals and the proliferation of profitability, the top flight still remains a division characterised by significant debt. At the end of the 2017/18 season, Premier League clubs' net debt was £3bn, up almost £1bn on the summer 2017 position. Soft loans remain the largest component of clubs' net debt, accounting for nearly three-quarters of the total. Everton are a good recent example of how this works.

'In the last few years, the cost of acquiring and paying for the squad has been greater than turnover. That is not sustainable for more than a few seasons. The only reason that Everton have been able to do this is because of the club's new owner, Farhad Moshiri, who arrived back in

2014. Since arriving he has been willing to loan the club ever increasing amounts of money, thought to be around £250m at the last count,' says Paul Quinn of the *Everton Business Matters* podcast.

There are times when seeking loans from an owner, or any other outside source, are unavoidable. If Everton ever get around to building their new stadium at Bramley Moore Dock, the cost is likely to be around £500m, a sum way beyond a club that is consistently trading at a loss. The club will have to further increase its debt obligations to secure the move.

'Debt for investment in real assets that generate additional income is a very normal business practice. All major stadium developments in the UK in recent times have been funded by a combination of internal resources and debt,' says Quinn.

Liverpool recently borrowed £110m from its owners, FSG, to redevelop the Main Stand. And Spurs took out a massive £637m loan to build its new stadium. Despite the debt, in the longer term both developments will pay dividends. Liverpool are already earning an extra £12m per season from the new stand, and it's believed that Spurs are generating a staggering £800,000 from each game at their new home.

'But debt for the purchase of players and general running costs is not sustainable,' says Quinn. 'It's acceptable in the short term to assist with cash flow, but ultimately a business cannot continue to spend more than it earns. Everton's current business model is unsustainable and requires a reduction in costs and a large increase in income. The club has become dangerously reliant on an owner who could, at any point, decide to stop funding the club.'

Yet it's easy to see why clubs do this. 'What you have in the Premier League is essentially three mini leagues,' says Rob Wilson. 'At the top you have the big six, who will generally dominate the higher positions in the table. Then, after that, you have a middle band, clubs like Everton, Wolves and Leicester, clubs that will have a decent shot at a Europa League place. Although these clubs will rarely get into the Champions League, they are usually fairly certain to not be involved in a relegation scrap. After this you have a third mini league, which probably includes about ten clubs, all of whom could theoretically get relegated.'

At every level, the temptation to throw more and more money at the club is palpable. Whether it's the tantalising prospect of winning the league, the idea of crashing the elite or simply the need to stay up, the Premier League will always offer an owner the chance to burn through their savings. But there is no guarantee that it will work. Just look at Sunderland.

For Ellis Short, the US-based private equity billionaire, a meeting with Niall Quinn at the 2006 Ryder Cup near Dublin must rank as one of the worst chance encounters in his life. At the time, Quinn was part of the Drumaville Consortium, owners of Sunderland. Largely made up of Irish investors, Drumaville were looking to offload the club as the Irish economy began to tank. Short, with a £2bn fortune, seemed the ideal candidate.

In 2008 he gained a controlling interest in the club and for the next seven years effectively underwrote Sunderland's revolving door of players and managers. Up until the 2014/15 campaign, Short supported an investment minimum of £20m every season.

Although the 'Sky' deals that the Premier League enjoyed during this time were not as generous as the amounts seen today, while Sunderland competed in the top flight under Short's ownership, millions still came to the club. Despite this, he had to continually dip into his own pocket. When his time with Sunderland drew to a conclusion in 2018, after he agreed to sell to a group led by the former Eastleigh chairman Stewart Donald, Short had sunk around £200m into his Mackem adventure.

In fact, Short was only able to palm the Black Cats off to Donald on the proviso that he agreed to pay off all of Sunderland's remaining debt, which stood at around £110m (£70m of which was owed to himself).

By this point, Sunderland had joined an unwanted club, one populated by the likes of Bolton Wanderers, Portsmouth, Blackpool, Wigan Athletic and Blackburn Rovers, clubs who had reached the promised land of the Premier League only to slip downwards to the third tier in a spiral of failure and debt.

'Our last season in the Premier League under David Moyes had been terrible. But we thought that was as bad as it would get. Although Short had made it clear he wanted out and had turned the cash tap off, we all believed that the club still had enough about it to have a go at promotion. I don't think anybody thought we'd end the season in the relegation places, going down to League One. And yet, that's exactly what happened,' says Paul Dobson of the Sunderland fanzine *A Love Supreme*.

The club's dismal campaign in the Championship was captured in all its horror in *Sunderland 'Til I Die*, a series that broadcast on Netflix in 2018. The behind-the-scenes documentary showed a club in near perpetual crisis. With the 'cash tap' turned off and the hangover of relegation weighing heavy over the Stadium of Light, Sunderland seemed like a zombie club, shuffling its way to oblivion. The fact that we the viewer already knew the club's eventual destination merely added to the sense of tragedy that permeated the series. We knew that every bombastic boast, every claim of a 'corner turned', every ray of hope would ultimately count for nothing. Relegation and League One was waiting. There was nothing they could do or say to stop that destination being reached.

Within football there is a pervading sense running through the game that all that matters for success is money. And there is truth in that. Throughout the pyramid, the ability to achieve upward momentum is very often made much easier with a few quid.

'But it's not all that matters,' says Dobson. 'You need to have the right people in place. You need to build a team and a club that works. You need to have patience and you need to be organised. If you want a template for the way in which having money is not enough for success, then looking at what happened at Sunderland would be really instructive. We are a great example of how not to run a football club.'

It's hard to pinpoint one factor that caused Sunderland's unravelling. Certainly, Short turned out to have something of an itchy trigger finger when it came to managers, rattling through seven during his tenure. 'And the problem with that is that you never got to build anything,' explains Dobson. 'As each new manager arrived, a raft of players came with them. But the managers never hung around for long, so the club ended up clogging up the squad with signings bought by a predecessor, often on lengthy and lucrative contracts, making them impossible for the next incumbent to shift on.'

The club's transfer policy was chaotic, perhaps best exemplified by the case of Ricky Álvarez. The Argentine midfielder arrived at the Stadium of Light on an initial loan deal from Inter Milan in August 2014 but made only a handful of appearances as a knee injury limited his involvement.

Sunderland wanted the player to undergo surgery but Inter held back. In response, partly motivated by the feeling that even a full fit Álvarez might lack what it took to compete in the Premier League, Sunderland then attempted to pull out of a mandatory agreement to make Álvarez's transfer permanent after they had secured Premier League status that season.

The battle that followed, which involved FIFA and the court of arbitration for sport hearings, resulted in defeat for Sunderland, who were ultimately hit with a €10.5m bill for a player who was no longer on their books. Álvarez joined the Italian club Sampdoria in January 2016.

'Álvarez might have been the worst example of a chaotic transfer policy but he was not the only mistake the club made. We had the ill-fated tenure of director of football Roberto de Fanti, which saddled the club with a host of expensive failures. We had players brought in for one style of play who were then unsuitable after a managerial change. And we had players, like Jack Rodwell, who were just there for a payday, waiting out their contracts, happy to just sit on the bench. The transfer policy was just a mess.'

In terms of lumbering Sunderland with inadequate players on vastly inflated wages, much of the overall blame is pinned on the club's former chief executive, Margaret Byrne. Under her watch, Sunderland's wage bill ballooned to become one of the ten highest in the Premier League, yet Sunderland achieved just one top-ten finish during a decade in the top flight.

A prime example of Byrne's inability to get value for money is former England international Rodwell. She was the person who negotiated a five-year contract, paying Manchester City £10m to sign him, without a relegation clause that would reduce his wages. Rodwell, an injury-plagued player, only managed 76 (mostly lacklustre) appearances for the club, which, according to *The Chronicle*, ended up costing Sunderland around £299,000 per outing.

'For me, Byrne's role as chief executive is a fine example of the half-arsed manner in which Ellis Short conducted his football business – in stark contrast to how he worked as a venture capitalist. The role of chief executive should be reserved for footballing experts and not somebody who got the job simply because they happened to be working at the club, in this instance as legal director,' says Dobson.

As much as what happened at Sunderland can be attributed to incompetence, an equally strong factor in the club's protracted death spiral was fear. Fear, in short, of relegation. The 'drop' haunted the club during much of its time in the top flight, contributing to Short's itchy trigger finger when it came to managers.

'We always seemed to be fighting relegation. And that meant the club never had any breathing space. Going down to the second tier was so financially catastrophic, that, inevitably, as soon as it looked like we might be dropping, the manager was shown the door,' says Dobson.

Relegation has never been something that any club would welcome. Football is about upward momentum, so the 'drop', with its associated humiliation and a coming season spent battling lesser lights, goes against everything that playing for, managing, owning or supporting a club is about.

But, in the pre-Premier League era, going down into the second tier did not carry with it the same financial penalty that it does today. And it's this that has turned relegation into something that clubs and fans truly dread.

Down in the Championship, the financial rewards are nowhere near those of the Premier League.

'Along with the drop in TV money, relegation is obviously also often accompanied by a reduction in other aspects of a club's revenue-generating potential. So, you'll likely see attendances drop a bit, commercial revenue contract and retail sales go down,' says Rob Wilson.

To ease the transition and help clubs adapt, the Premier League provides parachute payments to those sides that are relegated. Currently, in the first year, the payment is 55 per cent of the amount that each Premier League club receives as part of its equal share of broadcast revenue. Based on the most recent figures, that percentage is roughly worth £40m. The percentage is reduced to 45 per cent in the second year (roughly £35m) and, if the club was in the Premier League for more than one season before relegation, 20 per cent in the third year (roughly £15m).

'Although parachute payments really help, on the business side relegation is a shock to the system. It's hard to anticipate just what a challenge it can be when you go down,' says Jonathan Jackson, chief executive of Wigan Athletic, who were relegated from the Premier League in 2013.

'I think that, as a smaller club,' he continues, 'if you don't plan for the possibility of relegation then you are taking a huge risk. When we were in the Premier League, we were always skirting with danger and the possibility of dropping loomed large. And so we made sure that relegation clauses were written into every contract [and wouldn't consider players who weren't open to this] and were very careful with spending.'

According to Jackson, holding on to the above principles is not always easy, specifically during the winter transfer window. 'If by January it looks like you're in for a relegation dogfight, the temptation is there to go and spend, to buy your way out of trouble. And that can work but it is a huge risk. If it doesn't come off then potentially you've wasted a huge amount of money and that could become a massive problem when you start life in the Championship because relegation always means a reduction in income. As hard as it is, you have to try and stick to your guns and just hope that enough quality exists in the squad to see you through.'

QPR, who went down with Wigan that season, provided a cautionary example of what happens when a club does gamble on staying up. During the campaign, the club splurged tens of millions on new players, including a £20m roll of the dice during the January window. It was ultimately to no avail, as Harry Redknapp's men finished rock bottom of the league.

The cost of the club's desperate attempt to avoid relegation was laid bare when it confirmed losses of £65m the following year. As well as losses almost trebling, the club's net debt virtually doubled from £91m to £177m. QPR had gambled everything on staying up. When that didn't happen it was faced with the reality of Premier

League levels of expenditure but without Premier League levels of income (even with the assistance of parachute payments).

'But even when you *do* prepare for relegation like we did, it's still a huge challenge,' admits Jackson. 'Despite the relegation clauses, the players who left on free transfers and the players who were sold, we still had one of the biggest wage bills in the Championship and I'd say that it took about four years to get it down to a level that we were comfortable with. And don't forget, it's not just about a profit and loss account and the balance sheet. While you're trying to make this huge financial adjustment, the loss of TV money, the decline in attendances, the decline in commercial revenue, reduction in media exposure, you're also having to rebuild a team too. Players and sometimes coaches inevitably leave, partly because you can't afford them anymore but also because they want top-flight football. It all amounts to a hugely difficult and turbulent process.'

In fact, according to Jackson, despite the financial assistance provided by the Premier League, he thinks the drop from the top flight to the second tier is arguably the hardest in the game.

'We have been in the unenviable position of recently experiencing what it's like to not just drop from the Premier League but also going down from the Championship to League One.'

In fact, Wigan have been relegated to League One twice in recent seasons. The FA Cup victory over Manchester City back in 2013 ended up being the high-water mark for the club, a point after which life has been tough.

'From a footballing perspective, dropping to the third tier is obviously hard on everyone involved,' Jackson admits.

'Fans who in recent years have been enjoying Premier League football initially did not want to experience life in the third tier, even if it meant us winning more games. But, financially, the impact of dropping from tier two to tier three is not as dramatic as being relegated from the Premier League. It's not good, obviously, but when it comes to the financial environment, things like transfer costs, wages and broadcasting revenues, it is not too dissimilar across the various levels of the EFL. Obviously, the Championship is at the higher end of the financial scale in the EFL but it's nothing like the Premier League and that gap continues to widen.'

The desire for a club like Wigan, and others that have found themselves excluded from the top table, is to get back into the Premier League as soon as possible. But as palpable as that desire is, it's not straightforward.

Recent research by Jonathan Liew, a writer at *The Telegraph*, found that of the 85 teams relegated from the top tier over the past 28 seasons, only 20 were promoted back the following campaign. That proportion remained unchanged even after the introduction of parachute payments in 2004.

If a less-than-one-in-four chance of getting back into the top flight immediately seems slim, then in following seasons the chances deteriorate. Former Premier League clubs spending a second year in the second tier have just a 14 per cent chance of promotion. By the time they begin a third campaign, they are actually slightly worse than the average team in the division, usually finishing the campaign in the bottom half of the table.

'It's an incredibly hard league to get out of,' says Nigel Howe of Reading. 'We play more games per season than those in the league above, the division is filled with high-quality teams, many of whom have recently played in the Premier League, and the calibre of managers and players that are attracted to the league is increasingly getting better and better.'

During the 2018/19 campaign, 31 second-tier players had recently represented their country in that summer's World Cup. And the division boasted an array of talent, old and young, who had either enjoyed decent careers in the top flight or who would go on to thrive there during the following campaign. For the former, this would include the likes of Joe Allen, Jay Rodriguez and Jack Butland, and for the latter players such as Jack Grealish, Daniel James and Tammy Abraham.

'And it's also a division that demands a lot financially from clubs,' Howe continues. 'I've been involved with Reading since the mid-1990s and I've watched as this league has become progressively more expensive to compete in. The figures now that surround things like transfers and players' wages wouldn't have been believable 20 years ago.'

One of the factors behind this are those parachute payments. In the Championship, during the 2017/18 season, parachute payments from the Premier League accounted for a third of total revenue.

'The clubs who are in receipt of these payments start with a financial advantage, which means they can spend more on players and wages,' says Brentford's co-director of football Phil Giles. 'The pervasive thinking amongst a lot of clubs is that if they are to compete with those in receipt of parachute payments then they have to spend big as well. So, you end up with an upward spiral on costs, in part caused by this huge injection of money.'

The riches on offer in the Premier League would always mean that owners are tempted to overspend. When Newcastle, Brighton and Huddersfield were promoted in 2016/17, during the following year the combined operating profits of the three stood at £130m, which represented a £237m turnaround on their collective operating loss of £107m the year before. Entry into the top flight does not just bring with it footballing glamour, it also papers over all manner of financial cracks.

'But the money from parachute payments is exacerbating the problem,' says Rob Wilson. 'It causes those with access to this money to overspend and encourages those without to indulge in risky spending in the hope of keeping up with their better-off neighbours. Collectively, it's creating a league that is beset with financial problems.'

2017/18 saw a fifth successive season of revenue growth in the Championship, with record revenues of £749m. But, alongside this came record wage costs of £795m. The wages/revenue ratio increased from 99 per cent to 106 per cent, highlighting the increasing level of financial risk that Championship clubs are willing to take in order to chase success.

Given record wage spending, it is no surprise that Championship clubs regularly record losses. According to Deloitte, in 2017/18 the collective pre-tax losses increased by 54 per cent to £320m, the second-highest level ever recorded.

Inevitably, as with other levels of the Football League, debt has become a fact of life in the Championship. For 2017/18, it came in at just under £1bn. Of the existing debt, 78 per cent came in the form of 'soft loans', illustrating that Championship clubs continue to be heavily funded by their owners.

'The amount of money that is available in the Premier League, combined with the amount that comes down with relegated clubs via parachute payments, is creating something that is essentially unsustainable,' says Nigel Howe. 'Clubs are rolling the dice, spending more than they can afford. You hear of clubs borrowing against future parachute payments, going into debt over a revenue stream that might never come to fruition. It's a ridiculous way to run a league and, as we have seen recently on a number of occasions, when it gets out of hand the very existence of the club is put at risk.'

For those who lack both parachute payments and the desire (or ability) to vastly overspend, life in the Championship is hard.

Paul Warne, manager of League One Rotherham, summed it up in 2019 when he told *Training Ground Guru (TGG)* that the Championship has become distorted and uncompetitive because of the 'obscene amounts of money' being spent.

Warne had led the Millers to promotion via the League One play-offs but found his side fighting the prospect of relegation all season, a fight they would ultimately lose.

Warne told *TGG*: 'We've virtually got the same League One side together that finished fourth last year. Anyone coming up from League One will find the divide is massive. If the smaller teams come up, the task is getting greater and greater and it's turning into a Premier League 2 and the rest in my opinion. The parachute payments are crucial, they make a massive difference … I think now the divide is getting bigger and bigger.'

Although overspending is common, not all have been lured into the same trap. Often touted as the model for how a football club should be run in the upper reaches of the pyramid, Burnley have spent the past decade illustrating that 'success' need not go hand-in-hand with debt. Speaking to ESPN FC in 2017, chairman Mike Garlick summed up the club's thinking:

'If we acted in an oligarch's way during one transfer window, the damage done could last for five years. It doesn't just damage you for one season. Bradford City is probably the best example: They had 14 to 21 days of summer madness [in 2000], and it took the club five to ten years to turn around from that. We simply don't want that to happen. We want to be as ambitious as we can, but we have to live within our means, and whatever we do has to be sustainable.'

After being relegated to the Championship in 2014/15, an event that can sometimes prove to be financially catastrophic for clubs, not only did the Clarets bounce back at the first time of trying, they also did so without indulging in some kind of reckless gamble. Yes, the club had parachute payments to both ease transition and provide a competitive edge, but in contrast to many of Burnley's peers, the club eased through the campaign financially, emerging debt free.

Once back in the top flight, the same prudent approach to the game has continued. The club's last published accounts, for 2017/18, showed a record profit of £45m and no outstanding bank or directors' loans.

The key to this success? Management continuity plays its part. In the trigger-happy world of the Premier League and the Championship, where managers are lucky if they are able to hang around for a few seasons, Burnley has stood by Sean Dyche, never wobbling in its commitment.

This was even the case following relegation, a time when most bosses tend to get the chop. Dyche repaid the club's faith in that instance by not only earning an immediate promotion but also going on to provide Burnley's highest finish in the Premier League era a few seasons later, when they finished seventh, meaning qualification for the Europa League.

With relative longevity, Dyche, alongside a receptive board, has also been able to change the way that the club approaches the game. At his very first board meeting in 2012, the new manager told the board they could not repeat the mistakes made after the club's 2009/10 Premier League campaign (a solitary season that had ended in relegation). Burnley had squandered most of the TV money received on players, failing to invest in the club's infrastructure.

That mistake has been put right. Two years ago, for example, the club's academy was Category Three, with the youth teams training on pitches prone to flooding and using facilities that were essentially just a handful of fairly tired Portakabins. The youth section was also separated from the senior side.

After significant redevelopment, the club will soon become the 25th in the country to be elevated to Category One status. Dyche has been the driving force behind this transformation, ensuring that the money earned from recent campaigns has not been squandered and invested instead in infrastructure and facilities. Now all the players, irrespective of age, work at the same state-of-the-art £10m Barnfield Training Centre.

Alongside this, the club has also operated a transfer policy that, by top-flight standards, remains remarkably modest. During Dyche's time in charge, Burnley have signed 57 players, at an average amount spend of £1.9m per player. With a clear identity on the pitch, one that runs through the club, Burnley have been able to buy accordingly, recruiting to 'try and get the best players possible for what we are', as Dyche puts it. It might be a more 'reductive' style of play compared to many in the top flight, but it remains consistent and brutally effective for a club of Burnley's means.

Burnley are not alone in swimming against the tide. Not all clubs in the top two tiers regard playing in the top flight as the only measure of success. And not every club is willing to bet the farm to make it to the promised land of the Premier League.

On recent entry into the top flight, Norwich City Sporting Director Stuart Webber insisted that the club will continue to stick to the values that got it promoted, an emphasis on youth and development, combined with a specific style of play.

When Webber was appointed as Norwich City's first sporting director in April 2017, he arrived at a club with a massive wage bill, which had also failed to bounce back to the promised land of the Premier League at its first attempt.

What followed was a ruthless restructuring, both on and off the pitch. The squad was completely revamped, and almost every head of department was replaced. Emphasis has been placed on developing youth, of committing the club to a playing philosophy and recruiting players who suit both this and the club's ethos. And underpinning it all, a revamped, state-of-the-art training ground that cost £6m, one that replaced the 49 Portakabins that had previously constituted the club's base.

On promotion to the Premier League, the club has largely stuck to its guns, tying down much of the existing squad to longer-term contracts and promoting from the academy, with former youth players, such as Max Aarons, Jamal Lewis and Ben Godfrey, getting their chance to play on the biggest domestic stage.

Whether this will enable them to remain competitive in the top flight, only time will tell. At the time of writing, after a spirited opening that saw the club claim the scalp of champions Manchester City, Norwich appeared to splutter and deflate, a seemingly inevitable fight against relegation looming ahead.

But should the club remain true to the values and ethos espoused by Webber, relegation need not be the devastating watershed moment that it can often be for some clubs. Relatively free of debt and possessed of first-class facilities, plus an approach to the game that looks beyond the short term, there seems little chance of Norwich becoming another Bolton, Portsmouth or Sunderland.

A similar tale, albeit with a slightly different twist, is on offer in west London. Eight years ago, Brentford was bought by lifelong supporter Matthew Benham.

Benham is the owner of Smartodds, which provides statistical research and sports modelling services, and is a minority shareholder in Matchbook, a sports betting exchange. Through his business ventures, Benham has learned how the power of numbers can be used to beat gut instinct. At Brentford, he has set about proving the same thing, using data analytics to transform the club, to give it a competitive edge against better-funded rivals.

'Since Matthew took control, the idea has been to do things differently to how most other clubs do things. If we did things the same way as everyone else, then with the budget we have and the size of the club, we're going to have a hard time competing in the Championship,' says Phil Giles.

One of the most obvious areas where this innovative approach to the game has been felt is in the area of recruitment. And possibly its most headline-grabbing move came in 2016 when Brentford made the controversial decision to close its academy.

As with all academies, most players didn't make the grade at the club – but for some time Brentford hadn't even been able to benefit from the best players the academy did produce. Brentford's last youth player to feature regularly for the first team had made his debut in 2005.

'We were becoming a feeder club for bigger sides, losing our most talented young players for next to nothing,' says Giles.

Not long before the academy was scrapped, Brentford lost two promising U16s to Premier League clubs: Ian Carlo to Manchester City and Josh Bohui to Manchester United. In both cases, these talented youngsters left for very little in terms of compensation because players can't sign professional contracts until their 17th birthday. Brentford had no way to protect their investment in players from the ages of 8 to 16.

'Even before the two departures, the club was doubting whether the academy represented good value. Despite the £500,000 we got in subsidy from the Premier League, to maintain it was costing us £1.5m each year. And so, alternatives were sought.'

The alternative is the current set-up. With the money saved from scrapping the academy, the club decided to create a B team focussed on players aged 17 to early 20s.

The new strategy was created with two targets in mind: to recruit 'the rejects', players released or unwanted by other English clubs, alongside 'underrated' overseas players, who would see Brentford as a path to English football, and ultimately the Premier League.

Today, it is a team made up of talented teenagers plucked from 'undervalued' countries, including Sweden, Denmark and Finland, plus young recruits from the likes of Manchester City, Chelsea and Norwich City, all moulded together with a handful of former Bees academy players.

'The idea was to use analytics and our understanding of what kind of player can be successful in England to find value. In England, for example, Premier League academies make mistakes, often because they're making decisions on who to keep and who to release at an age when relative age, for example, still plays a role. We use our data to try and capitalise on those mistakes,' says Giles.

Outside of England, part of the club's recruitment process involves using analytics to identify leagues where physical qualities are often overlooked in favour of tactical qualities.

'Physicality is important in England. There are players abroad who already have the physical attributes to do well here but are often not highly regarded in their own country because they lack tactical or technical attributes. We think the tactical side of things can be taught and we are confident we can provide an environment where that happens. So, our aim is to bring these players here, players who might go under the radar, and develop them in the B team, with an aim to get them into the first team or sell them on at a profit at a later date.'

Freed from the confines of the traditional youth system, Brentford's B team has been able to set its own agenda, playing the matches it wants, whether that's games against the U23 sides of London's Premier League giants or more exotic matches against European teams. In the past season this approach saw the side play the U23 sides of Arsenal, Chelsea and West Ham, alongside more far-flung fixtures, such as those against Grasshopper Zürich U23s, Albacete U19s and FC Cartagena.

'Our players are getting a much broader football education,' says Giles. 'We can play the games we want to play, exposing them to different styles of football, to different kinds of opposition, to an array of different challenges. It's a more realistic football environment, one that offers a greater test than the traditional U23 system. And that, plus the research we undertake, is probably the reason why we're finally seeing players coming through into the first team with more regularity than was the case under the old set-up.'

The Brentford B team is less than three years old and already 12 players have progressed to make first-team debuts.

'Not all of these will become first-team regulars. And of those who do, there remains the chance that they will be sold on. But compared to the situation in the past, when the club would invest in young players who never made it to the first team, you can see how much more beneficial to the club the B Team has become. And it's an example of how doing things differently, of how using the information that is out there to find value, can enable smaller clubs to compete against those with much bigger budgets,' says Giles.

But just how long those 'bigger budgets' will remain in such rude health is a question that seems to permanently hang over football in the higher reaches of the game.

Football at this level seems to always rest on the assumption that the good times will keep rolling. Since inception, in financial terms, the Premier League has been a huge success story, smothering all in its path and gradually coming to be the most watched league in the world (by some distance). Within English football, the received wisdom remains that in a fracturing media landscape, elite level live sport is one of the few examples of bankable content, an event that viewers will make an appointment to view. And, importantly, one for which punters are willing to constantly put their hands in their pockets.

But despite the undoubted success of the Premier League, as both a medium for enriching its members and a global viewing phenomenon, there are hints that perhaps the days of endless growth might be coming to an end.

In recent years, the Premier League has reported negative fluctuations in domestic viewing figures, with a few of these dips alarmingly large. While some of this can be attributed to seasonal factors (bigger clubs like Newcastle and Aston Villa being relegated from the top flight), such sizable dips are new, suggesting that this is more than a blip. After all, big clubs have dropped before without an accompanying decline.

Part of this reflects demographics that younger audiences are, for example, more likely to watch highlights on social media than they are a full, 90-minute match on Sky Sports. One reason Sky has recently decided to broadcast free highlights on YouTube shortly after matches is in acknowledgement of this trend, the realisation that younger audiences consume football content differently to those from older age groups.

'But cost is also playing a part too,' thinks Rob Wilson. 'One of the consequences of Sky losing its monopoly over the broadcasting of the Premier League has actually been to increase what it costs to watch live football on TV.'

During the 2019/20 season, Sky broadcast 112 games live, BT showed 52 and Amazon covered 20 games over just two game weeks. According to the *Daily Mail,* fans would have had to pay over £900 to watch the lot.

'Watching live football on your TV is not cheap,' says Wilson. 'To cover it all, you are asking people to hand over almost a grand per season. That's more than the cost of any average season ticket in the league. You're getting to watch more games, of course, but it's still very expensive. In tougher economic times, it's perhaps inevitable that there are some people who can no longer afford it, or other people who perhaps only buy one of the packages.'

And for those who don't want to pay yet still want to watch it, 'illegal streaming' is increasingly an option. A recent survey of 1,000 people for 5 Live found that 47 per cent of those asked had watched a match through an illegal provider at least once in the past, while 36 per cent claimed to stream matches at least once per month.

Worryingly for Sky, BT and the Premier League, the charge towards illegal streaming was led by the young. 65 per cent of those aged 18–34 confessed to streaming a match at least once per month, against 33 per cent of the 35–54 demographic. The figure dropped to just 13 per cent of those over the age of 55.

Decent broadband, the proliferation of sites that offer easy-to-access games (such as VipBox) and social media communities who share streaming sites have made it easier for supporters to access games. And this includes matches that take place during the FA blackout, that period between 2:45pm and 5:15pm on a Saturday afternoon when no live broadcast is permitted domestically. Through illegal streaming it's now entirely possible to watch a Premier League side's entire season, all from the comfort of your own home, and it not cost a penny (as long as you don't mind all manner of 'adult' pop-ups and the commentary delivered in Arabic or Yoruba).

Inevitably, in response, the Premier League has attempted to fight back. During the 2018/19 season, its specialist anti-piracy unit blocked and disrupted over 200,000 illegal streams.

And it has gone after providers too. Back in 2019, three men, who had traded as Dreambox, Dreambox TV Limited and Digital Switchover Limited, providing illegal access to Premier League football to more than 1,000 pubs, clubs, and homes throughout England and Wales, were jailed for a total of 17 years for conspiracy to defraud.

'The fact that the Premier League has ramped up its efforts to stem pirating illustrates that they do see it as a real threat to what they do. And, certainly, its growth, combined with the slight decline in the domestic broadcast deal, do suggest that perhaps the days of endless growth might be on the wane. But has the bubble burst? Probably not yet,' argues Rob Wilson.

The Premier League has, so far, been able to accommodate its problem areas, like piracy and fluctuating domestic demand, by its hugely impressive overseas growth. The 'product' the league is promoting has been gobbled up by overseas football fans. During the 2018/19 season, the Premier League revealed that it reached a cumulative global audience of 3.2 billion for all programming watched. In total, the Premier League was shown in 188 of the world's 193 countries recognised by the United Nations. The five countries without coverage in the 2018/19 campaign were Afghanistan, Moldova, Turkmenistan, North Korea and Cuba.

'The Premier League has been better able to push its product internationally than other leagues in Europe,' says Wilson. 'In part it's a reflection on how well the league markets itself. But equally, the clubs themselves, through their summer tours, through how they engage on social media, through their own marketing, have helped this trend. Physical engagement in particular is very important to geographically remote fans. Managers might moan about summer tours in China or the US, but they are hugely important in building a club's and the League's international brand.'

And so, for the foreseeable future at least, the top flight as we have come to recognise it, staggeringly wealthy, awash with millionaires and filled with the brightest and best from across world football, looks set to continue.

Before the Premier League was created, and even for the early years of its life, the divide that existed between the divisions of the old Football League were measurable but not vast. The top tier was always the place that hosted the biggest clubs, that drew the most attention, that made the most money. But a relative minnow, such as a Wimbledon or a Watford, eking out a life in the lower tiers could still dream of one day, with the right manager and a bit of luck, making it all the way to the top. The rungs of the ladder were easier to climb back then.

But that is clearly not the case anymore. When the Premier League was created back in the early 1990s, nobody could have foreseen the success/monster it would become. The changes that have occurred, much of it powered by broadcast money, have enabled the top tier to pull away from its foundations. It might technically be regarded as the top of the English pyramid but can it really be described in that way when it is barely tethered to the structure beneath?

And the links that do remain are hardly beneficial ones. The wealth at the top appears to poison much of what exists below, distorting and twisting what remains of the old Football League, changing what it means to run a club, infusing the game with an unhealthy amount of risk. Its reach is even being felt further down, its trickle-down riches infecting the previously immune upper regions of the non-league world.

Will anything change in the coming years? For all the talk of the Premier League bubble bursting, talk that has been around in the top flight longer than James Milner, it doesn't seem likely any time soon. The Premier League rolls on regardless, immune to the economic forces that appear to afflict other industries. An economic marvel.

But it doesn't shape every aspect of English football. Although it might distort the pyramid as we have known it, modern football amounts to more than that pyramid. In recent years new forms of the game have emerged in the digital world. Some interact with 'traditional' football, some don't at all. And where and how they fit in with the existing structure in the game is uncertain. It's the world of Football 2.0, a place inhabited by new and innovative football clubs, a place that, for many, represents the future of the game.

Chapter Nine
Football 2.0

I T'S football, but just not as you might know it. It's a world of YouTube teams, streamed content and digital sides. A world of 'tekkerz', 'worldies' and 'hashtags'. A world where a non-league minnow can pull in more fans than a Premier League giant, where a digital league can grab more viewers than the National League, where the lines between broadcaster and club have become blurred.

When pundits and journalists talk about the state of the national game, their focus tends to be fairly narrow. As earlier chapters highlighted, just because 'traditional' forms of the sport, such as junior football and Sunday league, are facing challenges, and in some parts of the country declining it, does not mean that football, if seen from a wider perspective, is struggling.

If you widen that perspective a bit further, stand well back and embrace the digital world then you encounter Football 2.0, for many not just a rapidly growing alternative to the 'traditional' game but also possibly its future. And at its heart is *FIFA*, the video game that went from indifference to dominance.

FIFA has been around in various formats since 1993, when it was first released by the US games giant EA Sports. Initially, not much faith was placed in the new game. Neil Thewarapperuma, EA Sports' marketing manager back in 2013, candidly summed up the company's attitude to the video game when it was being developed, claiming that, 'EA didn't give a shit about *FIFA*'.

For the US-based EA, football (or 'soccer' for them) was seen as a marginal sport for children, likely those not good enough to play American football. Their roster of games at that point embraced the mainstays of US sporting life, basketball, ice-hockey and American football, and this was where the budget, in both development and marketing, was concentrated.

Fast forward a quarter of a century and this little-regarded game, based on a sport that Americans have never really taken to their hearts, has become a global behemoth that now accounts for over a third of EA's annual income.

On any given Sunday, the day on which it is played most often, more than 200 million matches of *FIFA* take place across the world. *FIFA 19* (the 'International Soccer' was quickly dropped) sold 20 million copies worldwide last year. And overall, *FIFA* is the world's highest-ever-selling sports game, with around 260 million copies sold since it was first released back in the early 1990s.

Why it's proven to be so popular owes a lot to the game's authenticity. Not that this would've been overly apparent to anyone playing *FIFA*'s first incarnation. In those days, the game did not look much like real football. Aside from the slightly static gameplay, the virtual players were also not based on real footballers. David Platt, the England midfielder and Serie A star, featured on the cover of the first edition of *FIFA*, but that's where he stayed. Within the game, you could choose from 48 international sides, each of which consisted of 20 players. But every player looked identical, bar respective team kits and varying shades of skin tone.

Over the following years, EA has worked hard to change this, pushing realism with every new edition. Key to this has been licensing, both of club names and of player images. The most recent version of the game boasts 700+ teams from 30 leagues across the world, with nearly every player faithfully replicated digitally (that's over 17,000 players).

For the young and excitable, those in awe of today's elite, that means Champions League fixtures with the likes of Real Madrid, Bayern Munich and Barcelona. To the hipsters and the more mature audience, the latter of which I'd include myself in the ranks of the latter, it means unlikely ties between footballing minnows, like Carl Zeiss Jena, San Martin de Tucumán and Vejle Boldklub.

This sense of realism also extends to how the digital players play. EA works with a 9,000-member network of data reviewers, led by the German statistician Michael Müller-Möhring. They ensure that each player profile, which includes more than 30 statistics, embracing attributes such as speed, stamina and temperament, is as accurate as possible. So Bernardo Silva is as skilful as you'd imagine, Mo Salah as potent in front of goal and Granit Xhaka as insensibly reckless as he is in real life.

Because of this, the gameplay has also grown and matured year-on-year. Matt Prior, *FIFA*'s current creative director, has said that, 'Until *FIFA* is indistinguishable from football in real life and plays exactly like football, we'll always have more to do.' This commitment to realism has seen defenders develop terrible first touches (where once they would control the ball like Pirlo), certain centre-forwards make half-hearted tackles and wingers fail to track back, just like they do in real life.

Beyond the play itself, the developers have also kept a keen eye on realism for the wider match experience. Teams shake hands in front of true-to-life sponsor boards, inside perfectly recreated digital versions of real-world stadiums, from Anfield to the Weserstadion. Virtual fans, now highly individualised in appearance, sing true-to-life chants and hurl abuse at the officials – irrespective of whether the calls are right or wrong. Of course, this being the 'digital' world, the calls are always correct.

This sense of realism is the main reason why the game has seen off so many rivals over the years. Playing *FIFA* is as close as it gets to playing football without actually getting off your arse. Perhaps this is best felt in its grasping of the uncertainty of the game. The ball will ricochet, players will collide, passes will go astray, mistakes will be made, players will tire, form will dip. Everything that makes real football so engaging, the fact that the ball is round and anything can happen, is included in the multitude of algorithms spinning in action as the match unfolds.

'It can move you in the same way as real football too,' says long-time devotee Bevan King. 'I've been playing it for about 18 years and it still surprises me what an emotional game it is. When you win, it feels great, just like the feeling when the clubs I have played for have won games. And when you lose, it can frustrate the fuck out of you. There is even a thing called "*FIFA* Rage" that anyone who has played it will be familiar with. It's that moment of pure fury when a game doesn't go your way and some jammy sod online has nicked a win. I'm pretty sure that a fair few Xbox controllers across the country have bitten the dust because of a moment of *FIFA* Rage.'

A sense of one-upmanship courses through the game. You can talk to (and smugly goad) people online as you play, message them outlining your 'brilliance' once games have finished and, after every goal scored, players can access an array of celebrations, ranging from a sedate and simplistic Brazilian fist-pump to the more ostentatious and deeply irritating 'Giddy Up'.

'Getting bragging rights matters to people,' says King. 'There's a mate of mine I play regularly in a league over the course of each edition of the game. I remember one year it came down to the last game, which I won with a penalty in the dying minutes. It's been about three years and he's still annoyed. I bring it up now and then for badness, because it's so funny to see just how much that penalty winds him up.'

So ubiquitous has *FIFA* become, so much a part of the footballing landscape, that inevitably it has also begun to bleed into 'traditional' football. Many players now indulge in the game and the Borussia Dortmund defender Mats Hummels has even been quoted as saying that he and other players use what they learn in *FIFA* to develop their performance on the pitch.

You'd imagine that you can't learn that much from a video game, and yet back in 2008 the Parma goalkeeper, Marco Amelia, was adamant that it was hours of playing *FIFA* that helped him save a penalty from Ronaldinho. He claimed after the match that 'it was just like playing against him on PlayStation. He had the same run-up. It was very strange.'

The headline ratings the players receive (measuring attributes such as pace, physicality and shooting) have also come to be prized by professionals. So much so that according to *The New York Times* some agents have even called up EA to beg for upgrades for their players' scores. When *FIFA 20* arrived last year, Everton's forward Richarlison took to Instagram to complain about his overall player rating of 79, which was considerably lower than those of his team-mates. And a few years ago Romelu Lukaku reportedly used a ratings snub as fuel to continue improving in real life (presumably his first touch wasn't included in the snub).

Despite *FIFA* replicating what is essentially a team sport, within the game's various modes much of the play is individual. Whether playing against the console, playing a mate in person, or playing a stranger online, in most instances the user controls the team and directs the play (along with a bit of help from the game's active intelligence system).

But one part of *FIFA* that does differ, a part that enables multiple people to enter the gameplay, is Pro Clubs – a mode that lets its users to create a virtual football club.

'Pro Clubs is the closest you can get in this virtual world to actual 11v11 football,' says Jerrell Silva, the man behind the Virtual Pro League (VPG), one of several virtual divisions where these clubs compete.

Pro Clubs operates like a real football club. You create your own club from scratch, picking a name, a stadium and creating a kit. Then, you invite people to come and play together online using your own created players against other similarly constructed teams.

In the format of the game that EA offers within *FIFA*, there are ten divisions in total, with intermittent cup windows sprinkled throughout the year. League matches are played across ten-game seasons, with point thresholds for relegation, promotion and title wins. The format ensures that you're always playing for something.

Although organised sides do play in the EA leagues, there is a large 'drop in' element to it too, where individual players can join others in ad hoc teams. It's a way of playing Pro Clubs that inevitably attracts showboaters and ball-hoggers, with the 'team-play' element of the game receding like a half-forgotten memory. Putting in a disciplined performance as a centre-half is a fairly joyless experience when the rest of the side has spent 12 minutes elasticoing their way around the pitch.

'To be honest, not only are the EA leagues a bit messy, they are also really easy. Any half decent, properly organised Pro Club could power up the divisions and win the top title without breaking a sweat. It's far better instead to join up with an external league,' says @WorldofJCC, who plays Pro Clubs and regularly broadcasts about this format of the game on YouTube.

One such league is the VPG (which covers gamers playing on the Xbox One). This has four leagues, with 12 teams in each. There is promotion and relegation, a domestic cup in the season and a European competition at the end of the campaign. Along with basic rules that are common to all leagues, such as no racism, sexism and homophobia, the VPG has additional rules covering swearing and other forms of offensive language (so, in this at least, it does differ from the average Sunday league game).

'We also have transfers,' says Jerrell Silva. 'Clubs start out with £5m. They can get more by buying coins, selling players for a profit or winning leagues, cups and tournaments. When they want to sign a new player, they have to meet a release clause in the contract, just like real football.'

In the same way that managing a Sunday league side necessitates lots of administrative and organisational skills, so too does running a Pro Club, as Dan Savage, who runs Port Vale Esports FC, explains:

'You've got to recruit players, which takes time. You come across a lot of players now on Twitter, where people upload clips that advertise themselves. When you've identified somebody, you invite them for a trial. Partly this is to see if they have what it takes in a game. But also you want to see if they will gel with the team. During matches and training we are all chatting on headsets and so chemistry is really important. If you can't get on with other players, then you aren't going to make it with our side.'

The majority of play (matches and training) takes place in the evening, when players have come home from school or work.

'For a manager like me, organising all of this is no different to a normal game of football. You have to organise availability, work on a formation, tactics and in the game, as the manager, provide instructions about what should be going on. After the game I will watch the performance back and try to pick out things to work on. And before the next game I will also watch our upcoming opponent and organise our approach to that game accordingly. It's a lot of work and probably the reason why so many players are reluctant to step up and become managers,' says Savage.

But playing is no walk in the park either. Having been an avid *FIFA* player for eight years, and immodestly thinking myself pretty handy, I was kindly given a chance to play for a side in the VPG. It's fair to say that I didn't set the world alight. The halves might be shorter and the levels of physical exertion negligible, but the mental effort involved in holding your position, following the manager's instructions and contributing to the play is as taxing as the most frenetic of Sunday league fixtures.

'New players can take a time to settle in,' explains Savage, 'and sometimes Pro Clubs is not for everyone. Equally, we have players who, for whatever reason, go through a dip in form. And just like any other football club, that means they might get dropped. In general, most get the form back. We are a community here, so we give people time.'

The arrival of professional football clubs, such as Port Vale, into the world of Pro Clubs illustrates a new phase of its development. The VPG now boasts several esports teams that are associated with Football League clubs, such as Port Vale, Fleetwood Town and Scunthorpe United.

'It has been impossible to ignore the growth of the esports industry over recent years,' says Robb Noble, media manager at Scunthorpe. 'And in order to engage with the future generations of supporters we need the club to continue to evolve in this area. Esports provides a great opportunity to engage with both existing fans as well as a new digital audience around the Scunthorpe United brand. Whether that is playing as the team, competing against us or watching the streams and following the coverage on social media.'

The broadcast side of esports, those 'streams' that Noble refers to, represent a growing phenomenon. Although there might only be 22 people playing in a match, there are many more watching the action online. Streaming, provided by host sites, such as VPG, or external ones, like Twitch, can bring viewers in their thousands to these matches.

'Streaming is a huge part of the Pro Clubs world,' says @WorldofJCC, whose own Pro Clubs highlights (and related content) is broadcast to his 95,000 subscribers on YouTube. 'The audience out there is growing all the time. A lot of people who are into *FIFA* like the idea of watching two clubs competing against each other. And they also like the idea of communicating with players via sites like Twitch and YouTube. That sense of an online community is not something that "traditional" football can offer you in the same way. With something like Pro Clubs, fans are getting the chance to communicate with the actual players.'

Streaming of *FIFA* content has boomed in recent years. In part, it has been helped by the ease with which players can edit, upload and share their own content via broadcasting sites or through social media. Every worldy, every bicycle kick, every piece of outrageous 'tekkers' can now be shared with your followers. But, equally, there has been a growing demand for that game content too.

Although part of this has manifested itself in a bigger audience for Pro Clubs, there has also been an explosion in the numbers choosing to watch 'traditional' one-v-one *FIFA* games. Esports tournaments, which pit individual players against each other, have expanded in recent years, a trend that has brought with it a corresponding boom in those tuning in. In 2019, for example, the FIFA eWorld Cup managed to rack up 47 million views across online platforms during the three-day event.

The global esports audience, of which *FIFA* is an important part, grew to 453 million worldwide in 2019, made up of 201 million esports enthusiasts and 252 million occasional viewers. As more money has flowed into the market, drawn through advertising to this growing audience, professional *FIFA* players have emerged. Some, such as Kai Wollin, who represents Manchester City, are attached to professional clubs, while many others are attached to new esports clubs, several created by current and former pros, such as Ruud Gullit (Team Gullit), Mesut Özil (Team Özil) and Christian Fuchs (NoFuchsGiven).

'There is a huge audience out there, people who love football but want something different from what's being served up by "traditional" broadcasters and the "traditional" game,' says @WorldofJCC. 'Although they still follow clubs like Liverpool, Manchester City and Chelsea, and go to matches or watch games on Sky and BT, they also might support a player like Kai Wollin or an esports club. Or, like the millions out there who just watch "traditional" football because they enjoy the content, they'll do the same on Twitch with something like esports. When you consider the total football audience out there, you have to now include esports. It might not be football as some people know it, but it is a growing part of the football world.'

How people consume football, and how people define 'football', is clearly changing. But while the interest in Pro Clubs and esports is one way that this change is manifesting itself within Football 2.0, another has its origins in the rough and ready world of Essex Sunday league.

It's a squally morning in Braintree. At 'The Fortress', a few acres of parkland on the outskirts of the town, a scrub of rec surrounded by post-war council houses, Braintree Iron are taking on Palmers FC for a place in the Essex Premier Cup Final.

For the few who have braved the elements to watch, this is football at its most elemental; an experience devoid of comfort, as far away as it's possible to be from the corporate world of the top flight. Through wind and rain they will watch the unfancied visitors run out 3-1 victors and then trudge home, kicking the claggy mud from their shoes as they do.

But the attendance figures for this fixture are not restricted to those hardy souls hugging the touchline. Tens of thousands of fans will watch this game later from the comfort of their own homes, liberated from the harsh realities of Sunday league. This is the world of YouTube football.

It all started back in 2013 when a group of mates from Thurrock in Essex, who had known each other since school (and who had played together in their youth), floated the idea of starting their own Sunday league team.

'The motivation,' says founder member Matt Smith (or 'Smiv' as he is more widely known by his online followers), 'was to see if we still had what it took to compete, and also to have a day each week where we knew we'd be able to catch up with each other.'

More friends soon jumped on board and bit by bit a team was cobbled together and a ground was found to call home. Dreams of adopting a similar name to their boyhood club (East Thurrock Juniors) were thwarted by league rules. And so, they opted for Palmers FC, named in homage to their new home, Palmers College in Grays. With everything in place, their journey began, the club taking its first steps in the Thurrock Association Sunday League.

So far, so unremarkable. Teams such as Palmers emerge across the country every year, often from a nostalgic urge to tap back into the feeling that playing with your mates used to give you in the days of junior football (with booze generally acting as the catalyst for the nostalgia trip). But it's what followed next that made the story of Palmers FC a bit different, turning its narrative from a run-of-the-mill tale of mates playing football again to one that would mark the club out as true footballing pioneers.

At the time, Smiv was trying to get a video production company off the ground: 'I've always been a believer of brand awareness and planting a seed in people's head, so I decided to sponsor the team and plaster my company's logo over the front of the shirt. I figured if local people needed a video for a wedding, event or even within the job they worked in, they'd subconsciously think of me.'

Smiv also had a YouTube channel (he had been an early pioneer of content creation on the platform) with several thousand subscribers. 'It struck me that I could widen the impact of my sponsorship if I started filming the boys on a Sunday and sticking a bit of the content on my channel. I hoped people would see the logo and that would get me more work. In the early days, it was more about me getting commissions than it was about the football. So, what happened next was a bit of a happy accident.'

Smiv took a camera down to the side's next fixture and filmed the game. 'The boys allowed me to do it but, like myself, didn't really see what it could become. I managed to get enough to put together a highlights reel but thought that on its own it seemed a bit flat, so I put a bit of, admittedly dodgy, commentary over it.'

The response was instant. 'People seemed to love it,' says Smiv. 'I was getting hit after hit on YouTube, with more and more people tuning in as the weeks went by.'

It soon became clear to Smiv that he had tapped into something: 'When you watch it, it's obvious that the quality of football isn't great. Just looking at it and comparing it to something like the Premier League highlights, you question why anyone would watch it. But it seemed to tap into this audience who loved it. Something about the sight of a few mates playing together just struck a chord with people.'

Viewing numbers steadily rose and then, midway through the second season, took off, thanks in part to a boozy night out, an inspired substitution and some on-field martial arts.

'It was a game where everything aligned perfectly,' explains Smiv. 'The night before, we went out for a quiz night and got absolutely pissed [which was included in the highlight]. Then in the game, our manager at the time, who was still pissed, brought himself on and scored. And finally, one of the opposition players got himself sent off after he decided to roundhouse one of ours. Luckily for us, he wanted that kept in the video!'

The video, or more specifically the roundhouse, got picked up by *The Sun's* online content, bringing what Palmers FC was doing to a much wider audience. Ultimately, 'Thug Life', as the video was named, clocked up nearly 1,000,000 views.

Six years on, the Palmers FC story stands as an example of what can be achieved at this level through innovation. Over that time, the club managed to clock up 232,000 subscribers on YouTube, and the content that Smiv created, some 600-plus videos, was regularly viewed by over 100,000 eager fans.

Dave Macey, one of those subscribers, has a theory as to why so many people have tuned in to watch the club over the years:

'When you watch something like Sky, it's all very serious, like football is a matter of life and death. But most football is just a laugh. And Palmers capture that. Yes, the players involved want to win, like we all do when we play weekend football or five-a-side, but it's also clear that they are in it for the simple joy of getting together with your mates and just playing the game.'

There is also a sense of familiarity and intimacy to the videos that has added to their appeal. On that squally morning in Braintree, we get to see the pre-match routine, which involves stopping off at a McDonalds drive-through (complete with order confusion), the fleet of car shares getting lost on the way to Braintree, and the joys of rocking up to a game and finding nowhere to park. To anyone who has ever played Sunday or Saturday football, or even just taken their kids to play junior football, all of the above will strike a chord.

'And underpinning all of this,' says Macey, 'is the production itself. It's rough and ready, mirroring the reality of Sunday football. And Smiv's commentary is a thing to behold. Rapid, knowing and always funny, the likes of Martin Tyler and Darren Fletcher could learn a thing or two from him. I love the fact that it's filled with nicknames, cut-aways and references to the non-football world that occasionally intrudes, like a dog running on to the pitch.'

The social media side of the club has been another part of its appeal. On Twitter (30,000 followers), Instagram (40,000 followers) and YouTube, those who follow Palmers have not only been provided with content, but have also had the chance to communicate with the club and the players. Palmers have enjoyed the kind of social media following more akin to a National League side but, unlike clubs in that division, they have interacted on a personal level with people choosing to follow them. It's a sense of inclusivity that 'traditional' football clubs often lack, the feeling that you can be part of the story.

For the players at Palmers, Smiv's innovation has broadened their football world: 'At a club level, we have been lucky enough to be invited to some great events [in exchange for a plug here and there on the socials], played at Premier League grounds and been involved in plenty of charity events. The players also got a taste of what it's like to gain a bit of footballing notoriety. When you play Sunday league you don't expect to have thousands of followers on Twitter or Instagram. But for our players, that was the case.'

Their local league has also benefitted. At the time of Palmers' inception, like many across the country, the Thurrock Association Sunday League was struggling for numbers. But the growth of Palmers' online presence has coincided with an upturn in its fortunes. In contrast to other local leagues, many of whom are struggling to maintain one or two divisions, the Thurrock Association Sunday League now boasts five.

'I think other people have got involved in Sunday league because of what we've done. And I know for a fact that the clubs we played against loved it,' says Smiv.

'Initially they laughed and thought I was a bit of a geek, but over time they came to appreciate the benefits. After all, imagine turning up on a Sunday, scoring a worldy and knowing it was caught on camera, you'd want to see it back wouldn't you?'

Although, according to Smiv, this level of popularity did put the club at a slight disadvantage every week. 'When the fixtures were released, everyone looked out for Palmers, because that was their 15 minutes of fame. They were going to be viewed by thousands so each player was always on the ball and ready to go. We very rarely went up against an unprepared side!'

At the time of writing, the club has found itself at something of a crossroads. The transitory nature of amateur football has meant a good deal of upheaval at Palmers, with many of the original band of mates who formed the club moving on. This, combined with other changes within his personal life, has led to Smiv stepping back from the project. Right now, Palmers FC still exist, but the YouTube element of the club is on hiatus.

But, although the original trailblazers of YouTube football are no longer with us, their example lives on. Indeed, perhaps the most significant impact of what Palmers FC have done concerns those who have followed in the club's footsteps. Some, such as SE Dons and Kitchener FC, have adopted, with varying success, the model established by Palmers. But others, like Hashtag United, have taken the idea and run with it.

Spencer Owen, the man behind Hashtag United, made his name on YouTube creating videos about *FIFA*, tapping into the same expanding audience that has emerged within the esports world in recent years. As he explained to *The*

Warm Down back in 2018, he recognised the potential the game represented in his attempts to build an online audience.

'When I started making football videos on YouTube, I used to film documentaries about East Thurrock, my local team. This was way before I had significant numbers of subscribers. I liked the content but I didn't have the audience. I wanted to get an audience and I was a big fan of *FIFA*, still am, and by making that gaming content it enabled me to have a voice.'

Although he covered various aspects of the game, his niche was FIFA Ultimate Team (FUT). In this mode, you form a squad from a selection of Panini-style playing cards, which include players from the past and present. You then compete with your ragtag band of players online. The more you win and the more you progress up the league structure (ten levels), the more coins you accrue, which enables you to either buy packs of players (tapping into that Panini-style aesthetic again) or individual players, the latter via their online market. If you ever wondered what it would be like to see a front line that contains Harry Kane, Alan Shearer and Gary Lineker, then FUT could be the mode for you. Since it was launched in 2009, FUT has grown to become the most popular element for the game's millions of users.

Back in 2013, viewers could watch Spencer online, via his channel Spencer FC, opening FUT packs, indulging in the slightly bizarre 'Wheel of FUTune', where Spencer would allow a wheel of fortune to dictate how he played FUT, or explaining his progress in Career Mode (*FIFA*'s mode whereby you play as a player or a manager for an entire career).

In three years, the channel attracted more than one million subscribers, and built an equally impressive following on other social media platforms. This meant that by 2016 Spencer had that audience he had always wanted. And with that achieved, his long-held desire to move back to original football content could be fulfilled. But rather than replicate what he had done before, he and his brother Seb had been working on an idea to do something a bit different.

'We had already, through the Wembley Cup, a competition played at Wembley that pitted two teams of content creators against each other, trailed the idea of creating a team for Spencer's subscribers to watch,' says Seb Carmichael Brown, one of the founders of the club and the current commercial director of Hashtag United.

The game had proven popular. 'But, as a format,' continues Carmichael Brown, 'you couldn't do it week-in, week-out. So, we thought we'd take things a bit more "grassroots". Spencer and I were convinced that regular people out there would like to watch regular players (players like them) play regular games, and so the idea formed of us starting our own team and creating content around that. We believed that we as a team made from tradespeople, office workers and salesmen could relate more easily to an audience rather than the millionaires playing in the Premier League. We were them, just ordinary fans who loved the game.'

He and Owen were able to convince enough mates to join their new enterprise and, with that, Hashtag United was born.

'The name was a deliberate nod to social media,' says Carmichael Brown. 'Not only were a lot of us working in social media, Hashtag was also going to be a club who from its very beginnings, was out there seeking an audience through social media.'

With a team on their hands, the challenge for the duo was what to do next. Although Spencer FC had an audience, the trick was now to create content that was more than just an average Sunday league side playing on dodgy pitches every week. A new generation of football fan was emerging, one focussed around gaming, the content Owen had built his channel upon.

'They were younger, and more into *FIFA*, specifically Ultimate Team,' says Carmichael Brown. 'That was the content they were used to from Spencer, so we had to keep that in mind when it came to Hashtag. To begin with at least.'

The solution was to borrow slightly from FUT, where players take on online opponents in friendlies but within a divisional structure, progressing to the next (more difficult) level only if they get sufficient points. Essentially, it's like a grading system, with opponents in division five being easier than opponents in division one.

With Hashtag United, each season would consist of ten games, in which they would play teams with a common theme – for example, Sunday league teams or staff teams of professional clubs. They would start in division five with the ultimate aim of finishing top of division one. In division five they would need 12 points (i.e. four wins) to be promoted, while they would need 24 points to win division one.

In further homage to FUT, there would be no other teams in their league – the teams they chose to play would not be competing for points, only for the glory of beating

Hashtag United and being watched on YouTube. In other words, Hashtag would compete in a league of their own, going up and down visualised divisions depending on their results.

Despite sharing DNA with what Palmers was doing, from the beginning Hashtag has looked like a more professional outfit, taking the original idea and polishing it for a wider audience. Although the early edited packages still came in at a similar 20 minutes, contained a familiar 'blokey' commentary (this time supplied by Owen) and were riven through with that same 'mates in it together' aesthetic, with Hashtag everything just looked slicker. With multiple camera angles, a higher degree of visual quality, player interviews and Spencer's changing room team talks bookending matters, the early videos were clearly an evolutionary step in the medium.

And it worked. Both on the pitch and off it, Hashtag United has been a huge success. In its division format, the club powered forwards, successively rising to every challenge presented and ultimately winning the division one title.

'Over the course of our climb up the divisions, we faced a huge variety of teams, such as the staff teams for West Ham United, Crystal Palace and Manchester City, and we also played fellow YouTube channels like COPA90, Ball Street and Dream Team FC. It was a brilliant experience, far better than we could've imagined,' says Carmichael Brown.

And in the non-football world, Hashtag's popularity has boomed. Today the club boasts 480,000 subscribers on YouTube, 450,000 followers on Instagram and 185,000 followers on Twitter. Recently, a social media table was put together based solely on YouTube official channel views for all UK clubs. Liverpool topped the list with over 42 million views, more than double any other. Then came the expected names such as Manchester City, Manchester United and Arsenal. However, in seventh place, ahead of many big Premier League clubs, was Hashtag United with just under 7.5 million views. Worldwide, its monthly numbers often translate to it being among the top 25 clubs, beating the likes of Everton, Spurs and Rangers.

'We are, without doubt, the most followed non-professional club in the world,' states Carmichael Brown. 'There are people walking around in Hashtag United shirts in South America, Australia and Africa. I don't know of any other club of our stature that can say that.'

How to explain such a phenomenon? 'First, you're watching people who are just like you,' says @ShawneyD, who has followed the club since its early days. 'You watch them and think "I could do that". But more than that, you imagine them going home and having lives like yours. You don't get that with the Premier League. I support Man Utd. But I don't think for a second that a player like Paul Pogba has a life that is anything like mine. When you look at his Instagram posts, it's all fancy living. When you look at those done by people who play for Hashtag, it's just normal stuff, like going to the pub, having a laugh with mates and that.'

And then there is the additional content. Hashtag has not confined itself to what happens on matchday. Viewers can log on to see videos such as 'Players Reading Mean YouTube Comments', 'How to Train in the Snow' and 'Freekick Challenge'.

'You get a look behind the scenes with stuff like that, see the players having a laugh, not taking things too seriously,' continues @ShawneyD. 'I know big clubs do similar things but with them you know that the players are only doing it because they have to and that when it's done, off they go back to their million-pound houses. With Hashtag, it's like you're watching your mates try a crossbar challenge.'

Hashtag United's expansion has enabled the club to monetise what it is doing, attracting commercial partners, sponsors and advertisers. And it's easy to see why they are flocking to the 'brand'. With hundreds of thousands of viewers tuning in, specifically those from the 16–25 'youth' demographic so beloved of advertisers, the club packs an increasingly sizable punch in the marketplace. Should the growth continue, it's not implausible to see Hashtag's channel as a potential rival to other sport broadcasters.

In fact, it's probably slightly 'analogue' to view what Owen and Carmichael Brown have created as a club in the conventional sense of the word.

'We are a football club but we are also a broadcaster,' says Carmichael Brown. 'I suppose it would be like a Premier League side, such as Manchester City, broadcasting its own games. That's what we're doing. And we need the money we bring in from advertising, commercial partnerships and merchandising to ensure that the broadcasting side, which is an increasingly expansive [and expensive] operation, grows and succeeds. We want to create the best, most original content possible to entertain our fans and grow the Hashtag brand.'

Inevitably, others have seen what Hashtag are doing and decided that they would like a slice of the action. One recent entrant into the market is Rebel FC.

According to its founder, the YouTube creator @Calfreezy (Callum Airey): 'Rebel FC is a team of passionate football fans who instead of choosing the traditional route to the top in football, are rebelling against the system and taking a chance on a different way in. They're aiming high and are committed to taking Rebel FC to the highest reaches of the footballing world.'

In a sign of the growing professionalism that has marked the development of 'YouTube football', Rebel FC represents a partnership between the club and the social video broadcaster Brave Bison. We are a long way from the rough and ready origins of Palmers FC.

'The idea with Rebel, as Callum envisioned it, was to do something creative. Although wanting to play more football was the main motivator for everyone involved, it had to be more than simply joining a normal club,' says Will Brophy, head of production at Rebel.

Largely drawn from the ranks of YouTube creators, Rebel now has 22 players on the books. It also boasts a kit deal with Under Armour and a two-year sponsorship deal with the energy provider Utilita.

To date, Rebel FC has restricted itself to friendlies, using the opportunity to build confidence against successively more challenging opponents, including Sunday league sides, university teams and representatives from other content providers, such as Arsenal Fan TV.

In many ways there is overlap between what it is doing and what Hashtag has done. There is match coverage, behind-the-scenes footage and the usual 'tekkers' based content, short videos or clips of skill moves, worldies and crossbar challenges, the kind that have proliferated online in recent years (both from amateur and professional clubs).

But, unlike Hashtag United, and the likes of Palmers FC, there is, understandably, less the sense of a group of lads simply playing football for the joy of doing it with your mates. Rebel FC, with its emphasis on the inclusion of 'influencers' and content creators, combined with its partnership with Brave Bison, feels more driven, less organic than its predecessors. This is a club, or rather a broadcaster, that looks to firmly have its eye on the bottom line.

And yet, the less organic feel has not dimmed the club's appeal. The appetite for this kind of football, if judged by the many thousands of young people who have followed the Rebel story is anything to go by, appears inexhaustible at the moment.

This 'younger' demographic was certainly evident at Wembley Stadium on an overcast November afternoon back in 2018. I might be a rare visitor to the home of football (Evertonians are infrequent patrons after all), but I've been enough times to get a taste of the average experience. And in a word, like much of top-flight football, it tends to be old. Men of a certain age, between 30 and 50, dominate the match-going demographic. And they set the mood music, less singing, less enthusiasm, more swearing. Football as pageantry it is not.

The EE Wembley Cup is very much the antithesis of that. To most fans (those more likely to be at Wembley for a 'Football 1.0' match), it's an event that will have passed them by. And yet, there are nearly 35,000 here today and 230,000 viewers tuning in live.

The event, the brainchild of Spencer Owen, started as that original match back in 2015 between Spencer FC and Sidemen United, two teams made up of YouTube creators.

Over the following years, Owen's original idea has grown. The number of teams involved has gradually expanded, ex-pros, such as Robert Pires, David Trezeguet and Cafu, have got involved in games and the public, in their tens of thousands, are now part of the live experience.

Despite the growth, the event remains very much rooted in its YouTube origins. The most recent Wembley Cup saw Rebel FC compete for the first time. And they were joined by XO FC (part of the Ball Street Network, a hub of football content) and F2 FC (from the F2 Freestylers, a hugely popular 'tekkerz' channel on YouTube). Completing the quartet in 2018's expanded competition was Hashtag United.

'The weird thing is,' explains Andy Garrett, who brought his son to the event, 'the kids who come to watch are much more excited to see their YouTube heroes, like Billy and Jeremy from F2, than they are to see an actual football legend like Trezeguet. I imagine most older fans would have no idea who Bill and Jeremy are, but to millions of younger people they are a huge deal.'

This tallies with an event that Carmichael Brown recalls from a few years ago when his brother was lucky enough to snag an interview with Gareth Bale for his channel.

'About halfway through the interview a load of local kids came running over. Spencer was fully expecting them to flock to Gareth Bale for autographs. But it was him that they wanted to talk to. He was a bit embarrassed by it and asked one of the kids why they would rather get his autograph than Bale's and he replied that Spencer was more like his mate. And I think that's the key to all of this. We are accessible in a way that millionaire footballers simply aren't.'

The autonomy of this alternative football world has given the likes of Hashtag United a large degree of freedom. It has been able to choose the format it participates in and the opponents it faces. And all this free from the usual burdensome regulations (from the league and FA) that 'conventional' clubs face.

This was evident at the Wembley Cup, where in 2018 the organisers were able to tinker with the format to an extent that would have made reform-minded administrators at UEFA green with envy. Along with a shorter, 30-minute game length, an innovation called 'Man Down Time' was brought in, which, should the scores be level at full time, would see a player removed from each team every minute until one of them scores.

And yet despite enjoying such autonomy, and ever-growing popularity, in 2017 Hashtag United took the surprise step to enter the far more regulated world of non-league football, bringing together the worlds of Football 1.0 and Football 2.0 in the process. The club regards this new adventure as 'chapter two' of the journey (with 'chapter one' being Hashtag's rise up those self-created 'divisions').

'What we had done with Hashtag was great,' Owen outlined on *The Warm Down*, 'but there was a cap on it. It was always an ambition of ours to make a club and take it in this sort of direction. We didn't know how it was going to go, whether we would merge with an existing club or go it alone. As it is, we have been able to do it ourselves and, because of the restructuring that has happened in non-league football, jump in straight to Step 6.'

Initially, Hashtag was admitted to the Spartan South Midlands Division One, hundreds of miles from the Essex base where the majority of the team reside. But the club faced resistance from rival clubs, who claimed its arrival forced other sides out of the division.

'We didn't want that,' explains Carmichael Brown. 'We were aware from the very beginning that we had to win people over. What we are is something different from the norm. We are not a conventional club. We don't have a rich history going back years, we don't have a base, like a village or a town. So, when we joined non-league football, it absolutely couldn't be at the expense of an existing club because that wouldn't have just been unfair, it would also have made our job of winning people over so much harder.'

Eventually, after liaising with various football authorities, Hashtag United was invited to join the Eastern Senior League Division One South.

Prior to entry into this level the club underwent some necessary changes to its model. First came a home. Until this point Hashtag had been a rootless club. Although games were played in north London, it had no ground or local infrastructure to speak of. The first job was to remedy this.

The club initially entered into a groundshare with Haringey Borough at Coles Park in Tottenham, not too far from where Hashtag used to play in north London. But with the side mostly based in Essex, this was far from ideal. The club remedied this at the end of its inaugural campaign, moving east into Essex to groundshare at Chadfields, home of Tilbury FC.

The club also underwent a change to the playing side too, perhaps the biggest of which was the appointment of an experienced manager, in the form of East Thurrock's former assistant coach Jay Devereux.

'I left East Thurrock at the end of the 2016/17 season – just to have a break and spend a bit of time with the family,' he recently told *The Bootiful Game*. 'Earlier on in the year, Spencer contacted me and asked me if I would be interested in managing Hashtag and, at the time, I was loosely aware of what they were doing on YouTube.'

As someone who had been coaching in the National League South with East Thurrock, Devereux was initially unsure of the wisdom of taking a job that was such a drop down the pyramid.

'I went to a couple of games they had with them and just went along to watch from the side-lines really. I really enjoyed it and I thought it's different, very different to what I've been used to. A chance to look at things from a different angle, but by the same token, wanting to operate in the traditional football world. The more I spent time around them, the more they knew what they wanted to do, the more excited I was by it and I agreed to be their manager.'

Along with the hiring of a manager with more experience, the club has also had to bring in players more suited to this level of the pyramid. The switch meant that some of the founding players, such as Spencer Owen (who is now on permanent commentary duties), have made way for several players with non-league experience.

'The aim is for us to take this club as far as it's possible to go, so inevitably that will always mean new players, players who are more suitable to the level we are at, coming to the club. But we are very much a community at Hashtag, so we've tried to retain as many of our original players as possible. And several of those who couldn't continue with the first team have moved across to our Sunday league side.

We are always keen to keep people as part of the Hashtag community,' says Carmichael Brown.

Hashtag United are like no other club at this level. Harry Honesty, who came to the club from East Thurrock United, probably sums it up best, describing playing for them 'like being a professional footballer but not being a pro!'

'Getting used to having a camera in your face and being under a microphone took a bit of getting used to,' says Jay Devereaux. 'The main difference between this club and others I would say is probably the scrutiny and the expectation. Whilst you don't get many coming to our games, if you lose a game you've got nearly half a million followers on YouTube, of which most videos get around 200,000 views, you're getting lots of comments on that. You can kind of get a little bit of a taste of what the managers managing big clubs are facing.'

There are very few clubs, and certainly none at this level, for whom content is their lifeblood. Hashtag are a uniquely rootless club in non-league football. Without a local fanbase, its source of income is entirely dependent on the content created (and its ability to drive advertising revenue and attract corporate partners). The move into 'real' football has represented a challenge for how this content is created, as Carmichael Brown explains:

'How we tell the story has had to change completely. In the past, our games have been less frequent and afterwards we've had two or three weeks to turn around match edits. And to a certain extent it was all about keeping the result a secret until the video went live, to give people an extra reason to log on. Non-league football has changed that. There are more games, sometimes two in a week, and as there are fans at the match [albeit limited numbers of them] we have to get that content out quickly because the result gets out. And we can't just live stream it because of the FA's blackout on Saturday afternoon football.'

The club's dependence on content creation for its survival undermines one of the myths that has surrounded Hashtag United since the club first announced its intentions to enter non-league football, that it was like a smaller version of AFC Fylde or Salford City, a moneyed club trying to buy success.

'It's understandable why some people might have thought that but it's not true,' explains Carmichael Brown. 'A lot of the money we make goes into content creation. We have significant overheads here that other clubs don't have, like paying people to create the best video content possible. On the playing side, although our manager is remunerated, we've got a very limited playing budget. I don't always think that people outside the club appreciate just what goes into creating our content. It involves a lot of people and a lot of hard work. And we certainly don't have an endless source of income to simply bankroll the playing side and 'buy' our way up the pyramid.'

To date, the move to non-league football has gone well. On the playing side, the club secured promotion out of the division at its first attempt. This has then been complemented by continual growth on social media too, with the club expanding subscribers and followers throughout the season.

'Enjoying success so early is really good. But we realise that there is a long way to go. I know that, when we launched, Spencer said that we could be in the Premier League in ten years. However, he was only saying that to illustrate what is theoretically possible. We know that getting to the Premier League in that timeframe is not realistic. I think what we really want is sustainability. So many clubs at this level don't have sustainable business models and rely on benefactors. Some do that well, but others throw money at it and fall apart. We don't want that. If we're around in five years and making a profit, I think that will be defined as a success.'

Football in England today, and what it means to run a football club, requires a much broader definition than was the case even ten years ago. A whole generation of kids are growing up seeing non-traditional forms of the game, like esports or YouTube football, as being equally worthy of their time as the Premier League.

A 90-minute fixture between Liverpool and Manchester City might take millions of pounds to create and be ram-jammed with the biggest names in the game, but to a ten-year-old sitting at home with the choice of watching that or his favourite content creators battle it out in a 12-minute *FIFA* head-to-head on Twitch, it's very possible that the latter might win out.

The game as we have known it is changing and the new generation of fans coming through no longer consume football as we once did. Football 2.0 doesn't just represent a new and vibrant form of the sport, it also reshaped the very definition of what a football club actually is.

Chapter Ten

Epilogue

THERE'S a commonly held view in English
football that money is the most important thing
in the game. And, indeed, it's hard to have taken
the journey I have over the past year and not come to a
similar conclusion.

There might seem to be a chasm separating a club like
Liverpool FC and a club like Stuart Day's Roma, who
play nearby. But in reality, their needs and challenges
are not dissimilar. Both face costs and both need to raise
income to cover them. Liverpool's costs might be more
considerable and its array of money-making avenues
greater, but fundamentally the economics are the same.
And if costs consistently exceed income, then you're in
trouble.

Money defines English football. And for the majority
of those who are involved, there is never enough of it.
This might be the strangest aspect of our modern game.
At no point in football's long history has the sport created
so much wealth. The national game is a huge success
story, specifically the Premier League. The top flight

contributes £7.6bn to the British economy each year, it is one of the country's leading entertainment exports and locally Premier League clubs are worth millions to their surrounding economies.

Yet, despite this, the sport is also one that is irredeemably hard up. At the extreme end of this problem is football at the very bottom. This is where the lack of money is most keenly felt. It's there in the Sunday league teams paying exorbitant fees to play, it's there in the junior clubs facing week upon week of cancelled fixtures and it's there in the Saturday sides struggling to afford a ground to play in.

But it's elsewhere too. Throughout the pyramid, despite the money that exists within English football, so many clubs are struggling just to survive. So much so, that permanence is becoming less common. Clubs are folding, or threatening to fold, at a rate that should not be happening in a sport as rich as our national game is.

Beyond the promised land of the Premier League, so many clubs live a precarious life, often only a few bad decisions away from disaster. Or, as the recent coronavirus crisis has illustrated, at grave danger should an external event undermine their ability to get people through the gate.

The shutdown of football that occurred in response to the virus illustrated the fact that many clubs lack the finance to cover even short periods of time when planned income is no longer available. For a lot of clubs, football is a hand-to-mouth existence, where the absence of weekly income makes survival a challenge. Postponements due to bad weather can be damaging enough. The succession of postponements created because of the pandemic possesses the potential to ruin clubs.

At the time of writing, the shutdown is in its infancy. But already the EFL has had to create a £50m short-term relief fund to help clubs with cash-flow issues because of the coronavirus outbreak. Below its divisions, the rest of the pyramid has no such safety net. Those with contracts to honour will find life tough. In mid-March, not long after the shutdown, National League side Barnet were forced to put all the club's non-playing staff, some 60 people, on immediate notice of redundancy. The feeling amongst those playing at Steps 1 and 2 is that Barnet will just be the first of many.

And lower down, even amongst those whose wage bills are more modest or non-existent, the impact could be profound. So much of the budgets of the clubs in the National League system and below rely on social activities: quiz nights, sportsman's dinners, football fiestas. In the short term at least, these will be cancelled, meaning that clubs will be faced with the prospect of significant funding shortfalls once football resumes.

Although the coronavirus pandemic represents an extreme and unprecedented external shock, clubs might have been better able to withstand both it and the manifold other issues they face during an average season had the vast wealth created by English football been more equitably shared. But it isn't. And it's a problem that's essentially one of concentration.

In unfettered, free-market capitalist economies, economic power tends to concentrate in a tiny elite. Since the 1980s, as social and fiscal controls have been increasingly rolled back in the UK, and trade union powers neutered, attacked by a succession of market-friendly governments, this trend has become more and more pronounced. Today, Britain's richest one per cent own as much as the poorest 55 per cent of the population. And that concentration is only heading one way.

Over the past 30 years, English football has not just mirrored the wider economy, it has acted like a steroid-fuelled microcosm of it; a largely unrestricted form of turbo-capitalism. And it's an industry in which an economic elite has taken an ever-increasing share of the wealth that has been produced.

Like an Eton-and-Oxford-educated scion of a moneyed family, who no doubt points to their own endeavours and apparent brilliance as proof that their position of dominance is deserved, the members of football's elite do something similar. By their reckoning, it is they, and their stars, who produce the product that people really pay to see, it is they who power the game forward, it is they who have made English football the success story it is.

But like those same privileged heirs who forget the society beneath them that makes everything possible, the society that gave them the opportunity to work so hard and to be so 'brilliant', the members of football's elite forget the pyramid that supports them too. The Premier League does not exist in a vacuum. Its history and its success is in part derived from the vast network of clubs, players and coaches that exist beneath it and without whom the national game would look very different indeed.

But short of the arrival of some kind of brave new socialist dawn, little of the above is going to change any time soon. And so, the game as we know it will continue to rely on love to keep it going, on passion to cover the shortfall between what is needed and what is available.

Irrespective of what kind of club it is, what is clear as you travel up the pyramid, from the soggy pitches and run-down clubhouses at grassroots and even up to the bright lights of the Premier League, is how much of the national game is dependent on people getting involved for the sheer love of the sport.

'It's just football isn't it?' says Andy Garrett. 'It gets in your blood from a young age and you can't shake it off, that need to watch it, to follow it, to play it. I still remember being a young kid and having a ball at my feet at all times, kicking it around the house and forever annoying my mum. In the years that have passed, the love of the game that I had back then has never left me. I might be coaching now rather than playing but I still have the same level of enthusiasm and excitement on a Saturday morning today as I did when I played all those years ago.'

And it's through people giving their time or their money that English football boasts not just a vast and extensive pyramid but also so many clubs.

'If tomorrow, people stopped volunteering, stopped paying to play and stopping putting their hands in their pockets to keep clubs afloat, whether that be fans kicking in a few quid to keep a club going, a businessman funding his local non-league club, or somebody higher up the food chain investing millions in a professional side, the pyramid would look very different. We have so many clubs in this country because so many people do give their time and their money freely. There is a huge amount of goodwill underwriting the national game. Without it, the majority of our clubs would be in serious trouble,' says John Allman.

And these are clubs that often represent so much more than just a medium for football.

'The game nowadays is about a lot more than what happens on the pitch. For fans and volunteers, it's a place to come and socialise, a place where they can be part of a community, a place where they can feel a sense of belonging. Many of the bonds that unite communities have been fractured in recent decades. Football clubs represent one of the few remaining examples of a medium that can bring people together, a place where we can be as one,' says Andy Higgins of the Blackpool Supporters' Trust.

And, increasingly, it's not a one-way relationship. The idea of football clubs as agents for change within their communities has now taken hold, at multiple levels within the game. Although football clubs, to their credit, have a long history of putting their hands in their pocket when it comes to charitable causes, of getting involved to help the local community, this feels like something different, as Jonathan Jackson of Wigan Athletic explains:

'What I think you're seeing now is a more consistent approach to the "community" aspect of football. Clubs are now permanently involved in the community, using the power of football to positively impact on people's lives, year-in, year-out. It's about being there for the long term and bringing consistent investment to address some of the issues people in our community face. As clubs we can't solve every problem, but we recognise that we are part of the local area, that this community supports us and so, in turn, we can do what we can to make people's lives that bit better.'

This sense of clubs changing, of evolving to adapt with the times, illustrates something else about English football too: its restless nature. This is a sport that, in recent years, has been in a state of constant flux; declining in some areas, expanding in others, embracing new communities and age groups as it changes.

The charge often levelled against the sport in the past, that it was characterised by a kind of small 'c' conservatism, that it was often slow to change and hostile to modern notions of inclusivity, is one that is harder to make stick than was once the case. Although the sport is far from perfect, and still has problems with racism, misogyny and homophobia, it is much more inclusive than it used to be. Whatever your gender, your race, your age or your ability, football is now a sport that offers you a place, whether that be within the confines of the 'traditional game' or within the digital world of Football 2.0.

'Football is meant to be the nation's sport, but for too long it wasn't a sport that opened its doors to everyone. But as you have seen with the huge leaps forward that have taken place in women's football and in the creation of new forms of the game that cater for the elderly and the disabled, this is now a sport better suited to England as it is today. There is still work to be done but we are on the right path,' says Jen O'Neill.

In the past few years, I've got to experience much of the above first hand. My own son has been playing junior football since he was five and, as a dutiful parent, I spent years watching him from the touchline.

Almost from the very beginning, he plagued me with requests to get involved in the coaching, pointing out with regularity examples of other dads who had stepped in to lend a hand. As I'm a long-time devotee to the concept of not volunteering, he had his work cut out.

In the end, it took three years of nagging before I eventually relented, in part due to genuine respect at how dogged he was but equally I've been inspired by the people I have met during this journey.

If you ever wanted to get a taste of the realities of football in this country, then a spell coaching with a grassroots club would provide you with an illuminating crash course. I've experienced the atrocious pitches, the knackered facilities, the tired, often basic equipment. The disparity between the matches that take place in the top flight on a Saturday afternoon at the nearby Amex in Brighton and the games that take place in the surrounding towns and villages where we play on a Saturday morning is as large as it is depressing.

But you also get to experience the positive side of football too. The parents making the effort to shape the footballers of tomorrow, the teenagers giving up their time to referee games, the mums and dads forgoing their Saturday morning to serve tea in the bar. And they do it all just to see the smiles on kids' faces and the chance to be part of something that matters to this community.

And I have got to experience the reality of a sport in transition too. We have girls playing in mixed-gender sides, we have boys with disabilities playing mainstream football and we have teams venturing out into new forms of the game, such as futsal. Although football at the club might largely be rooted in the traditions of the game, there is enough variety here to give even the casual observer an insight into modern football's innovative nature.

So, I'll end this journey with a snapshot of my own part in the pyramid, my own contribution to the national sporting narrative.

It's a cold Saturday morning in January in the heart of the Kent countryside. Our side is 7-0 down and there are just two minutes left on the clock. Call me pessimistic, but I don't see a way back into this game.

The kids are away from home against Sevenoaks Town. If ever a game was designed to test the resilience of the modern football philosophy, one based on inclusivity, positivity and child-focussed learning, it would be this one. The opponents are streamed, rooted in fixed positions and notions such as 'equal time' and 'mixed ability' have been thrown to the wind. The coaches bark instructions from the touchline, command and control still very much evident.

In response, our players look slightly shell-shocked. The harshness of the opposition coaches, the physicality of a ruthlessly competitive opponent and the gulf in ability has left them shaken, humbled by a 30-minute mauling in which the scoreline could've been so much worse.

When the final whistle rings out, they leave the pitch dejected, the cheers of their opponents subduing them further.

But the head coach's faith in the philosophy he has espoused all season is undimmed. For him, this match is just part of a learning curve, another stop on a journey that will take years in the making. And that's what he tries to impart to the kids after the game, the sense that the scoreline is of no consequence and what matters instead is how they played, what they learned and what they can take away from the morning.

To his eternal credit, he gets the kids leaving with smiles on their faces. Impossible as it might seem from watching what has just occurred, he wrings positives out of the experiences, shifting their perspective, turning what could have been a disastrous memory into a valuable learning experience. Weirdly, they leave in better spirits than the other team.

This is our contribution to the pyramid. We're attempting to give these kids the best football journey possible. Will we get it right? Probably not all of the time. But we'll try our best, doing what we can to navigate them through the ups and downs of life at the bottom, making up for the terrible pitches, the absent facilities, the coaches and teams who still think it's the 1970s.

And hopefully, in the future, these kids will continue to love the sport as much as they do right now. Because it is obviously a love. Why else would they turn up week-in, week-out, suffering the wind, the driving rain and the cold? Our side loses way more than it wins and yet the kids come back every Saturday.

If that love continues then these will be the players, coaches and administrators of tomorrow. They'll be the ones propping up the pyramid, keeping clubs alive, making sure that English football continues to be thrive.

Bibliography

Clubs

Accrington Stanley
www.accringtonstanley.co.uk/

AFC Fylde
www.afcfylde.co.uk/

AFC Wimbledon
www.afcwimbledon.co.uk/

Binfield FC
www.binfieldfc.com/

Bolton Wanderers
www.bwfc.co.uk/

Blyth Spartans
www.blythspartans.com/

Bromley
www.bromleyfc.tv/site/

Billericay
www.billericaytownfc.co.uk

Birmingham Walking Football Club
www.walkingfootballbirmingham.co.uk/

Brighton and Hove Walking Football Club
www.brightonwfc.com/

Brentford FC
www.brentfordfc.com/

Bury
www.buryfc.co.uk/

Bottesford
www.bottesfordfc.co.uk/

Burnley
www.burnleyfootballclub.com/

Carlisle Futsal Club
www.carlislefutsal.com/cfc/

Chichester Ladies
www.pitchero.com/clubs/chichesterladiesfc/teams/26102

Corinthian-Casuals
www.corinthian-casuals.com/

Crowborough Athletic
www.pitchero.com/clubs/crowboroughathletic

Dexter Sports
www.dextersportsyfc.org.uk

Dulwich Hamlet
www.pitchero.com/clubs/dulwichhamlet

Ebbsfleet United
www.ebbsfleetunited.co.uk

Exeter City
www.exetercityfc.co.uk

Fletcher Moss Rangers
www.fletchermossrangers.com

Gateshead fc
www.gateshead-fc.com

Grimsby Ancient Mariners
www.grimsbyancientmariners.co.uk/about.html

Hartlepool United
www.hartlepoolunited.co.uk

Helvecia
www.londonhelveciafutsal.com

Hashtag United
www.youtube.com/user/spencerbets

Hough End Griffins
www.houghendgriffins.com

Horden CW
www.pitchero.com/clubs/hordencollierywelfare

Lowestoft Town
www.lowestofttownfc.co.uk

Leyton Orient
www.leytonorient.com

Lewes FC
www.lewesfc.com

MHS@MHSJFC (Twitter)

Mendip Broadwalk Sundays FC
@MBWsundays (Twitter)

North Ferriby
www.northferribyfc.co.uk

Norwich City
www.canaries.co.uk

Oxford City
www.oxfordcityfc.co.uk

Palmers FC
www.youtube.com/user/smivadee/featured

Rebel FC
www.youtube.com/channel/UCi0AtmAUs1z4WAScpMt83EQ

Reading FC
www.readingfc.co.uk

Rotherfield FC
www.rfc1893.com/

Saltdean United
www.pitchero.com/clubs/saltdeanunited

South Shields
www.southshieldsfc.co.uk

South Tyneside Ability FC
www.southtynesideability.co.uk

Sutton United
www.suttonunited.net

St Francis Rangers
@StFrancisRanger (Twitter)

Scarborough Athletic
www.scarboroughathletic.com

Tranmere Rovers
www.tranmererovers.co.uk

Tadley Calleva
www.tcyfc.co.uk

Tooting and Mitcham United
www.tmunited.org

Whitchurch Alport
www.whitchurchalportfc.co.uk

World of JCC
www.youtube.com/user/WorldofJcc

Wigan Athletic
wiganathletic.com

Yeovil Town Women
www.yeoviltownwomenfc.co.uk

York City
www.yorkcityfootballclub.co.uk

Books

Dunn, C., *Roar of the Lionesses* (Pitch Publishing Ltd, 2016).

Szymanski, S. and Kuper, S. *Soccernomics: Why England Loses, Why Spain, Germany and Brazil Win, and Why the US, Japan, Australia, Turkey and even Iraq are Destined to Become Kings of the World's Most Popular Sport* (HarperSport, 2012).

Young, P., *History of British Football* (Stanley Paul & Co Ltd, 1968).

Conn, D., *The Football Business* (Mainstream Publishing, 2002).

Conn, D., *The Beautiful Game? Searching for the Soul of Football* (Yellow Jersey Press, 2005).

Websites

Aloia, A., Derby County v Aston Villa: Championship play-off a £170m 'roll of the dice' (www.bbc.co.uk/sport/football/48399061)

Ziegler, M., Premier League to make record £9bn from TV deals (www.thetimes.co.uk/article/premier-league-to-make-record-9bn-from-tv-deals-dr6fhkk9h)

Gibson, O., Premier League lands £3bn TV rights bonanza from Sky and BT (www.theguardian.com/media/2012/jun/13/premier-league-tv-rights-3-billion-sky-bt)

Premier League, Premier League value of central payments to clubs 2018/19 (www.premierleague.com/news/1225126)

Wigmore, T., Premier League 'Big Six' cash in as overseas TV rights rise 35 per cent (www.telegraph.co.uk/football/2019/08/03/premier-league-big-six-cash-overseas-tv-rights-rise-35-per-cent)

Dalleras, F., Champions League final prize money 2018/19: What Liverpool and Tottenham can earn and how winnings have trebled in a decade (www.cityam.com/champions-league-final-prize-money-2018-19-liverpool-and)

Glenday, J., Premier League smashes shirt sponsorship record for tenth successive season (www.thedrum.com/news/2019/07/23/premier-league-smashes-shirt-sponsorship-record-10th-successive-season)

Jensen, N., How Manchester United's commercial diversification increased their market presence (www.tifofootball.com/features/manchester-united-commercial-market-presence/)

Wang, B., Esports audience is over four times bigger than NFL audience (www.nextbigfuture.com/2019/08/esports-audience-is-over-four-times-bigger-than-nfl-audience.html)

Conn, C., Premier League finances: The full club-by-club breakdown and verdict (www.theguardian.com/football/2019/may/22/premier-league-finances-club-guide-2017-18-accounts-manchester-united-city)

TheTicketBusiness, Aston Villa lead the way in Premier League season ticket price rises (www.theticketingbusiness.com/2019/07/15/aston-villa-lead-way-premier-league-season-ticket-price-rises/)

Lampkin, J., Perplexing transfer fee inflation in the Premier League (www.medium.com/@jlampkin19/perplexing-transfer-fee-inflation-in-the-premier-league-62c677dce686)

Wilson, S., Ellis Short – 'Man who lost £200m while running Sunderland into ground' (www.thenorthernecho.co.uk/

sport/16192274.ellis-short-man-who-lost-200m-while-running-sunderland-into-ground)

Hunter, A., Miracle of Burnley: Inside the Premier League's most unlikely success story (www.theguardian.com/football/2019/oct/25/burnley-miracle-premier-league-success-story-poorest-owner)

Conn, D., QPR debt rises to £177m after reporting £65.4m loss last season (www.theguardian.com/football/2014/mar/06/qpr-debt-177m-report-premier-league-relegation)

Keegan, M., Bury expelled from the Football League after no viable takeover offer emerged for the 134-year-old club (www.dailymail.co.uk/sport/football/article-7400775/Bury-expelled-football-league.ht)

Traf69, Ken Anderson: Saint, Sinner, Hero or Villain? (www.lionofviennasuite.sbnation.com/2019/2/28/18244983/ken-anderson-saint-sinner-hero-or-villain)

Conn, D., Bolton's 'rogue chairman' Ken Anderson puts EFL ownership rules under scrutiny (www.theguardian.com/football/2019/jan/09/bolton-ken-anderson-efl-ownership-forest-green-christian-doidge)

Wilson, P., Bolton Wanderers saved after Football Ventures complete takeover deal (www.theguardian.com/football/2019/aug/28/bolton-wanderers-football-ventures-takeover)

Conn, D., Oystons ordered to buy out Blackpool shareholder for £31m after losing court battle (www.theguardian.com/football/2017/nov/06/oystons-blackpool-ordered-pay-shareholder-high-court-valeri-belokon)

Pike, R., A Growing Gap: Analysing the Championship's new financial realities (outsideoftheboot.com/2017/10/18/a-growing-gap-analysing-the-championships-new-financial-realities/)

Consultancy.uk, Gap widens between have and have-nots of English football (www.consultancy.uk/news/22303/gap-widens-between-have-and-have-nots-of-english-football)

BBC, Gateshead: From brink of National League play-offs to possible oblivion? (www.bbc.co.uk/sport/football/48134461)

Gary, T., Women's Super League: How much have big stadiums helped clubs? (www.bbc.co.uk/sport/football/50308454)

Wrack, S., Salary cap losing its relevance in changing landscape of women's football (www.theguardian.com/football/blog/2019/nov/21/salary-cap-losing-its-relevance-in-changing-landscape-of-womens-football)

Gibson, E., Sexism in football: The beautiful game's ugly secret? (touchstoneblog.org.uk/2016/11/the-beautiful-game)

Jackson, J., Peter Lim to buy 50% stake in Salford City from Class of '92 (www.theguardian.com/football/2014/sep/22/salford-city-peter-lim-class-of-92)

Young, J., Corinthians-Casuals return to Brazil for historic friendly with Corinthians (www.espn.co.uk/football/blog/name/68/post/2265807/headline)

Magee, W., How Non-League Day was born out of a QPR friendly, Facebook friends and the financial crash (www.inews.co.uk/sport/football/non-league-day-2018-facebook-premier-league-international-break-506428)

King, I., The return – not for the first time – of South Shields FC (www.twohundredpercent.net/south-shields-return)

English football league system (www.en.wikipedia.org/wiki/English_football_league_system)

Groundhoppers, Horden C.W. and the quest for salvation (www.groundhoppers.blog/2016/02/21/horden-cw-and-the-quest-for-salvation/)

Walker, M., Horden Colliery Welfare were the first club of the great Colin Bell ... here is why we can't let clubs like this die (www.dailymail.co.uk/sport/football/article-3496014/Horden-Colliery-Welfare-club-great-Colin-Bell-t-let-clubs-like-die.html)

Cowlishaw, D., The rise and rise of AFC Fylde (www.thesetpieces.com/features/rise-rise-afc-fylde/)

Davis, C., Chichester and Sunday League disbanded after half a century (www.chichester.co.uk/sport/football/local/chichester-and-sunday-league-disbanded-after-half-a-century-1-8557914)

Manchester Evening News, Middleton loses Sunday league football after 50 years (www.manchestereveningnews.co.uk/sport/football/football-news/middleton-loses-sunday-league-football-688731)

Steel, A., Oldest Sunday league in country closes (www. gazettelive.co.uk/sport/other-sport/oldest-sunday-league-country-closes-3701493)

Campbell, D. and Green, F., The long term pay-off from working longer hours (www.kent.ac.uk/economics/documents/research/papers/2002/0205.pdf)

Foster, R., From five-a-side to futsal and Star Sixes: How football's small forms went big (www.theguardian.com/football/the-agony-and-the-ecstasy/2017/mar/28/five-a-side-futsal-star-sixes-football-tournament

The FA, Fast Forward with Futsal (www.thefa.com/media/files/get-involved/fa-futsal-strategy-2018-24)

Pye, S., When Soccer Six was the perfect Christmas present for football fans (www.theguardian.com/football/that-1980s-sports-blog/2018/dec/22/soccer-sixes-perfect-christmas-present-football-fans)

Booth, R. and Butler, P., UK austerity has inflicted 'great misery' on citizens, UN says (www.theguardian.com/society/2018/nov/16/uk-austerity-has-inflicted-great-misery-on-citizens-un-says)

Press Release: It Will Take Up to 11 Years for the Government to reverse Austerity (www.neweconomics.org/2019/09/it-will-take-up-to-11-years-for-the-government-to-reverse-austerity)

Press Release: Councils will need billions of pounds in additional funding to meet the rising costs of adult social care (www.ifs.org.uk/publications/14559)

Naylor, M., Wokingham Borough Council hikes price of junior football pitches (www.getreading.co.uk/news/reading-berkshire-news/wokingham-borough-council-hikes-price-10735305)

Pyman, T. Tunbridge Wells: Grassroots football clubs brand 67% increase in football pitch hire costs a 'total disgrace' (www.kentonline.co.uk/tunbridge-wells/news/football-pitch-price-hike-branded-total-disgrace-194078/)

Bond, D., Sport England cuts FA funding by £1.6m after grassroots decline (www.bbc.co.uk/sport/football/26760067)

Tyrrell, N., Liverpool and Everton to make major grassroots football investment for City's poorest children (www.

liverpoolecho.co.uk/news/liverpool-news/lfc-everton-clubs-make-major-17089748)

Blanchard, S., England's lazy children: A third of youngsters are doing less than 30 minutes of physical activity a day, world's biggest study reveals (www.dailymail.co.uk/health/article-6467017/One-three-children-30-minutes-exercise-day.html)

Child in the City, Children spend half the time playing outside in comparison to their parents (www.childinthecity.org/2018/01/15/children-spend-half-the-time-playing-outside-in-comparison-to-their-parents)

BBC, Premier League should be 'taxed' to improve grassroots facilities – former FA chairman (www.bbc.co.uk/sport/football/45901164)

Broomfield, M., Hundreds of English playgrounds have been closed due to Tory budget cuts (www.independent.co.uk/news/uk/politics/playgrounds-closed-england-conservative-budget-cuts-tory-government-children-public-spaces-councils-a7682141.html)

Doward, J., As British teams conquer Europe, cuts force sale of 710 local football pitches (www.theguardian.com/society/2019/jun/02/tory-cuts-force-sale-710-local-football-pitches)

Cole, S., What happened to MyFootballClub – the club where fans decided everything? (www.theguardian.com/football/2017/oct/26/what-happened-to-myfootballclub-ebbsfleet-united)

Plummer, G., King's Lynn and District Sunday League forced to fold after almost six decades (www.lynnnews.co.uk/sport/sunday-league-stalwart-talks-about-league-folding-after-56-years-9074732/)

Ogden, M., Burnley Chairman Mike Garlick committed to Premier League Success (www.espn.co.uk/football/english-premier-league/23/blog/post/3307399/burnley-chairman-mike-garlick-talks-espn-fc-about-premier-league-sustainance)

Austin, S., Paul Warne: 'Obscene' finances are dividing Championship (www.trainingground.guru/articles/paul-warne-obscene-finances-are-dividing-championship)

Delaney, M., The death of the 72? Why football outside the Premier League is on its knees (www.independent.co.uk/sport/football/football-league/premier-league-epl-efl-league-one-two-championship-miguel-delaney-a8926126.html)

Grassroots Football Survey (www.thesoccerstore.co.uk/blog/latest-news/the-results-of-the-2017-fa-grassroots-football-survey-are-in/)

Press Release, Record Revenues of £4.5bn Power Premier League Clubs to Operating Profits of Over £1 billion (www2.deloitte.com/uk/en/pages/press-releases/articles/premier-league-clubs-generates-combined-profile-of-1bn-pounds-2016-2017.html)

Moore, R., The End of Parklife as we know it? The Battle for Britain's Green Spaces (www.theguardian.com/uk-news/2017/jul/09/the-end-of-park-life-as-we-know-it-the-battle-for-britains-green-spaces-rowan-moore)

ITV Report, Is there evidence of a crisis in grassroots football? (www.itv.com/news/central/2016-08-30/is-there-evidence-of-a-crisis-in-grassroots-football)

The rapid decline of 11-a-side football, why exactly are we seeing it die a death in the UK (www.footyaccumulators.com/news/the-rapid-decline-of-11-a-side-football-why-exactly-are-we-seeing-it-die-a-death-in-the-uk)

Hughes, S., As the Merseyside Derby looms large, has the city of Liverpool lost touch with its football roots? (www.independent.co.uk/sport/football/news-and-comment/everton-liverpool-merseyside-sad-to-see-losing-touch-footballing-roots-a8291526.html)

Dmitracova, O., UK Working hours would be shorter if pre-1980 trend had not been derailed, new study says (www.independent.co.uk/news/business/news/uk-working-hours-productivity-pay-new-economics-foundation-a9102446.html)

Brierley, O., The true costs of setting up a grassroots football team (www.kitlocker.com/blog/the-true-costs-of-setting-up-a-grassroots-football-team/)

Davies, R. and Partington, R., More than 25% of UK pubs have closed since 2001 (www.theguardian.com/business/2018/nov/26/uk-pub-closures-financial-crisis-birmingham-ons-figures)

Hollis, S, Meet the worst football team in England (www.
theargus.co.uk/sport/sportsnews/14142074.meet-the-worst-
football-team-in-england)

Foster, R., How North Ferriby's village football team made it
to the National League (www.theguardian.com/football/
the-agony-and-the-ecstasy/2016/jul/15/north-ferriby-village-
football-national-league)

@ThatsLiquid, Riders on the storm (www.thatsliquidfootball.
com/2019/04/14/riders-on-the-storm-assessing-
the-wreckage-of-north-ferriby-united-and-the-
hope-that-remains)

Nesbit, D., The Football League and 'the old pals act' (www.
taleoftwohalves.uk/featured/football-league-old-pals-act)

Attendances (www.footballwebpages.co.uk)

Butler, A., In Salford City, the new 'most controversial club'
in England (www.dreamteamfc.com/c/news-gossip/418300/
inside-salford-city-the-new-most-controversial-
club-in-england)

Johnston, N., FA Cup: Billericay Town owner aiming for the
Premier League (www.bbc.co.uk/sport/football/40997071)

The Bootiful Game, FA release fees paid to agents by non-
league clubs … even a Step 4 side is on the list! (www.
thebootifulgame.co.uk/2019/04/04/fa-release-fees-paid-to-
agents-by-non-league-clubs-even-a-step-4-side-is-on-the-list)

Williams, A., How a battle for the very soul of Gateshead
ousted some of the National League's worst owners (www.
thesefootballtimes.co/2019/08/12/how-a-battle-for-the-
very-soul-of-gateshead-ousted-some-of-the-national-
leagues-worst-owners)

Brooks, C., Gateshead under transfer embargo (www.
nonleaguedaily.com/gateshead-under-transfer-embargo)

Davies, G., England Lionesses World Cup semi-final becomes
most-watched TV show of 2019 (www.telegraph.co.uk/
news/2019/07/03/england-lionesses-world-cup-semi-final-
becomes-most-watched)

Middleton, L., Record amount of girls and women playing
football after World Cup (www.metro.co.uk/2019/07/09/
record-amount-girls-women-playing-football-
world-cup-10136975)

Weeks, J., 1921: The year when football banned women (www.historyextra.com/period/first-world-war/1921-when-football-association-banned-women-soccer-dick-kerr-ladies-lily-parr)

Press Agency, All-Girls junior team wins boys' football league (www.independent.co.uk/news/uk/home-news/girls-football-team-junior-league-sb-frankfort-fc-plymouth-devon-a8898696.html)

Sportblog, Cost-cutting Charlton scrap women's team (www.theguardian.com/sport/blog/2007/jun/23/costcuttingcharltonscrapwom)

Thompson, A. and Kopczyk, K., Women's Sport Week 2017: Gender prize money gap narrowing, new study show (www.bbc.co.uk/sport/40299469)

Deloitte Annual Review of Football Finance 2019 (www2.deloitte.com/uk/en/pages/sports-business-group/articles/annual-review-of-football-finance.html)

Halliday, J., Bury FC: despair as club is expelled from Football League after 125 years (www.theguardian.com/football/2019/aug/27/bury-and-bolton-two-of-englands-oldest-clubs-face-tuesday-expulsion)

Conn, D., 'We never got that money': the inside story of Bury's road to financial ruin (www.theguardian.com/football/2019/jun/18/bury-inside-story-financial-ruin-winding-up-petition-loans-car-park)

Conn, D., Bury financial crisis deepens amid pressure over £4.2m loan (www.theguardian.com/football/2019/may/29/bury-financial-crisis-loan-former-owner-stewart-day-winding-up-petition-debt)

BBC, Bury: Shakers given 12-point deduction by EFL after creditors approve rescue bid (www.bbc.co.uk/sport/football/49034775)

BBC, Bury Takeover: C&N Sporting Risk 'unable to proceed' with bid for League One club (www.bbc.co.uk/sport/football/49486208)

Foster, R., Maidstone's revival after going bust in the Football League offers Bury hope (www.theguardian.com/football/the-agony-and-the-ecstasy/2019/sep/06/maidstone-united-bury-football-league-bust-liquidated)

Press Assoc., Bolton Wanderers takeover completed by Sports Shield consortium (www.theguardian.com/football/2016/mar/10/bolton-wanderers-takeover-completed-sports-shield-consortium-dean-holdsworth)

Press Assoc., Bolton placed into administration after rejecting Bassini takeover (www.theguardian.com/football/2019/may/08/bolton-placed-into-administration-after-rejecting-bassini-takeover)

Conn, D., Oystons ousted as high court brings in the receiver at Blackpool (www.theguardian.com/football/2019/feb/13/blackpool-receivership-sale-risk-12-point-deduction)

Wilson, J., Morgan, T. and Percy, J., Experts warned EFL two years ago that clubs like Bolton and Bury faced financial turmoil (www.telegraph.co.uk/football/2019/08/20/experts-warned-efl-two-years-ago-clubs-like-bolton-bury-faced)

Gap widens between have and have-nots of English football (www.consultancy.uk/news/22303/gap-widens-between-have-and-have-nots-of-english-football)

Everly, J., How much Championship promotion is worth to Rotherham United and League One teams (www.bristolpost.co.uk/sport/football/football-news/league-one-promotion-championship-worth-1396662)

Pike, R., A look at the finances of the English Football League, specifically the Championship's new financial realities (outsideoftheboot.com/2017/10/18/a-growing-gap-analysing-the-championships-new-financial-realities/)

Saunders Smith, N., Editorial: The end of football (www.argyle.life/analysis/editorial-the-end-of-football/

BBC, English Football League: Attendances reach 60-year high of almost 18.4m (www.bbc.co.uk/sport/football/48206875)

Phantis, Fifa: The video game that changed football (www.phantis.com/2016/12/28/fifa-the-video-game-that-changed-football/)

Grubb, J., EA Sports' FIFA franchise surpasses 260m copies sold (www.venturebeat.com/2018/09/05/ea-sports-fifa-franchise-surpasses-260-million-copies-sold)

Varley, C., Can computer games make you better at sport in real life? (www.bbc.co.uk/bbcthree/article/008d2e50-81c9-4352-bfb8-c37379d8553a)

FIFA eWorld Cup 2019 Grand Final generates record viewership (www.fifa.com/fifaeworldcup/news/fifa-eworld-cup-2019-grand-final-generates-record-viewership)

The Warm Down, Interview with Spencer Owen (www.youtube.com/channel/UCmX3073pl-9ASXYaWDrEAHw)

Hahn, S., Hashtag United proving the doubters wrong in non-league (www.itsroundanditswhite.co.uk/articles/hashtag-united-proving-doubters-wrong-non-league)

Derisz, J., Hashtag United: The future of football? (alloutfootball.co.uk/hashtag-united-the-future-of-football)

Carruthers, M., Mike Coulson opens up on why he quit Gateshead, Joseph Cala, Richard Bennett and off-field controversies (www.sunderlandecho.com/sport/football/mike-coulson-opens-why-he-quit-gateshead-joseph-cala-richard-bennett-and-field-controversies-80593)

The Bootiful Game, From selection dilemmas to Youtube scrutiny – an extensive chat with Hashtag Utd's manager Jay Devereux! (thebootifulgame.co.uk/2018/10/14/from-selection-dilemmas-to-youtube-scrutiny-an-extensive-chat-with-hashtag-uds-manager-jay-deveraux/)